The End of the World
and Other Teachable Moments

John D. Caputo, *series editor*

PERSPECTIVES IN
CONTINENTAL
PHILOSOPHY

MICHAEL NAAS

The End of the World
and Other Teachable Moments

Jacques Derrida's Final Seminar

FORDHAM UNIVERSITY PRESS
New York ■ 2015

Copyright © 2015 Fordham University Press

All rights reserved. No part of this publication may be reproduced, stored in a retrieval system, or transmitted in any form or by any means—electronic, mechanical, photocopy, recording, or any other—except for brief quotations in printed reviews, without the prior permission of the publisher.

Fordham University Press has no responsibility for the persistence or accuracy of URLs for external or third-party Internet websites referred to in this publication and does not guarantee that any content on such websites is, or will remain, accurate or appropriate.

Fordham University Press also publishes its books in a variety of electronic formats. Some content that appears in print may not be available in electronic books.

Library of Congress Cataloging-in-Publication Data is available from the publisher.

Printed in the United States of America
17 16 15   5 4 3 2 1
First edition

In memory of Helen Tartar

Contents

Abbreviations of Works by Jacques Derrida

"AANJ"   "Above All, No Journalists!" Trans. Samuel Weber. In *Religion and Media*, ed. Hent de Vries and Samuel Weber, 56–93. Stanford, Calif.: Stanford University Press, 2001. (In *Cahier de l'Herne: Derrida*, ed. Marie-Louise Mallet and Ginette Michaud, 35–49. Paris: Éditions de l'Herne, 2004; rpt. as *Surtout pas de journalistes!* Paris: Éditions de L'Herne, 2005.)

AEL   *Adieu: To Emmanuel Levinas.* Trans. Pascale-Anne Brault and Michael Naas. Stanford, Calif.: Stanford University Press, 1999. (*Adieu à Emmanuel Lévinas.* Paris: Éditions Galilée, 1997.)

AF   *Archive Fever.* Trans. Eric Prenowitz. Chicago: University of Chicago Press, 1996. (*Mal d'archive.* Paris: Éditions Galilée, 1995.)

AL   *Acts of Literature.* Ed. Derek Attridge. London: Routledge, 1992.

AP   *Aporias.* Trans. Thomas Dutoit. Stanford, Calif.: Stanford University Press, 1993. (*Apories.* Paris: Éditions Galilée, 1996.)

AR   *Acts of Religion.* Ed. Gil Anidjar. New York: Routledge, 2002.

ATT   *The Animal That Therefore I Am.* Trans. David Wills. New York: Fordham University Press, 2008. (*L'animal que donc je suis.* Ed. Marie-Louise Mallet. Paris: Éditions Galilée, 2006.)

BS 1	*The Beast and the Sovereign*. Vol. 1, *Seminar of 2001–2002*. Trans. Geoffrey Bennington. Chicago: University of Chicago Press, 2009. (*La bête et le souverain*. Vol. 1, *2001–2002*. Ed. Michel Lisse, Marie-Louise Mallet, and Ginette Michaud. Paris: Éditions Galilée, 2008.)
BS 2	*The Beast and the Sovereign*. Vol. 2, *Seminar of 2002–2003*. Trans. Geoffrey Bennington. Chicago: University of Chicago Press, 2010. (*La bête et le souverain*. Vol. 2, *2002–2003*. Ed. Michel Lisse, Marie-Louise Mallet, and Ginette Michaud. Paris: Éditions Galilée, 2009.)
"CF"	"Le cinéma et ses fantômes." Interview with Antoine de Baecque and Thierry Jousse. *Les cahiers du cinéma* 556 (April 2001): 74–85.
CFU	*Chaque fois unique, la fin du monde*. Ed. Pascale-Anne Brault and Michael Naas. Paris: Éditions Galilée, 2003. (For the English edition, see *WM*.)
"CHM"	"Cogito and the History of Madness." Trans. Alan Bass. In *Writing and Difference*. Chicago: University of Chicago Press, 1978, 31–63. ("Cogito et historie de la folie." In *L'écriture et la différence*. Paris: Éditions du seuil, 1967, 51–97.)
"CS"	"Countersignature." Trans. Mairéad Hanrahan. *Paragraph* 27, no. 2 (2004): 7–42. ("Contresignature." In *Poétiques de Jean Genet: La traversée des genres*. Actes du Colloque Cerisy-la-Salle 2000. Ed. Albert Dichy et Patrick Bougon, Paris: IMEC, 2004.)
D	*Demeure: Fiction and Testimony*. Trans. Elizabeth Rottenberg. Stanford, Calif.: Stanford University Press, 2000.
"D"	"Différance." Trans. Alan Bass. In *Margins of Philosophy* (Chicago: University of Chicago Press, 1982), 1–27.
"EF"	"Epochē and Faith: An Interview with Jacques Derrida." An interview with John D. Caputo, Kevin Hart, and Yvonne Sherwood. In *Derrida and Religion: Other Testaments*, ed. Yvonne Sherwood and Kevin Hart, 27–50. New York: Routledge, 2005.
ET	*Echographies of Television*. With Bernard Stiegler. Trans. Jennifer Bajorek. Cambridge: Polity Press, 2002. (*Échographies de la télévision: Entretiens filmés*. Paris: Éditions Galilée/Institut National de l'Audiovisuel, 1996.)
"FK"	"Faith and Knowledge: The Two Sources of 'Religion' at the Limits of Reason Alone." Trans. Samuel Weber. In *Religion*, ed.

Jacques Derrida and Gianni Vattimo, 1–78. Stanford, Calif.: Stanford University Press, 1998. ("Foi et savoir." In *La religion*, ed. Jacques Derrida et Gianni Vattimo, 9–86. Paris: Éditions du Seuil, 1996.)

"FL"   "Force of Law: The 'Mystical Foundation of Authority.'" Trans. Mary Quaintance. In *AR*, 230–298. (*Force de loi*. Paris: Éditions Galilée, 1994.)

"FOR"   "*Fors*: The Anglish Words of Nicolas Abraham and Maria Torok." Trans. Barbara Johnson. Preface to *The Wolf Man's Magic Word: A Cryptonymy*, by Nicolas Abraham and Maria Torok. Trans. Nicholas Rand. Minneapolis: University of Minnesota, 1986, xi–xlviii. ("Fors," preface to Nicolas Abraham and Maria Torok, *Le verbier de l'Homme aux loups*. Paris: Aubier-Flammarion, 1976.)

FS   *For Strasbourg: Conversations of Friendship and Philosophy*. Ed. and trans. Pascale-Anne Brault and Michael Naas. New York: Fordham University Press, 2014.

"G 1"   "*Geschlecht I*: Sexual Difference, Ontological Difference." Trans. Ruben Bevezdivin and Elizabeth Rottenberg. *PSY 2* 7–26. ("*Différence sexuelle, différence ontologique*: [*Geschlecht I*], in *Heidegger et la question: De l'esprit et autres essais*. Paris: Flammarion, 1990, 145–172; first published in the *Cahier de l'Herne* devoted to Heidegger.)

"G 2"   "*Geschlecht* II: Heidegger's Hand." Trans. John P. Leavey, Jr. and Elizabeth Rottenberg. In *PSY 2* 27–62; first published in *Deconstruction and Philosophy*, ed. John Sallis. Chicago: University of Chicago Press, 1987, 161–196. ("*La main de Heidegger*: [*Geschlecht* II], in *Heidegger et la question: De l'esprit et autres essais*. Paris: Flammarion, 1990, 173–222.)

"G 4"   "Heidegger's Ear: Philopolemology (*Geschlecht* IV)." Trans. John P. Leavey, Jr. In *Reading Heidegger: Commemorations*, ed. John Sallis, 163–218. Bloomington: Indiana University Press, 1993. ("L'oreille de Heidegger: Philopolémologie [*Geschlecht* IV]." In *Politiques de l'amitié*. Paris: Éditions Galilée, 1994, 343–419.)

IW   *Islam & the West: A Conversation with Jacques Derrida*. Mustapha Chérif. Trans. Teresa Lavender Fagan. Chicago: University of Chicago Press, 2008. ("L'Islam et l'Occident: Rencontre avec Jacques Derrida." Mustapha Chérif. Paris: Odile Jacob, 2006.)

"J"   "Justices." Trans. Peggy Kamuf. In *Critical Inquiry* 31,
           no. 3 (Spring 2005): 689–721.

"LJF"   "Letter to a Japanese Friend." Trans. David Wood and
           Andrew Benjamin. In *PSY 2*, 1–6; first published in *Derrida
           & Différance*. Warwick: Parousia Press, 1985, 1–8.

LLF   *Learning to Live Finally: The Last Interview.* Trans. Pascale-Anne
           Brault and Michael Naas. Hoboken, N.J.: Melville House,
           2007. (*Apprendre à vivre enfin: Entretien avec Jean Birnbaum.*
           Paris: Éditions Galilée/Le Monde, 2005.)

"LO"   "Living On: Border Lines." Trans. James Hulbert. In
           Deconstruction and Criticism. New York: Seabury Press/
           Continuum Press, 1979, 62–142. ("Survivre." In *PAR*,
           117–218.)

MB   *Memoirs of the Blind: The Self-Portrait and Other Ruins.*
           Trans. Pascale-Anne Brault and Michael Naas. Chicago:
           University of Chicago Press, 1993. (*Mémoires d'aveugle:
           L'autoportrait et autres ruines.* Paris: Éditions de la Réunion
           des musées nationaux, 1990.)

N   *Negotiations: Interventions and Interviews, 1971–2001.* Ed.
           Elizabeth Rottenberg. Stanford, Calif.: Stanford University
           Press, 2002.

"NA"   "No Apocalypse, Not Now: Full Speed Ahead, Seven
           Missiles, Seven Missives." Trans. Catherine Porter and Philip
           Lewis. In *PSY 1* 387–409. ("No apocalypse, not now (à
           toute vitesse, sept missiles, sept missives," in *Psyché 1*
           395–418.)

OG   *Of Grammatology.* Trans. with a preface by Gayatri
           Chakravorty Spivak. Baltimore: Johns Hopkins University
           Press, 1976. (*De la grammatologie.* Paris: Éditions de Minuit,
           1967.)

OS   *Of Spirit: Heidegger and the Question.* Trans. Geoffrey
           Bennington and Rachel Bowlby. Chicago: University of
           Chicago Press, 1991. (*De l'esprit: Heidegger et la question.*
           Paris: Éditions Galilée, 1987.)

P   *Points . . . Interviews, 1974–1994.* Ed. Elisabeth Weber.
           Trans. Peggy Kamuf and others. Stanford, Calif.: Stanford
           University Press, 1995. (*Points de suspension: Entretiens.*
           Edited and presented by Elisabeth Weber. Paris: Éditions
           Galilée, 1992.)

PAR   *Parages.* Ed. John P. Leavey Jr. Trans. Tom Conley, James
           Hulbert, John P. Leavey, and Avital Ronell. Stanford, Calif.:

Acknowledgments

Early versions of several chapters of this book have been presented at conferences or given as lectures, and some have been published in shortened versions elsewhere. This work has benefited enormously from the questions and conversations that followed each lecture or conference presentation and from the careful attention of copyeditors and editors. Those who read or heard those earlier versions will recognize here the traces of their questions, comments, and suggestions. I would like to thank these friends and colleagues for their hospitality and kind attention: Gianfranco Dalmasso at the Università di Bergamo, Kevin Newmark at Boston College, Ted Jennings, Virgil Brower, Tony Hoshaw, and Kuni Sakai at Chicago Theological Seminary, Keith Peterson at Colby College, Joshua Ben David Nichols and Amy Swiffen at Concordia University, Pablo Lazo Briones at Universidad Iberoamericana in Mexico City, Marc Crépon at the École Normale Supérieure in Paris, David Jones at Kennesaw State University, Carmine DiMartino at the Università di Milano, Andrew Benjamin at Monash University, Ben Vedder and Gert-Jan van der Heiden at Radboud University in Nijmegen, Patrick Gamez and Tony Mills at the University of Notre Dame, Penelope Deutscher, Michael Loriaux, and Nasrin Qader at Northwestern University, Ted Toadvine, Alejandro Vallega, Daniela Vallega-Neu, and Peter Warnek at the University of Oregon, Leonard Lawlor, Jennifer Mensch, and Dennis Schmidt at Penn State University, Kas Saghafi (and the sponsors of the 2011 Spindel Conference) at the University of Memphis, Andrew Lazella, Crina Gschwandtner, and

Sharon Meagher at the University of Scranton, Allison Tyndall Locke, Laura James, and Eduardo Mendieta at Stony Brook University, Nicholas Royle at the University of Sussex (along with my other co-editors of the *Oxford Literary Review*, who joined me at Sussex in a series of conferences on Derrida's seminars: Geoffrey Bennington, Timothy Clark, Peggy Kamuf, and Sarah Wood), and Shannon Mussett and Michael Shaw at Utah Valley University. I am particularly grateful to Jeffrey Nealon at Penn State University and Kelly Oliver at Vanderbilt University, who both offered me many excellent suggestions and much-needed encouragement on an earlier draft of this work. I would like to offer a special word of thanks to Jeffrey McCurry and John Sallis for their generous invitation to present an early version of the final chapter of the book as the André Schuwer Memorial Lecture, sponsored by the Simon Silverman Phenomenology Center at Duquesne University, at the 2011 meeting of the Society for Phenomenology and Existential Philosophy. This invitation was for me all the more precious insofar as I had the good fortune of meeting André Schuwer on several occasions and so was able to experience firsthand his kindness, generosity, and good humor, as well as his formidable but always self-effacing intelligence.

Chapters 1 and 7 were originally published in *Research in Phenomenology*, the first in volume 40, no. 2 (2010): 219–242 and the second in volume 44, no. 1 (2014): 1–27. I am grateful to the journal's editor, John Sallis, for allowing me to republish revised versions of these essays. An early version of Chapter 2 was published in *The Ends of History: Questioning the Stakes of Historical Reason*, ed. Joshua Nichols and Amy Swiffen (New York: Routledge, 2013), 161–178. A version of Chapter 3 first appeared in *Societies*, 2 (2012): 317–331. A revised version of Chapter 4 appeared in *Thinking Plurality*, ed. Gert-Jan van der Heiden (Leiden: Brill, 2014). An abbreviated version of Chapter 5 was published in *L'a-venire di Derrida*, ed. Gianfranco Dalmasso, Carmine DiMartino, and Caterina Resta (2014). Finally, a shorter version of Chapter 6 appeared in a special issue of *SubStance* devoted to Derrida's *The Beast and the Sovereign* (2014).

I would like to thank here my friends and colleagues in the Derrida Seminar Translation Project, who have taught me so much over the last five years about the seminars at our annual week-long meeting at IMEC (Institut Mémoires de l'édition contemporaine) in Normandy, France: Geoffrey Bennington (Emory University), Peggy Kamuf (University of Southern California), Kir Kuiken (SUNY at Albany), Kas Saghafi (University of Memphis), David Wills (Brown University), and, at DePaul, Elizabeth Rottenberg and Pascale-Anne Brault. I am also very grateful to my students and other colleagues at DePaul, especially Will McNeill, whose graduate seminar in autumn 2011 on Heidegger's *Fundamental Concepts of Metaphysics* was truly invaluable as I myself was teaching a seminar on Derrida's *The Beast and the Sovereign*.

Finally, I would like to express my deep gratitude to David Farrell Krell, for his unparalleled knowledge of Heidegger and Derrida, to be sure, but especially for so many years of conversation and friendship. The discerning reader will be able to trace the influence of his work, his generosity, and his friendship on just about every page of this book.

Introduction: Derrida's Other Corpus

Those who had the good fortune to attend even a single session of a Jacques Derrida seminar know just what a chance, what a boon—just what an event—the project to publish the entire series of his seminars represents for anyone interested in his work. Admired by readers and scholars the world over at the time of his death in October 2004 for the more than seventy books he had published during his lifetime, Derrida was known to his students perhaps first and foremost as an engaging lecturer and an exemplary pedagogue who, every Wednesday afternoon in his seminar in Paris, presented readings of works from the entire history of philosophy and literature. As rigorous and careful as they were innovative and inspiring, these readings taught generations of students not only about various philosophical and literary themes, figures, and problems but also, and more important, about how to read, how to question, and, thus, how to teach in turn. The publication of the seminars will thus bring to fuller awareness a very different aspect of Derrida's philosophical practice. Since the seminars differ greatly from Derrida's published works, and since only a mere fraction of the seminar materials has been made available before now, the result will be what can only be characterized as a wholly *other corpus* besides the one we already know, a second corpus that will no doubt cause us to reconsider everything we know or think we know about Jacques Derrida.

For more than forty years, Derrida held a weekly, two-hour seminar in Paris, first at the Sorbonne (1960–64), then at the École Normale Supérieure

(1964–84), and finally at the École des Hautes Études en Sciences Sociales (1984–2003). For each session, Derrida would prepare some thirty to forty double-spaced pages, at first by hand—in a nearly illegible script—then on a typewriter, and finally on a word processor or computer.[1] With between ten and fifteen sessions a year, a single seminar thus runs up to five or six hundred double-spaced pages (between three hundred and four hundred printed pages), each carefully written out in complete sentences and paragraphs by Derrida himself, none of them thus needing to be reconstituted on the basis of outlines or student notes.[2] The decision to publish what were already quite polished and nearly publishable works had thus in many ways been prepared by Derrida himself during his lifetime, even if the decision was ultimately made not by Derrida but by those close to him after his death.[3] Projected to run some fourteen thousand printed pages in just over forty volumes (more or less one for each year), the publication of the collected seminars of Jacques Derrida represents a major event in contemporary philosophy and literary theory, one that will inevitably lead to a full reappraisal of Derrida's work and of his place in twentieth century philosophy and literary theory. With the recent publication of the first volumes of the seminars, those of 2001–2002 and 2002–2003 under the title *The Beast and the Sovereign*, and, even more recently, the seminar of 1999–2000 on *The Death Penalty*, this rethinking or reappraisal is already underway.[4]

The central aim of this book is to show that there is no better place to begin such a reappraisal of Derrida's work than the two-year *The Beast and the Sovereign*, Derrida's final seminar, where questions of death, mourning, solitude, and the end of the world come to mark the seminar—and, as a result, Derrida's entire corpus, his published works as well as his other seminars—in a unique and rather uncanny way. *The End of the World and Other Teachable Moments* is an attempt to give an account of this very singular seminar at the end of Derrida's remarkable writing and teaching career. It attempts to show how Derrida always worked with and within the constraints of the seminar format, constraints that differ greatly from those of publishing or even lecturing, and it will demonstrate how Derrida was forced in the course of this final seminar to take account of some rather unique and earth-shattering events in the world around him and in his own life. If the seminar was thus never just one forum or format among others for Derrida, *The Beast and the Sovereign* will prove to have been not just one seminar among others in this other corpus.

One of the points of interest for Derrida scholars in the coming years will be to analyze how different discursive contexts always dictated different writing strategies, differences in both the form and content of Derrida's work.[5] There are very noticeable differences in tone, style, approach, subject matter, and so on, between published texts, conference presentations, interviews or improvised discussions, and, now, the seminars.[6] Those who may have struggled in the past with some of Derrida's more difficult published works will thus be pleased to find in the seminars an often more accessible and straightforward style. Though still demanding, the seminars were written to be presented orally to a rather wide and diverse audience, from friends and intellectually inclined and curious Parisians to students preparing to take the *agrégation*, the state examination that would allow them to teach philosophy in French high schools or universities, and to students from abroad who traveled to Paris just to attend Derrida's seminar. The seminars were thus written with a very clear pedagogical purpose; they were meant to be understood by those hearing them for the first time, not necessarily read and reread, studied and analyzed, like many of his published works.

We thus see Derrida in the seminars teaching students how to *read* works throughout the history of philosophy and literature, how to read texts closely and patiently, in their letter, and then how to read them in relation to other texts, themes, and questions from the history of philosophy and literature. If interviews and discussions were almost always devoted to explicating what had *already* been said or previously published, the seminars were usually places for Derrida to forge more or less new trails or paths, even if it was often by returning to material he had treated under a different light in earlier works. This is certainly the case of the two years of *The Beast and the Sovereign* seminar, where Derrida takes up texts on the animal and on sovereignty that he had not treated before, at the same time as he returns to questions he had posed elsewhere and even rereads texts he had read before. As we will see, these two seminars—Derrida's final two seminars—will be at once continuous with his other seminars and very different than them, at once part of the series and absolutely unique in their genre.

While much will need to be said in the future about the style of the seminars themselves, about their unique pedagogical purpose, about the way they changed as the institutions for which Derrida taught changed, about the themes, figures, and questions Derrida took up, the seminars both call out to be read as works in their own right and invite comparison with the works Derrida himself published during his lifetime.[7] Because the seminars were often the basis for Derrida's published works—even though, as I said, very few seminar sessions have been published in anything close to their original form—it should come as no surprise that many connections exist between the seminars and almost all of Derrida's work.[8] Such connections can be drawn both synchronically, by comparing a seminar with the works that were published at more or less the same time the seminar was given, or diachronically, either by tracing a theme or notion from a late seminar back to very early published works, or by following a theme or question from an early seminar forward to later published works. Because the seminars are in general more prosaic, less elliptical, and more pedagogically minded than many of Derrida's published works, they will be a tremendous resource to scholars hoping to gain further insight into Derrida's published works.

The End of the World and Other Teachable Moments is an attempt to read and analyze Derrida's final two seminars and, for reasons that will become clear, the second year in particular, by heeding this double injunction to read the seminars in their own right and in relation to works that were published around the same time as the seminar or, in some cases, long before. The two volumes of *The Beast and the Sovereign*, which correspond to Derrida's final two seminars at the École des Hautes Études en Sciences Sociales, are perfectly suited for such synchronic and diachronic readings, for they telescope together two strands or themes that became prominent in many of Derrida's published works of the 1990s but that can be traced back to some of his earliest works. As the title *The Beast and the Sovereign* alone suggests, these seminars bring together material about the animal in works such as *The Animal That Therefore I Am* with Derrida's parallel thinking of the question of sovereignty during this very same period. One can thus look at these two themes in isolation and then at the kinds of questions opened up when they are conjoined.

Though one could, of course, trace the theme of sovereignty under this or other names all the way back to the very beginning of Derrida's work, insofar as deconstruction is perhaps always the deconstruction of some putatively *sovereign* formation, principle, or ideal, it could be argued that there is a ten- to twelve-year period where this theme is marked in a particularly insistent way, beginning with "Force of Law" (1990) or *The Other Heading* (1991) and including the 1995 essay "Faith and Knowledge" (where Derrida looks at the Greek origins of the concept of sovereignty), right up through the essay "Unconditionality and Sovereignty" (1999) and *Rogues*— the first part of which was delivered at the 2002 Cerisy-la-Salle conference devoted to Derrida's work under the title *The Democracy to Come*.[9] In the first year of the seminar *The Beast and the Sovereign*, the seminar that immediately precedes the writing of *Rogues*, Derrida develops in a particularly powerful way the reading that is sketched out in *Rogues* of the history of the concept of sovereignty from Plato and Aristotle to Bodin, Hobbes, and Schmitt. He also defends in this seminar even more vigorously than elsewhere the thesis that the concept of an indivisible and unconditional sovereignty remains in its essence theological in its premises and its origins. This is true, Derrida insists, even in Hobbes, where the human covenant of the *Leviathan* initially appears to be thoroughly secular and modern in its exclusion of both the animal and God but where, he argues, an essentially theological notion of sovereignty nonetheless remains the model for all political rule. The question of sovereignty in *The Beast and the Sovereign* must thus be thought in relation to Derrida's thoroughgoing critique of this theological model of sovereignty and his skepticism with regard to so-called secular conceptions of sovereignty, along with a series of other seemingly secular notions that Derrida shows to be rooted just as firmly in the theologico-political, notions such as work, literature, cosmopolitanism, religion, tolerance, the death penalty, and so on. We also come to see in the seminar, as Derrida suggests in *Rogues*, that such a theological notion of sovereignty is inextricably related to the very concept of self-identity, to what Derrida, using Benveniste's etymologies, refers to as *ipseity*, that is, the power of an autonomous, self-same sovereign subject—whether this be an individual or a nation-state—to refer to or claim certain rights for itself and make *decisions* from out of itself.

The sovereignty of the self or of the nation-state is thus at the center of these two seminars, the very first sessions of which were written in the latter weeks of 2001, that is, just after 9/11, when the sovereignty of certain nation-states, and the United States in particular, appeared to have been shaken or threatened by, on the one hand, transnational "terrorist" organizations and networks and, on the other, international bodies such as the United Nations that were perceived or were at least presented as usurping the sovereign power of certain nation-states. The first volume of *The Beast and the Sovereign* can thus be read, among so much else, as a gauge or measure of Derrida's evolving response to the events of 9/11. It shows him responding on an almost weekly basis to, for example, the more and more resolute and inflexible assertion of the United States of its own national sovereignty as it was revving up the war machine for the invasion of Iraq. Derrida thus devotes several key passages to the events of 9/11 and the fear or terror that was created by them, or by their incessant repetition in the media—reflections that bear comparison with what Derrida says about the media in, for example, *Echographies of Television* and the interview on 9/11 in *Philosophy in a Time of Terror*. The very title *The Beast and the Sovereign*—a title that was proposed well before 9/11—already seemed at the time to have been ideally suited for questioning the strategic use in 2001–2002 of the phrase "the beast of Baghdad" to characterize the sovereign leader of Iraq in the weeks and months leading up to the American invasion of that sovereign country.

Important connections can and thus should be drawn between *The Beast and the Sovereign* seminar and Derrida's published works, between the seminar and what are called "world events" unfolding at the time of the seminar, and between this and earlier seminars. In his own summary of the seminar, included as part of the editorial note to the first volume (*BS 1* xiii), Derrida explains that the themes of the seminar developed in large part out of the previous year's seminar on the death penalty. In that earlier seminar, it was again the question of sovereignty that was central— the question, for example, of the sovereign's claim over the life and death of his subjects by pardoning or executing them. Derrida will thus take many of the insights regarding sovereignty from this previous seminar and rethink them in the context of the human's relationship to the animal, that is, the sovereign's relation to the beast. When we then draw these two different seminars together, along with the published texts that surround them, we see that what interested Derrida was always a structural relation between what might at first appear to be unrelated notions—for example, the death penalty, democracy, the question of the animal. But by rethinking each of these notions in the light of other, Derrida will demonstrate that it is a certain conception of the human and of sovereignty, a certain configuration of sovereignty, that connects these seemingly disparate themes and that can help explain why philosophy will have been throughout its history at once pro–death penalty, antidemocratic, and anthropocentric.

The Beast and the Sovereign brings together in a very explicit fashion a thinking of the sovereign *and* the beast, a thinking of the way the sovereign or man treats the beast, and a thinking of the sovereign *as* a beast, as either above the law or before or outside the law, as the exception that makes or lays down the law. This confrontation of the beast and the sovereign will lead to a critique not only of the very essence of sovereignty or of the sovereign's relation to the beast but also of the way the sovereign defines himself in opposition to the beast. What becomes central, then, to both volumes is not simply man's characterization of the beast but also the question of the property or the proper of man or the human. Such considerations then lead, of course, to a whole other nexus of texts, since the question of the proper of man can be found in works as early as *Of Grammatology* and "The Ends of Man" and it continues right on through the "Geschlecht" essays, *Aporias*, and so on.

In the first year of *The Beast and the Sovereign*, we thus see Derrida returning to themes and figures, beginning with the animal and question of sovereignty, he had treated elsewhere. As in the seminars on hospitality or testimony that preceded *The Beast and the Sovereign* by a few years, we see him taking up familiar themes and developing them in new directions through the reading and analysis of new material. Though Derrida rather uncharacteristically elected to include in some of the earlier sessions of the first year of *The Beast and Sovereign* seminar large portions of the ten-hour lecture he presented at Cerisy-la-Salle some five years before, pages that would be subsequently published in *The Animal That Therefore I Am*, this first year of the seminar is largely continuous in its themes, its approach, and its tone with previously published works and, especially, with earlier seminars.

But, as we will see, things change rather dramatically in the second year of the seminar, which is why this work concentrates primarily on the second volume of *The Beast and the Sovereign*. Indeed, only the first chapter of this work is devoted to the first year of the seminar (and to *The Animal That Therefore I Am*, with which it overlaps), while the subsequent six chapters and the conclusion are devoted to a series of rather surprising themes, interruptions, and ruptures in that second year. For if the second year of the seminar still resembles what came before it in many respects, it slowly begins to detach itself from the sequence of seminars it would bring to a conclusion.[10] While it can and should be read as a continuation of the previous year, as an analysis of the relationship between the beast and the sovereign, the human and the animal, other themes and questions related to death, mourning, survival, prayer, the archive, and, even, the end of the world begin to impose themselves on Derrida, thereby transforming the seminar into something more or different than a seminar, into a seminar unlike any other. This final seminar can thus be read, just like any other, as an attempt to treat a theme—the relationship between the beast and the sovereign—by reading and analyzing texts from history of philosophy and literature, but it can also be read, I will try to demonstrate, as a remarkable attempt to write a sort of autobiography otherwise, that is, as an attempt to chronicle a thinking of last things through a reading of other works. In other words, it can be read as a unique attempt to read oneself or one's life, to reread one's own work, through the *detour*—the necessary detour—of other lives and other texts. The second volume of *The Beast and the Sovereign* is a work like no other in either of Derrida's corpuses. It is a work that speaks of death as the end of the world and a work that, having been bequeathed or abandoned to the archive, now testifies on its own to that end—one of the many, though hardly the least, of its teachable moments.

Chapter 1, "Derrida's Flair (For the Animals to Follow . . .)," begins by tracing the history of Derrida's engagement with the question of the animal and the strategy he pursues in *The Animal That Therefore I Am* and *The Beast and the Sovereign*. Once again, what is at issue is philosophy's complicity with a certain conception of sovereignty. As I demonstrate, Derrida's strategy with regard to the question of the animal is always to question the ways in which philosophy has traditionally attributed a particular capacity to the human rather than the animal in order then to question the concept of sovereignty that is at the basis of this attribution. Whether it is a question of granting the human and denying the animal *logos* or a relationship to death, a capacity to mourn, to cry, to laugh, or to invent tools, philosophy has typically drawn a single, indivisible line between the human and the animal—all animals—on the basis of this trait or capacity. Derrida's strategy is to question the rigor and indivisibility of this line by suggesting in a first moment that the most advanced work in ethology or primatology seems to suggest that certain animals do seem to have the capacity to mourn, or have language, or use tools. But rather than press the point, Derrida typically turns very quickly in a second moment to the question of whether the human can really be said to possess fully or purely any of these capacities he so confidently assigns himself and denies the animal. For example, does the human really have a capacity to respond that can be clearly and rigorously distinguished from what is often considered to be mere animal or even machinelike reaction? Derrida thus begins by questioning the supposed fact that animals do not have such and such a capacity or attribute before going on to question the principle by which philosophers have claimed that humans do.

In all his work on the animal, we see Derrida questioning the confidence with which humans attribute certain capacities to themselves while denying them to animals, all in the name of a certain conception of human sovereignty that so often results in aggression and violence against the animal world and in a pervasive denial or denegation of this violence. All this raises, of course, the question of the relationship between deconstruction and psychoanalysis more generally, a question that Derrida first took up in 1966 in "Freud and the Scene of Writing" and that he would pursue in innumerable essays and books thereafter. From questions of the phantasm, repression, anxiety, and the uncanny to questions of cruelty and, as we will see in the final chapter, the relationship between Derridean *différance*, Heideggerian *Walten*, and Freudian *Trieb*, *The Beast and the Sovereign* conjoins deconstruction and psychoanalysis in a unique and particularly poignant way.

By drawing together the themes of the beast and the sovereign, animality and sovereignty, Derrida in the first year of the seminar *The Beast and the Sovereign* was ultimately led to question the legitimacy of all those attributes commonly granted by philosophers to humans but denied to animals: these include not only language, the trace, the capacity to respond rather than react, and so on, but also a relationship to death—a relationship that is often held to be unique to the human, or, for Heidegger, to Dasein. It is this relationship between sovereignty, animality, and death that comes to preoccupy the final pages of the first year of the seminar and that then comes to dominate the quasi-totality of the second. It is in large part for this reason that *The End of the World and Other Teachable Moments* places special emphasis on the second year of *The Beast and the Sovereign* seminar, the final year of Derrida's final seminar—obviously not just any seminar in Derrida's long teaching career.

The second year of *The Beast and the Sovereign* raises many of the same kinds of questions regarding the human and the animal that were raised in the first year. But very soon other themes begin creeping in that will come to dominate the entire year, among these, the themes of solitude, originary violence, dying a living death, survival—what Derrida calls *survivance*— various phantasm of survival, the alternative between inhumation and cremation, prayer, the archive, and so on. In addition to all these themes— themes that can also, of course, be found elsewhere in Derrida's work—a very different tone or pathos begins to make itself heard, one that wavers between melancholy and a remarkable sobriety or lucidity with regard to the end.

First presented in Paris from December 11, 2002, to March 26, 2003, the second year of *The Beast and the Sovereign* seminar revolves around two books that raise in different but very complementary ways all kinds of questions about the animal and the human, though also about solitude, dying a living death, survival, prayer, and an originary violence that seems to precede and to be at the origin of everything. Whereas the first year of the seminar treated a whole host of figures in some detail, from Machiavelli, Descartes, Hobbes, and Kant to Lacan, Levinas, and Deleuze, to name just a few, the second year of the seminar—some ten sessions in all—focuses almost exclusively on just two figures, or really, just two texts, Daniel Defoe's *Robinson Crusoe*—nothing more obvious or predictable than that!—and Heidegger's 1929–30 seminar, published in the *Gesamtausgabe* in 1983 and translated into English as *The Fundamental Concepts of Metaphysics: World, Finitude, Solitude*.[11] It is in this work that Heidegger famously claims that the stone is worldless, the animal poor in world, and the human world-forming or world-building. These and other remarks from Heidegger's seminar will lead Derrida in the second year of his own seminar to question not only, again, this attribution of world to man and its refusal to the animal but also the related claim that as the only being that has a world and that has *logos*, man would be the only being with a relationship to death as such. It is as a result of this relation that, for Heidegger, only the human can die, while the animal merely perishes. This meditation on death, on the possibility of thinking or having a relationship to death as such, this thinking of world, solitude, and finitude, will come to preoccupy this final seminar in a unique and truly uncanny way—as will the thinking of an originary violence in Heidegger's work that goes by the name of *Walten*, an originary and unmasterable violence that obsesses, dominates, and, in the end, consumes the seminar—and right up to its final word. That is the trajectory of the second year of Derrida's seminar *The Beast and the Sovereign* and that is, in essence, the trajectory of *The End of the World and Other Teachable Moments*.

Chapter 2 takes as its point of departure Derrida's choice to focus in this second year of *The Beast and the Sovereign* seminar on just two books. I ask there about the strategy behind this self-imposed restriction or isolation and I try to think it in relation to what Derrida says in the seminar itself about solitude, about the concept of world, and, especially, about the claim often made by philosophers that only the human being has a relationship to death as such or that only the human has the capacity to mourn. If, as Derrida argued in several places near the end of his life, death must be thought not simply as one event among others within a world whose horizon remains fundamentally unshaken by death but as an event that marks the end of the world itself, the end of the world as a whole and in its totality, then we must ask about the relationship between this end of the world in death and the end of the world that was threatening in February and March 2003 as the United States prepared for the invasion of Iraq in what promised to be another global or world war, another war that would threaten or put to the test the very notion of world.

Chapter 3, "To Die a Living Death: Phantasms of Burial and Cremation," attempts to follow the emergence in the Third Session and then the repeated deferral in subsequent sessions of an odd theme or question that arises out of Derrida's reading of *Robinson Crusoe* but that clearly has other, more personal origins as well. It is the question of what it means for a large and growing number of people in the Western world to have to decide, in a seemingly sovereign fashion, about how their bodies are to be treated after their deaths, that is, whether they are to be buried or cremated. The question is obviously related to the over-arching themes of the seminar, to the Heideggerian claim, for example, that only the human has a relationship to death as such while the animal simply perishes. But this question, which Derrida had treated in some detail back in *Aporias* in 1992, takes a very curious turn to the present—even the autobiographical—

in the seminar. Written just about a year and half before his death from complications of pancreatic cancer in October 2004, the seminar seems to be inflected in a rather unique way by these clearly motivated and interested ruminations about the fate of one's corpse—as well as one's corpus—after death. I thus look in some detail at Derrida's analyses in the latter parts of the seminar of Robinson Crusoe's obsession with being "buried alive" in the earth or "swallowed up" by wild beasts and then at Derrida's somewhat unexpected meditations on the different economies and phantasms attached to burial or cremation, that is, the various speculations and phantasmatic relations one might have with regard to the future of one's body after death. While these meditations clearly have their origin in Derrida's reading of *Robinson Crusoe* and Heidegger, I ask here about Derrida's decision to make this curious alternative between burial and cremation his own and his audience's, that is, *our* alternative, and I ask about the importance Derrida seems to attach to the fact that for the first time in human history a large and growing number of people across the globe are being confronted with the seemingly sovereign decision to have their bodies either buried in the earth, out of sight and yet still recoverable and readable—right down to the mitochondrial DNA—or else cremated, incinerated, with the ashes being collected and preserved in a movable container or simply scattered to the wind. What does this supposedly binary alternative between inhumation and cremation tell us, in Derrida's account, about Greco-European modernity and about certain modern conceptions of the subject and the subject's putative autonomy and sovereignty over its own life, body, and remains?

Placed at the center of the book, Chapter 4, "Reinventing the Wheel: Of Sovereignty, Autobiography, and Deconstruction," takes up Derrida's analysis of Robinson Crusoe's reinvention of the wheel and the questions of autobiography and world that emerge from this analysis. After recalling that the title of the Cerisy-la-Salle conference of 1997 that anticipates so much of *The Beast and the Sovereign* seminar was none other than "The Autobiographical Animal," I argue that, for Derrida, autobiography always takes on the figure of a wheel, that is, the figure of a self that must always take a detour through the world in order to return to itself, to a self that might appear the same as it once was but that will have been irremediably altered by that detour. This chapter thus begins with Derrida's very specific analyses of the wheel in *Robinson Crusoe*, and it expands outward, just like Derrida's analysis, to include questions of the relationship between reaction and response, automaticity and spontaneity, the nature of the *autos* on which our conception of autobiography depends, and, finally, the very work, movement, or historicity of deconstruction itself. I thus argue here that deconstruction will have always been a deconstruction of the wheel (as a figure of sovereignty and self-identity) and that every deconstructive reading must pass by way of a detour through the world, that is, it must venture out into other texts and other languages in order to return to itself altered, which is why every deconstructive reading always says at once the same thing and something very different. Since it is in this chapter that I look at the question of autobiography in *The Beast and the Sovereign* seminar, I allow myself in this chapter—and this chapter only—to begin and end with a couple of quintessentially American references, proof, once again, that every time the wheel of deconstruction turns round it takes us always at once back toward its point of departure and, inevitably, elsewhere.

Chapter 5, "Pray Tell: Derrida's Performative Justice," attempts to follow the theme of prayer through the entirety of the second year of *The Beast and the Sovereign* seminar. If, as Derrida shows, Robinson Crusoe's sojourn on the island can be characterized as a long "apprenticeship in prayer," then Derrida's seminar can itself be read as an equally long meditation on this same theme. Beginning with Derrida's critique in the 1970s of some of the central tenets of classical speech act theory—Derrida's insistence on iterability as the condition of the performative, his emphasis on the impossibility of completely distinguishing the serious from the etiolated performative, on the impossibility of grounding the performative in the intentions of a self-conscious ego or subject—I argue that Derrida develops the notion of an originary or elementary performative that conditions every utterance, constative or performative, and that is actually at the origin of the social bond. Prayer would be the name—or one of the names—of this originary performative. Every address to the other would be preceded by a sort of "pray tell," an originary request to the other to listen to what I am saying or to pay attention to what I am doing, in short, to *turn* toward me, even if it is to contest or reject me. The chapter concludes with the suggestion that once prayer has been relieved of the requirement that it be attached to a self-conscious, intentional, living being, once it has become coextensive with every speech act, then we might begin to consider every trace as a prayer, and the archive in general as the place of prayer.

The following chapter, "Derrida's Preoccupation with the Archive," demonstrates that the question of survival (*sur-vivance*) is posed in Derrida's final seminar by means of a radical rethinking of the trace and the archive. For Derrida, the archive must always be understood in relationship to two distinct sources, on the one hand, an attempt to protect and indemnify a unique past and, on the other, an attempt to preserve this unique past by opening it up to iteration, translation, and, thus, transformation. The archive is thus at once a chance, the only chance, in fact, for any trace to live on, and a threat both to that which is archived and, especially, to that which is not. As Derrida argues both in the seminar and in other texts from around the same time, there is an ineradicable violence in every act of archivization, as some things are kept and others are left to fall into oblivion.

Another thinking of protection or preservation is thus required to think the archive, as well as another conception of life. Because, as Derrida will argue, the category of life cannot be thought without appealing to a concept of repetition and, thus, of the trace, the possibility of the trace or of archivization begins not after life but already with the emergence of life itself—indeed, already "from the very first breath." This thus means that *survivance* does not simply follow upon life but is coextensive with it, that life and death must be thought together as survival and that any thinking of a life without death, like any thinking of speech or communication without the trace, is but a *phantasm*. *The Beast and the Sovereign* would be a prime example, the chapter concludes, of the very theory of survival or living-on, of life-death, of the trace and the archive, that is developed throughout Derrida's work but perhaps most pointedly in this final seminar.

In the concluding chapter, "'World, Finitude, Solitude': Derrida's *Walten*," I suggest that in addition to all these other relations and connections between the seminars and Derrida's previously published works, questions about the animal, about what is proper to man, about sovereignty, the trace, the archive, death, mourning, and so on, there is the need or the call to reconsider and reevaluate Derrida's long-standing relationship to Heidegger, a relationship that can be traced back to the very early 1960s and can be followed right up to the very end. In this chapter, I trace Derrida's previous references to or readings of Heidegger's seminar of 1929–30, and I try to explain the special importance or privilege Derrida seems to have granted it and the reasons for his repeated engagements with it, from the "Geschlecht" essays and *Of Spirit* to *The Animal That Therefore I Am* and the second year of *The Beast and the Sovereign*. Indeed this Heidegger seminar seems to have held a particular fascination for Derrida, and almost from the beginning, a fascination that would be apparent in *The Beast and the Sovereign* from the opening pages right up to its final word. We will see Derrida return almost obsessively, week after week, to the vocabulary of *Walten* in Heidegger's seminar, *Walten* as originary violence, as *physis* or as *différance*, characterizations that are rather striking in this final seminar but that might also profitably be read in light of certain claims or analyses from the 1968 essay "Différance" or, indeed, from some of Derrida's very first, handwritten, seminar lectures from the early 1960s on

Heidegger's "destruction of metaphysics." At the end of this chapter, I ask why Derrida "chose" to conclude and perhaps even sign this seminar—what would turn out to be his final seminar—with this notion of an originary or elemental violence that goes by the name, the German name, of *Walten*.

In *The End of the World and Other Teachable Moments*, I follow several different paths, several different questions (the end of the world, the alternative between cremation and burial, the archive, prayer, the human and the animal, *Walten*, and so on), though other questions and other themes, for example, sexual difference, poetry, the political, the secret, or psychoanalysis, to name just a few, were equally possible. The final six chapters of this book are devoted to following Derrida from week to week as he confronts these themes and questions through this final year of his final seminar. I have thus tried always to keep in mind that this is a seminar and not a book prepared for publication, a book that could have been rewritten and where the first chapter might have been written last or the last first. I try always to recall that while Derrida had a pretty good idea at the very beginning of the year what figures and texts he would be treating, the seminar inevitably developed, got inflected, and so was transformed from week to week. Derrida will keep to his initial plan to read Heidegger's 1929–30 seminar in conjunction with *Robinson Crusoe*, but he will constantly find himself being drawn or led elsewhere. We thus see Derrida responding week by week both to world events—9/11, the American invasion of Iraq in March 2003—and more personal ones, such as the death of Maurice Blanchot in February 2003. All this makes the seminar a very different genre than the book and lends it a very different tone, a very different temporality and relationship to history. What I say in Chapter 4 regarding the temporality of deconstruction in general finds, I believe, striking confirmation in this strange seminar, which begins with "I" (*je*) and ends with "*Walten*."

In *The Animal That Therefore I Am*, Derrida himself remarks on the unique genre of the seminar, in this case, once again, in reference to Heidegger's seminar of 1929–30, dates that, as I will remark upon again in this work, could well have interested Derrida or drawn his attention for other reasons:

> One can see how it advances in the final analysis: it is a seminar; one sees its different stages; one sees Heidegger coming back each week, writing his seminar, I suppose, from week to week—which means that I find this text at the same time very strong, obeying an unusual and somewhat baroque necessity, somewhat strange in its composi-

tion, and if I had time, I would have liked to do justice as much to the status, to the method, and to the most particular procedure employed by this text, which should be followed, as a result, stage by stage. (*ATT* 151)

Derrida goes on to say that he would "like to do justice to this text because it is so rich," to follow it "step by step," paying close attention, for example, to the role played by "the exclamation mark . . . throughout this enormous discourse" (*ATT* 159). The second year of *The Beast and the Sovereign* is not quite the elaborate commentary on Heidegger that Derrida once envisioned, but it is the closest we will ever get to such a commentary. While this book has no pretention to follow Derrida's seminar with this degree of rigor, right down, for example, to its use of punctuation marks, it does make an attempt to follow Derrida week by week as he interrogates and is himself interrogated by questions of originary violence, prayer, mourning, phantasms of burial and cremation, the archive, and survival, questions that always concerned Derrida but that came to press upon him all the more insistently and urgently in the winter and spring of 2003.

This, then, is where Derrida leaves us at the end of the second volume of *The Beast and the Sovereign*, at the end of some four decades of seminars, somewhere between burial and cremation, recuperation and loss, between what he calls, and not without some humor, as we will see, the clan or religious order of the *inhumants* and that of the *incinerants*. He leaves us with this alternative, at the same time as he sends us back to his prior works on Heidegger, as well as to all his other works on death and on mourning, though also—for these are always inextricably related—on the trace and the tradition, on inheritance and the archive, on life and survival, themes or questions that had preoccupied him from the very beginning and that cannot but concern us too as we continue to read, translate, and comment on these seminars, that is, as we continue to help inflect, transform, and disseminate this absolutely unique corpus and this truly remarkable and as yet barely explored archive.

From the corpse, then, to the corpus and the archive: I began this brief account of the first two published volumes of Derrida's seminars by recalling that it was not Derrida himself but those close to him, and ultimately his family, who ended up "deciding" to publish what I have characterized as his "other corpus." It was the "other"—not Derrida—who decided what should be done with Derrida's remains. And this was, perhaps, perfectly in keeping with Derrida's own wishes, for in the midst of the second volume of *The Beast and the Sovereign*, buried right in the middle of what would turn out to be his final seminar, we find this very strange but also very poignant definition of the "other"—this infamous "other" of French contemporary philosophy that Derrida had treated in various ways from the very beginning of his work right up to the end: "the other, the others, are precisely those who always might die after me, survive me, and have at their disposal what remains of me, my remains. . . . That's what is meant, has always been meant, by 'other'" (*BS 2* 126–127/188–189). The other is thus the one who is left to decide what to do with my remains, with my cadaver or my archive. No matter how clearly one expresses one's wishes, no matter how imperiously one tries to impose one's will through what is called a Last Will and Testament, the decision comes down always—without exception—to the other.

A year and a half after Derrida wrote and then spoke these words regarding the other during the second year of *The Beast and the Sovereign* seminar, the heirs of Derrida would be put to the test of this structural law by having to decide exactly how to proceed with both Derrida's body and his archive, his corpse and his corpus. With the publication of the seminars, we too are now among those "others" who are left to decide—what we call *decide*—just how and, first of all, whether to take up this other corpus and read it.

1

Derrida's Flair
(For the Animals to Follow . . .)

You have to hand it to him: He had a certain flair, Jacques Derrida did, and it was for that that he was often criticized, sometimes even denounced, and especially by other philosophers. He had a certain flair in his person, to be sure, but especially in his language, in the way he did philosophy, in what we naïvely like to call his *style*, and this is no doubt what drew the greatest fire from his detractors. He had a flair for language, true, but also for argument, for the ways in which philosophical argument must always be tracked through the thickets of language, and claims, no matter however universal or abstract, must always be ferreted out and picked apart through the idioms of particular languages, and in his case, for the most part, the French language. Thus Derrida demonstrated that even in philosophy the nets and snares we use to pursue our game, the signs we follow to pursue the objects of our chase, are always in some way complicit with and determined by what they seek. In other words, the hunter is always in part—though only in part—determined by the game he is pursuing and the game he is playing.

That is why Derrida had no illusions about the possibility of the philosopher ever simply surveying the objects of his or her pursuit from above, of observing objects from on high without having to put his or her nose to the ground in order to follow the traces. And he knew, of course, that when one is following a scent or reading a sign, rather than surveying a field or describing an object from above, the risk is always great of being thrown off the path or getting caught oneself along the way. That is why, for Derrida, the philosopher needs not only a capacity for clear and reasoned argument but also—and there is no better term here—a certain *flair*, that is, a particularly developed sense of olfaction, or let us just say it, a particularly keen sense of smell. While the French verb *flairer* means quite explicitly to sense, to sniff, to pick up a scent, or, as we might say, to follow one's nose, the English word *flair* retains at least some of the flavor or scent of the French from which it is derived when it suggests a knack, talent, or bent for something, as when we speak of a particularly good student having a flair for philosophy, a "keenness" or "instinctive discernment," a nose or sense for it.

In this first chapter, I would like to suggest that, in the last decade or so of his life and work, Derrida demonstrated a particularly keen sense for the animal, for the theme of the animal or of animals in philosophy, and that he followed this theme with an unparalleled doggedness in the book that was published after his death, *The Animal That Therefore I Am*, and in the two years of his seminar *The Beast and the Sovereign*. Derrida demonstrates in these works an extraordinarily developed sense, an extraordinary *flair*, for following or tracking the ways in which philosophy has traditionally treated the animal, opposing the animal—the entire animal world, as we will see, and not just particular animals—to the human by denying the animal and granting the human a series of attributes ranging from language, reason, culture, and technology to mourning and a relationship to death, from the capacity to respond or to weep to the ability to lie or to promise, attributes that will then be at the center of the human's definition of himself and, as a result, at the center of his philosophy.

I would thus like to follow Derrida here as he follows this argument regarding the animal in *The Animal That Therefore I Am* and in *The Beast and the Sovereign*. I will try to retrace Derrida's footsteps as he reads the traces of the animal in a philosophical tradition that runs from Plato and Aristotle to Heidegger and Levinas, a trail that Derrida himself could never have known he would end up taking when he set out but that, in retrospect, we can and, I think, we are now obliged to follow in the extraordinary corpus he has left us on this subject. If I have thus begun by recalling Derrida's relationship to language, and the differences between languages, between the French *flairer* and the English *flair*, for example, it is in order to suggest, along with Derrida, that language is never transparent in philosophy and that one must always follow Derrida's tracks in both English and in French, even when the translation is as intelligent, lucid, rigorous, and inventive as David Wills's translation of *The Animal That Therefore I Am* and Geoffrey Bennington's of *The Beast and the Sovereign*.

If Derrida follows what might appear to be a rather unorthodox theme for a philosopher—the question of the animal, and particularly of the animal in relation to human beings—it is because this theme is uncritically present, dogmatically present, indeed almost omnipresent in philosophy from the very beginning. The thickets and brambles through which Derrida will track down the presence of the animal will thus not be extraphilosophical but, precisely, intraphilosophical, not only contemporaries such as Levinas and Lacan but also Heidegger, Schmitt, Rousseau, Hobbes, Machiavelli, Descartes, Montaigne, Aristotle, and from the very beginning, therefore, Plato. Derrida thus did not invent this theme or trope for philosophy or go poaching animals outside philosophy in order to smuggle them in over its border. Though the animal appears oftentimes at the most uncritical moments of philosophical texts, and often without theoretical justification, it—they—populate philosophy from its very inception. One need only recall, for example, the enormous bestiary deployed by Plato to characterize Socrates alone, who is compared in the dialogues not only to a midwife, shepherd, captain, doctor, or philosopher king, but to everything from a gadfly, torpedo fish, bee, and snake to a goose, swan, stork, even a blood hound, as we see in the *Parmenides*, where Zeno says with obvious humor but also approval and admiration that Socrates follows the "argument with a scent as keen as a Laconian hound's" (*Parmenides* 128c), proof that Derrida was in good company in having a certain *flair* for philosophy. Or, again, one need only recall within the *Republic* the way in which the guardians are compared to watch dogs, the desiring part of the soul to a multiheaded beast, and the tyrant to a wolf—this latter example being at the center of the first year of *The Beast and the Sovereign* seminar. And then there would be Plato's pervasive use not only of the animal *in* his work but of the trope of the hunt *for* the very work of philosophy, not only, as we just saw, the necessity of having a certain flair for argument and dialectic but, in later dialogues such as *Phaedrus*, *Statesman*, and *Sophist*, the necessity prescribed by that method called *diairesis* or division of dividing concepts along their natural joints, as if the conceptual world or landscape were an enormous sacrificial beast that was to be divvied or carved up along its natural articulations.[1] It thus does not take too much digging or sniffing around to come to see that Derrida may not be overstating his case when he argues in *The Animal That Therefore I Am* that philosophy's incorporation of the animal within its own project, and the singular line it draws and redraws between the human and all other animals, is a "gesture" that seems "to constitute philosophy as such, the philosopheme itself" (*ATT* 40).

It is this dogmatic and for the most part uncritical and unjustified division between the human animal and all other animals that Derrida draws our attention to and takes aim at in *The Animal That Therefore I Am*. First published in French in 2006 and then in English translation in 2008, this posthumous work is the complete version of a long lecture Derrida delivered in July 1997 at a ten-day conference devoted to his work at Cerisy-la-Salle in Normandy, France.[2] As I recalled in the introduction, the general title for the Cerisy conference, chosen by Derrida himself, was "The Autobiographical Animal," and, as if to sign this conference with his own autobiographical flourish, the paper Derrida delivered as part of that conference was read on July 15, 1997, that is, on his sixty-seventh birthday, and it lasted an almost inhuman nine hours.[3] I recall all this as background for reading a work that was presented at a conference that was not just any conference for Derrida and on a theme that was, for him, not just any theme. Hence Derrida demonstrates in some of the earlier pages of *The Animal That Therefore I Am* that he had in effect been tracking the philosophical treatment of animals—as well as, I should add, the very notion or quasi-concept of *flair*—from almost the very beginning of his work.[4] One might be tempted to think that in these pages the author doth protest and self-justify too much were the list of texts treating the animal not so extensive, from early works such as "Plato's Pharmacy," *Signsponge*, "White Mythology," *Glas*, and *The Post Card* up through "Circumfession," "Fourmis," "Heidegger's Hand," *Politics of Friendship*, *Specters of Marx*, "A Silkworm of One's Own," and so on and so forth (*ATT* 35–39). And we can now say in retrospect that Derrida's meditations on the animal and on the relationship between the human and the animal would not end in 1997 but would continue right up to his death in 2004. Indeed these themes became constants in his work, not only in relationship to what is proper to man but also, and especially, in relationship to the theme of sovereignty, a theme that would become, as I argued in the introduction, dominant in the final decade of his work and, especially, in *The Beast and the Sovereign*. We will thus want to keep in mind that this work on the animal was hardly the first in Derrida's corpus and that it would develop into a long meditation on the proximity between the beast and the sovereign, both of whom are either above or before the law, who either see without being seen, with a sovereign gaze that makes the law insofar as it is above it, or who see and are seen seeing from a place that is outside or before the law—from what might be called "a wholly other origin," if not, as we will see, another origin of the world (*ATT* 13).

It is thus surely no accident that *The Animal That Therefore I Am* opens with a scene of seeing or of gazing, the unexpected and somewhat uncanny scene of Derrida describing the experience of suddenly finding himself being looked at naked by his cat. For many, this would be one of those moments when Derrida could rightly be accused of making a show of his flair, beginning a philosophical work with an autobiographical description of an experience that is prephilosophical and rather ordinary, the experience of coming out of the shower and being looked at naked by one's household cat. But Derrida could not be more serious in this opening scene, this sort of counter-Genesis that recounts the genesis of his work on animals, as the gaze of the other, in this case the animal other, is situated in relationship to the origin of shame or modesty as well as the culture and technics of clothing. What happens, asks Derrida, when a philosopher lets himself be gazed at naked by a cat and then tries to think this experience *philosophically*? This scene of a human being first *looked at* rather than looking, an object for the gaze of another rather than a subject whose gaze seeks to see and to know the object before it, sets the stage for the rest of Derrida's analysis and accounts for its many methodological reversals. In *The Animal That Therefore I Am*, it is the animal that is first seen seeing and the human that is first seen seen—a simple reversal that is enough to reorient an entire philosophical tradition of thinking the animal other.

Derrida thus treats the question of the animal and of the *flair* of the animal in philosophy, but he does so by rethinking philosophical argument and method in terms of that flair. By comparing his own way of proceeding in *The Animal That Therefore I Am* to that of an animal sniffing its way along, picking up a scent and following it wherever it leads, returning to its own tracks from time to time to pick up the trace or scent of another, even when that other is oneself, Derrida puts the very question of *flair* and its relative exclusion from philosophical interest at the center of his own work: "To put it differently, one would have to ask oneself *first of all* what there is about scent [*flair*] and smell in man's relation to the *animot*"—a neologism I will explain in a moment—"and why this zone of sensibility is so neglected or reduced to a secondary position in philosophy and in the arts" (*ATT* 55). In the opening scene of *The Animal That Therefore I Am*, it is the cat that looks and gazes and Derrida who is seen, Derrida who scratches and sniffs, who uses his flair to find his way through a philosophical tradition that attempts to understand and speak of the difference between the human and the animal. The original French title of the book, *L'animal que donc je suis*, means not only "the animal that therefore I am [*suis*]" but "the animal that therefore I follow [*suis*]," or, as in Genesis, "the animal that therefore I, the human, come after [*suis*]," the animal I follow, therefore, but then also the animal to which I, as man, will assign names and over which I—and this is where Derrida begins parting ways with the original Genesis—will have dominion.

While we have all probably had some version of this experience of being seen naked by an animal, seen and exposed, genitals and all, and while we have all probably felt the confused embarrassment that accompanies such an experience, the task for Derrida the philosopher is to think the experience of this gaze philosophically—something, he says in a rather bold claim, has never really been done in the history of philosophy since it would have called into question our very assurance of a singular and indivisible limit distinguishing the human from the animal. Listen to how Derrida couches this claim in the form of a challenge:

> At the risk of being mistaken and of having one day to make honorable amends (which I would willingly accept to do), I'll venture to say that never, on the part of any great philosopher from Plato to Heidegger, or anyone at all who takes on, *as a philosophical question in and of itself*, the question called that of the animal and of the limit between the animal and the human, have I noticed a protestation *based on principle*, and especially not a protestation that amounts to anything, against the general singular that is *the animal*. (*ATT* 40)[5]

This is, to be sure, a rather strong claim and a sweeping challenge. Derrida seems to leave himself some wiggle room, it should be noted, by suggesting that while certain philosophers might well have called the singular limit between the animal and the human into question, they would not have done so *as philosophers* but rather as poets, thinkers, or writers—anything but philosophers. This is not some historical contingency, therefore, but a necessity that stems from the very nature of philosophy itself. When it comes to the line or limit between the animal and the human, "*all* philosophers," Derrida writes and emphasizes, "have judged that limit to be single and indivisible"; it is, as we heard him say, a gesture that "constitutes philosophy as such" (*ATT* 40).

There would thus seem to be, according to Derrida, two types of thinkers about animals. First, there would seem to be those who have never been seen or who never saw themselves being seen by an animal gaze. Such thinkers would have thus never taken account of this gaze theoretically or philosophically because they would have never experienced themselves being seen from what Derrida calls "a wholly other origin" (*ATT* 13). This phrase "wholly other origin" at once anticipates the argument to come and recalls Derrida's early analyses in *Voice and Phenomenon* and elsewhere of Husserlian intersubjectivity, and particularly of the fifth *Cartesian Medi-*

tation in which the alter ego is said by Husserl to be accessible to the subject only by means of analogical appresentation. The suggestion already seems to be that the gaze of the animal recalls this other origin as much as, if not actually more than, the gaze of the other human being, since this wholly other would not be so easily understood as an alter ego or as a brother or member of the same community. This "wholly other origin," this origin that is at least as other as any other, might thus be even more appropriate for rethinking a certain humanistic and fraternalistic thought of community, more appropriate, perhaps, for thinking not only the animal other but the human one (see *ATT* 12).

The second type of thinker of the animal would consist of those "who admit to taking upon themselves the address that an animal addresses to them" but who do so as poets rather than as philosophers, since "thinking concerning the animal, if there is such a thing, derives from poetry" (*ATT*, 7). In other words, it is essentially in poetry or as a poet that one has traditionally addressed animals and allowed oneself to be addressed by them. It is thus surely no coincidence that the texts of Derrida where the animal is most prominent are among his most poetic and that in the one text where Derrida tries to address the very essence of poetry—"*Che cos'è la poesia?*" "What is poetry?"—an animal, the hedgehog, stands, or rather is rolled up in a ball, at its center (*ATT* 7). It is also surely no coincidence that, in both *The Animal That Therefore I Am* and *The Beast and the Sovereign*, poets and poetry are brought into the discussion even more than they usually are in Derrida's work, from the fables of La Fontaine to the works of Paul Celan, D. H. Lawrence, and Lewis Carroll.

Derrida thus approaches the question of the relationship between the human and the animal by using poetry and sometimes by being inventive like a poet, but he does this always by questioning and arguing *as a philosopher*, since it is only as a philosopher, I would argue, that he will be able to put into question a whole series of philosophical claims or principles on the basis of which the singular limit between the human and the animal has typically been drawn. In order, therefore, to intervene in the philosophical tradition and within its philosophemes, and in order to mark the fact that no philosopher *qua* philosopher has ever protested "the general singular that is *the animal*," that is, that no philosopher has protested against the violent grouping together of everything from the worm to the chimpanzee, the lizard to the dog, the protozoon to the elephant, under this general singular name *animal*, Derrida invents, in French, a word of his own—the *animot*. As Marie-Louise Mallet, the editor of *The Animal That Therefore I Am*, writes in her preface to the book:

As a response to that first violence Derrida invents the word *animot*, which, when spoken, has the plural *animaux*, heard within the singular, recalling the extreme diversity of animals that "the animal" erases, and which, when written, makes it plain that this word [*mot*] "the animal" is precisely only a word. (*ATT* x)

It is in response to the violence with which philosophers have grouped all these different kinds of creatures or critters under the label of "the animal" that Derrida invents a word that draws attention to the fact that "the animal" is not some natural category that has been simply picked out by human perception and language but, precisely, an age-old neologism and an invention of man. The neologism *animot* is thus not some play on words designed to display Derrida's linguistic inventiveness and flair; it is an invented or created word that reminds us that the French word *l'animal*—and the same would hold for the English *animal*—is, precisely, as a word, not natural, not simply the result of following some natural articulation between humans and all the other, incredibly diverse creatures in the world. Derrida writes, "The animal is a word, it is an appellation that men have instituted, a name they have given themselves the right and the authority to give to the living other" (*ATT* 23). Notice, then, that like that other invented word of the 1960s, *différance*, the difference between the two valences of the word can only be read and not heard, tracked through the written sign while being effaced in the spoken one. And while the word *différance* is itself both the name of and the effect of *différance*, the word *animot* both names the plurality of animals and draws attention to the process of naming of which it is an effect. Hence. the word *animot* is a name that describes and a word that performs what it describes, and unlike *l'animal*—which, we might say, conceals the *mal* (the evil) within it—*animot* makes absolutely no pretension to being natural or to being a unity. It wears its status as a hybrid right on its surface, in its letters. Fashioned out of two different words, the plural of animal, *animaux*, and the word for word, *mot*, it is not unlike those composite animals found in mythology that philosophers are so fond of invoking or reinventing in their meditations or thought experiments. It is itself, then, a sort of centaur, satyr, or chimera of language—yet another human invention with regard to the animal.[6]

But even before introducing this invented word and this thesis regarding the history of philosophy, Derrida begins *The Animal That Therefore I Am*, as I recalled earlier, with a sort of Edenic or primal scene, a scene of genesis, indeed a scene of the genesis of his thinking about the animal: the experience of being looked at naked by his cat, being looked at and feeling modesty or shame beneath the gaze of his cat, shame even for feeling shame.[7] Derrida suggests that this very experience of being seen naked leads to thinking itself and, as we will see, to philosophy. "The animal looks at us, and we are naked before it. Thinking perhaps begins there" (*ATT* 29). The question will thus be, in the end, whether this gaze of the animal, this interrogation of the human by the animal, or, rather, by this one absolutely unique animal other, is repressed or denied—a gesture that would be co-extensive, Derrida seems to suggest, with the entire history of philosophy—or whether it is what provokes a new thinking of the animal, of the animal in relationship to the human, and of a differential relationship between animals themselves. By broaching the question of the animal not by means of "the animal" in its generality, the animal as a concept, and not even by means of a particular species of animals, but by means of a very real and individual animal—Derrida's household cat, an absolutely singular, unique cat that will have one day surprised him naked with its gaze—Derrida quite literally reorients our philosophical gaze with regard to this question.

By opening *The Animal That Therefore I Am* with this primal scene, Derrida begins putting into question a whole series of attributes that are typically thought to be proper to man. He writes, for example: "It is thought that nudity is proper to man, an awareness of nudity, that which, in effect, transforms an absence of clothes into a veritable nudity" (*ATT* 4). Because animals are thought to be born naked without any consciousness of their nakedness, they would not really be naked at all. The human would be the only animal born truly naked because it is the only one with an awareness of its nakedness, the only one who feels shame for its nudity, and thus the only one who has to invent the supplement of clothing in order to hide that nakedness. As Plato's *Protagoras* already speculated, both nakedness and clothing would be proper to the human (see *Protagoras* 320c–328d).

Nakedness, clothing, shame—this is just the beginning of a very long and open-ended list of attributes that are regularly granted to the human and denied the animal, a list that includes everything from speech, reason, *logos*, history, laughter, imitation, lying, feigning to feign, a relation to death as such, mourning, tears, burying one's dead, gift-giving, technology, promising, the trace, and so on. For Derrida, this list of what is considered proper to man or to the human is not a mere aggregation of attributes or capacities but, precisely, a "configuration." "For that very reason," he writes, "it can never be limited to a single trait and it is never closed" (*ATT* 5). We will thus need to think how, in a given discourse, the animal's supposed inability to respond is related, for example, to its inability to laugh or to cry, or how a technology of clothing that is attributed to the human and human alone is related to shame, or how a supposed relationship to death and the animal's lack thereof defines the human's and the animal's respective relationships to the world.

How, then, does Derrida approach this configuration in order to begin to interrogate and destabilize it? To show this, let me begin by citing a rather lengthy passage from *The Animal That Therefore I Am*, repeated or republished in *The Beast and the Sovereign*, where Derrida lays out not only many of the themes of the book and of his subsequent seminar but, more importantly, the argumentative strategy he adopts in his analysis of them. Speaking here in the context of a reading of Lacan but expressing, it would seem, the approach he takes in the entire work, Derrida writes:

> It is *not just* a matter of asking whether one has the right to refuse the animal such and such a power (speech, reason, experience of death, mourning, culture, institutions, technics, clothing, lying, pretense of pretense, covering of tracks, gift, laugher, crying, respect, etc.—the list is necessarily without limit, and the most powerful philosophical tradition in which we live has refused the "animal" *all of that*). It *also* means asking whether what calls itself human has the right rigorously to attribute to man, which means therefore to attribute to himself, what he refuses the animal, and whether he can ever possess the *pure, rigorous, indivisible* concept, as such, of that attribution. (*ATT* 135; *BS 1* 130)

Two points about this passage—one about content and one about method. First, almost every one of these attributes denied the animal but granted to the human—the trace, technique, mourning, the gift, a relation to death—is treated by Derrida in some detail in other published texts, and often quite explicitly in relation to the animal. For example, this question of the nature of the trace, of whether the human alone is capable of the trace or whether the animal too can leave or efface traces, can be traced all the way back to the first part of *Of Grammatology*, published in article-form in *Critique* in 1965. In some of the most challenging passages of that work, Derrida suggested that the concept of the trace must first be liberated from the anthropocentric prejudice that restricts it to the human and then extended to all living beings.

With regard to method, we see Derrida in this passage deploying an argumentative strategy that can be found throughout *The Animal That Therefore I Am* and *The Beast and the Sovereign*. He begins by looking at a philosophical discourse that grants the human and denies the animal some attribute—language, technology, culture, mourning, a relationship to death, and so on. His next move is then to contest, briefly and sometimes with reference to ethology, primatology, or zoology, the supposed *fact* that the animal does not have such and such an ability or attribute. He argues that philosophers must begin to take seriously the progress that has been made in the sciences on these questions, since some of the most rigorous and thoughtful work in the sciences would suggest that some animals perhaps do respond and not just react, or do mourn, or have a culture, and so on (see *ATT* 89). Moreover, because such scientific work rarely claims that the animal as such has or does not have a particular attribute but that, for example, the *elephant* mourns or the *pigeon* can respond, taking such work seriously within philosophy would already have the effect of breaking up and multiplying the differences within that monolithic category called "the animal." Recent advances in ethology or primatology should thus cause us to hesitate to assert with such confidence that man has speech or technology and that the animal—the animal in general—does not.

But because Derrida is a philosopher and not a primatologist or ethologist, he does not want to rely too heavily on this kind of evidence or get himself into a debate in a field where he is hardly an expert and where the standards of argument and evidence are obviously much different from those in philosophy. Hence, Derrida typically moves very quickly to the other side of the question in order to contest not the *fact* that animals do not have such and such a capacity or attribute but the *principle* on the basis of which philosophers have claimed that humans *do*. He does this first by questioning the *confidence* with which philosophers attribute some capacity to the human while denying it to the animal. As he puts it, invoking once again that notion of flair, he tries "to track, to sniff [*flairer*], to trail, and to follow some of the reasons they [that is, philosophers] adduce for the so confident usage they make . . . of words such as, therefore, *animal* and *I*" (*ATT* 33). Derrida thus contests the confidence with which philosophers have used such words and supposedly secure concepts in order at once to distinguish in dogmatic fashion animals from the human and systematically efface the animal within man. "The critical or deconstructive reading" that Derrida calls for and tries to carry out would thus "seek less to restitute to the animal or to such an insect the powers that it is not certain to possess (even if that sometimes seems possible) than to wonder whether one could not claim as much relevance for this type of analysis in the case of the human" (*ATT* 173 n. 9). Derrida will therefore question, for example, the *fact* that certain animals cannot respond but only react, but he will quickly move on to question the philosophical *principle* behind the claim that humans themselves really can respond, that they possess a form of language that can really be distinguished from a mere code. He will thus challenge such a philosophical claim by arguing not simply that certain animals perhaps can respond but that even in the most seemingly spontaneous human response there is always an irreducible element of automatism, of machinelike or not fully conscious or intentional reaction, of expropriation into a language that is coded—elements or characteristics that would compromise from the start anything like a pure response.[8] It is this second move that allows Derrida then to question whether there is anything like a response *as such*, a response that would remain pure and uncontaminated by reaction. Hence, Derrida will call into question the purity and indivisibility of the line distinguishing response from reaction in a thinker such as Lacan, where a robust theory of the unconscious, a logic of repetition as iterability and automaticity, and an emphasis on the materiality of language—all traits of Lacanian psychoanalysis—should have caused that line to be fractured and multiplied.

This double questioning of both fact and principle forms what Derrida calls the "logical matrix" of his argument, and it leads to unsettling the assurance and confidence with which theorists draw the line between the human and the animal (*ATT* 95). Derrida thus writes, contesting the concepts of purity, rigor, and indivisibility that he had questioned in innumerable other contexts in relationship now to the line between humans and animals:

> My hesitation concerns only the purity, the rigor, and the indivisibility of the frontier that separates—already with respect to "us humans"—reaction from response and in consequence, especially, the purity, rigor, and indivisibility of the concept of responsibility that is derived from it. (*ATT* 125; *BS 1* 118–119)

We see something very similar in Derrida's reading of Heidegger one chapter later in *The Animal That Therefore I Am* and then in *The Beast and the Sovereign*. Faced with Heidegger's claim that only the human or Dasein can leave or let beings be, Derrida will go on to claim not that animals too can let beings be, that they too have access to the *as such* of beings, but that perhaps the human never has access to this *as such* or can never simply let beings be without some project, drive, desire, or design coming to intervene (*ATT* 159–160).[9] Derrida's strategy is thus to show that there is no pure and simple *as such*, a strategy, he adds, that "would presume a radical reinterpretation of what is living" (*ATT* 160).

Derrida repeats and rearticulates this strategy throughout both *The Animal That Therefore I Am* and the two years of his seminar *The Beast and the Sovereign*.[10] It tells us much, I think, about Derrida's approach to questions elsewhere and about some of the long-held methodological motivations behind deconstruction. As Derrida puts it near the opening of *The Animal That Therefore I Am*, "I have thus never believed in some homogeneous continuity between what calls *itself* man and what *he* calls the animal. I am not about to begin to do so now. That would be worse than sleepwalking, it would simply be too asinine [*bête*]" (*ATT* 30). Hence Derrida's strategy consists *not* in effacing or erasing the limit between the animal and the human but, rather, in "problematizing the purity and indivisibility of a line between [for example,] reaction and response" (*ATT* 126), "in multiplying its figures, in complicating, thickening, delinearizing, folding, and dividing the line precisely by making it increase and multiply" (*ATT* 29). His aim was thus always not to erase the limit between the human and the animal but to question that limit and multiply differences and distinctions between various animals, between animals and humans, and then—and perhaps especially—within the human itself (see *ATT* 159).

To break up the monolithic category "animal" and problematize the putatively singular and indivisible line between the human and the animal, one should thus ask not simply *whether* animals have language or culture or *whether* they can lie or erase their own traces but, for example, *which* animals couple, *which* dream or have a mirror stage, or indeed, *which* have a gaze before which I can feel myself to be naked and so feel shame (see *ATT* 62–63). Instead of simply asking whether the animal *can* respond and not just react, one should distinguish between different forms of reaction, different kinds of self-relation or autoaffection. When such distinctions are made, one can then begin to see that the human animal shares certain qualities with some animals and not others, and shares them to a greater degree with some rather than others. Rather than a single line distinguishing the human from the animal, multiple lines are thus drawn and differences of degree take the place of opposition, differences between animals and the human but also differences among animals and among humans. Derrida can therefore at once affirm that there is indeed "something like a discontinuity, rupture, or even abyss" between the human and the animal and yet also claim that when it comes to possessing language or having a relationship to death it is less a question of opposition than of difference (*ATT* 30).

We thus see Derrida here, as elsewhere, attempting to rethink binary oppositions in the name of difference. This is the case, as we have just seen, for species difference, but it is also the case for sexual difference. *The Beast and the Sovereign*, *La* bête *et le* souverain, begins in fact not with a sentence or even a fragment but with the two gendered pronouns *La* and *le*; "*La* . . . *le*," writes Derrida at the very beginning of the seminar, putting front and center the question of sexual difference that he will have pursued in innumerable texts since at least *Glas*, a book from 1974 that must be read, let me note in passing—since I spoke in the introduction of the relationship between Derrida's previously published works and his seminars—in conjunction with his 1971–72 seminar on "La Famille de Hegel."[11] One of the underlying arguments of the first volume of *The Beast and the Sovereign* is in fact that the relationship between the beast and the sovereign is inextricably related to the supposed opposition between what we call the sexes. Because, as Derrida has demonstrated in many different contexts, philosophical discourses are never made up of discrete, unrelated claims but always of a network or configuration of analogically established and hierarchically ordered relations, it is impossible to think the animal in relation to the human without also thinking the relationship and putative affinity in some of the most classical philosophical discourses of the West between the animal, women, children, and slaves, on the one hand, and the human and free adult male, on the other. Though this systematic configuration in Western thought is today hardly news, it is developed in a particularly striking and incisive way in *The Beast and the Sovereign*, teaching us much along the way not only about the function of language, and particularly analogy, in the construction of philosophical arguments but about the way Derrida goes about questioning this analogical structure.

Again, it is less the supposed fact of the animal not possessing some ability that Derrida contests but the confidence with which a line is drawn in principle and often with little regard to the facts between the human and the animal. This confidence, as we will see in a moment, has its own hidden origins, but for the moment it is important to underscore the way in which Derrida's questions with regard to the principles by which a philosopher has distinguished the animal from the human often end up putting into question that philosopher's entire ontological, epistemological, or ethical program.[12] For example, Levinas's apparent restriction of the category of the other to the human has repercussions, Derrida shows, for his entire ethical theory. By challenging Levinas's views regarding the animal, by posing the question of the animal other or the animal as other, the possibility, in short, of thinking the animal with a face, or the animal as being able to respond and say "Here I am," Derrida exposes the "profound anthropocentrism and humanism" of Levinas's thought and calls into the question the assumptions upon which Levinas's notions of alterity, exteriority, community, fraternity, and, thus, ethics rest.

The philosophical stakes and consequences of such questions could thus not be larger. As Élisabeth de Fontenay puts it in her excellent analysis of *The Animal That Therefore I Am* in *Sans offenser le genre humain*, the animal is a kind of "Trojan horse" that Derrida introduces into the citadel of metaphysics in order to question, if not overthrow, its philosophical oppositions and destabilize its structure.[13] By contesting the purity and rigor of the line between reaction and response, by introducing "a nonoppositional and infinitely differentiated, qualitative, and intensive difference between reaction and response," one ends up having to rethink the very basis of ethics, decision, and responsibility (*ATT* 126). By no longer drawing a single line between human response, on the one hand, and animal reaction, on the other, one is thereby forced to develop "another 'logic' of decision, of the response and of the event," a logic that would cause us to rethink the "historicity of ethical, juridical, or political responsibility, within another thinking of life" (*ATT* 126).

Derrida's analysis of the way philosophers have granted or denied certain capacities to animals or to humans thus leads to an even more far-reaching thesis regarding the history of philosophy itself.

> This question of the animal is not just interesting and serious in its own right. It also provides us with an indispensable intertwining thread for reading philosophers and for gaining access to a sort of secret "architectonics" in the construction—and therefore in the deconstruction—of a discursive apparatus, a coherence, if not a system. One understands a philosopher only by heeding closely what he means to demonstrate, and in reality fails to demonstrate, concerning the limit between human and animal. (*ATT* 106)

A "secret 'architectonics . . . a discursive apparatus, a coherence, if not a system": Derrida is suggesting here that the question of the animal holds not just an important but ultimately contingent place in the history of philosophy but that it is central to it and, thus, central to Derrida's reading or deconstruction of it. The question of the human or the animal having or not having language or the *logos*, or having or not having it purely, thus leads to a new take or twist on some very old themes: ever since the 1960s Derrida tracked what he called "logocentrism," that is, a privileging in Western philosophy and thought of language or of *logos*, and, depending on the context, of its relationship to phonocentrism, a privileging of speech over writing.[14] (I will return to this question of the human's privileged relation to *logos* in Chapter 5.) Elsewhere, he would speak, as is well known, of Eurocentrism, phallocentrism, or even carnophallogocentrism—neologisms that begin to look a little less precious or hyperbolic when considered in relationship to the argument advanced in *The Beast and the Sovereign* concerning the human's attribution of *logos* or the phallus to himself and his denial of it to the animal or the animal-machine, which then becomes a mere tool for human labor, experimentation, or consumption.[15] What Derrida referred to as a secret architectonics or coherence is but another aspect of this same logocentrism, that is, of the discursive apparatus that grants *logos* (speech, the symbolic, response versus reaction) to the human and not the animal. Derrida can thus argue that "logocentrism is first of all a thesis regarding the animal, the animal deprived of the *logos*" and that "this is the thesis, position, or presupposition maintained from Aristotle to Heidegger, from Descartes to Kant, Levinas, and Lacan" (*ATT* 27).[16] It is, in short, "an absolutely structuring operation throughout philosophy" (*ATT* 156).

Throughout *The Beast and the Sovereign*, Derrida will question at once this thesis or position with regard to the animal *and* the priority of the thesis or the question when it comes to engaging the animal—an approach that is reminiscent of his questioning in *Of Spirit* of the priority of the question in Heidegger and others. By questioning the priority of the thesis, Derrida is also questioning the priority of philosophy in its approach to the animal. That is no doubt why the seminar uses so many poetic examples and figures, from the fables of La Fontaine, particularly *The Wolf and the Lamb*, to Lewis Carroll and Paul Celan, whom Derrida had treated in *Shibboleth* and *Sovereignties in Question*, and whose "Meridian" raises, not coincidentally, the question of a "poetic sovereignty." This use of fables and poems then provokes additional questions about the fabular, the fantastic, and the phantasmatic, about poetry in relation to philosophy and, thus, about literature and language, idiom and translation—questions that become central to *The Beast and the Sovereign* and that I will explore more fully in Chapter 4.[17]

As for the six figures we just heard Derrida cite just a moment ago—"from Aristotle to Heidegger, from Descartes to Kant, Levinas, and Lacan" (*ATT* 27)—those are the ones Derrida treats in detail in *The Animal That Therefore I Am* and in some of the central sections of *The Beast and the Sovereign*. They are the privileged figures of the corpus that Derrida carves out within the history of philosophy or, rather, within what might be called a dominant line or lineage within that history. For there is, Derrida points out, another less prominent or dominant tradition, what might be called a countertradition within philosophy, that also needs to be recalled, revisited, and revived. Derrida will evoke, for example, Porphyry's "inexhaustible survey of the ethics of vegetarianism in Antiquity" (*ATT* 84–85) and, especially, Montaigne's "Apology for Raymond Sebond," "one of the greatest pre- or anti-Cartesian texts on the animal that exists" (*ATT* 6). It is in this latter that Montaigne questions what we earlier saw to be the focus of Derrida's critique, namely, the "naïve assurance of man" on the subject of the animal (*ATT* 6). In opposition to the dominant tradition before him and the even more dominant Cartesian tradition that would follow him, Montaigne grants the animal not only an ability to communicate but also "a capacity to respond" (*ATT* 163 n. 8).

Finally, Derrida credits Jeremy Bentham with radically transforming the terms of the debate surrounding the animal by asking not whether the animal has this or that capacity, this or that power or activity, but whether it has a certain affectivity or vulnerability, an exposure or a passion, that is, whether it—or they—can *suffer*. This question of Bentham's not only reorients or recalibrates a philosophical tradition bent on drawing a line between humans and animals on the basis of some capacity such as thought, language, or technology but allows us to rethink our relationship to the animal in terms of shared categories or experiences such as mortality, finitude, and suffering. It can also lead, Derrida seems to believe, to a new thinking and a new experience of "compassion" based on these shared experiences (see *ATT* 28).

Derrida thus evokes this countertradition throughout *The Animal That Therefore I Am*, but he spends much more time with the dominant tradition—the one that runs, as he sketches it out, from Aristotle to Descartes, Kant, Levinas, Heidegger, and Lacan—because it is this tradition, he believes, that is most widely reflected in our culture and its attitudes with regard to animals. It is here that Derrida at once widens and narrows the scope and stakes of his analysis in order to argue that what he takes to be a long-standing and quasi-pervasive attitude with regard to animals has entered a crucial phase. He does this by overlaying three additional temporal frames or epochal configurations onto the history of philosophy that has already been laid out, one frame that encompasses that history of philosophy from Aristotle to Heidegger or Levinas and two that are situated within it.

First, then, there is the much larger historical frame that encompasses much of the culture and thought of the West and Middle East (though no claims are made, it should be noted—for Derrida does draw limits even here—about the Far East). Because *The Animal That Therefore I Am* draws not only from the history of Western philosophy but also from Greek mythology and the Bible—Genesis in particular, as we have seen—Derrida speaks of a certain *sacrificial* logic that would be common to both the Greek and biblical traditions.[18] Though Derrida will tend to concentrate his analyses on a Cartesian tradition with regard to the animal, this Cartesianism will be understood as at once a profound mutation within Western philosophy and religion *and* a continuation and confirmation of that tradition. Hence, Derrida will claim that "Cartesianism belongs, beneath its mechanistic indifference, to the Judeo-Christiano-Islamic tradition of a war against the animal, of a sacrificial war that is as old as Genesis" (*ATT* 101). The hyphens that separate and join the three segments of this decasyllabic adjective are there to demonstrate that beyond all the differences there is a common tradition with regard to the animal, indeed, as he puts it elsewhere, adding a new segment to the beast, a common "Greco-Judeo-Christiano-Islamic tradition" (*ATT* 55) that would be "both Promethean and Adamic" (*ATT* 21).[19] In addition, therefore, to highlighting a philosophical tradition that privileges the human over the animal, Derrida links the story of man's dominion over animals in Genesis to God's preference for the offering of Abel, the herdsman, to that of Cain, the farmer, and to the Decalogue's silence on the question of the killing of animals. Derrida will speak of an "anthropocentric prejudice that comes down from Descartes," but comes down—and this would be the longest and most hyperbolic iteration of the bunch—"along the whole Epipromethean-Islamic-Judeo-Christian descendancy" (*ATT* 102). Surrounding and situating, then, the history of philosophy from Aristotle to Heidegger is this much larger historical and cultural frame. From the point of view of the human's relationship to and sacrifice of the animal, there is a common tradition that includes mythology, philosophy, and all three Western monotheisms or Abrahamic religions.

The second historical frame, this time within the history of philosophy, begins, as I suggested a moment ago, with Descartes. Though he puts the word in quotation marks, Derrida will nonetheless speak of a sort of "epoch" that runs "from Descartes to the present" (*ATT* 13). Diagnosing "a certain mutation between Montaigne and Descartes" (*ATT* 6), a transformation in the way we think of the animal or, indeed, of the "animal-machine," Derrida argues that this mutation is reflected in philosophy from Kant right on up to Heidegger, Levinas, and Lacan. Hence even those discourses that developed an explicit critique of the Cartesian cogito, discourses that might seem to be "the least Cartesian, the most heterogeneous vis-à-vis the mechanicism of the animal-machine, nevertheless belong to the filiation of the Cartesian *cogito*" (*ATT* 54). Derrida demonstrates in what are some of the most detailed analyses of the book that all of these figures share the belief, or what might be called the axiom, the prejudice, the presumption, or the presupposition that, for example, the animal can react but cannot respond (*ATT* 89). "The Cartesian animal, like its descendants (once again I'll try to recognize there Kant, Heidegger, Lacan, and Levinas, which also means so many others), would remain incapable of responding to true questioning" (*ATT* 84).

In a central chapter of *The Animal That Therefore I Am* entitled "And Say the Animal Responded," Derrida follows Lacan's claims regarding the capacity for language in humans and animals, and he concludes that Lacan too follows in the "Cartesian tradition of the animal-machine without language and without response" (*ATT* 119). Unable to pretend to pretend, unable to erase its traces, the animal cannot be a subject, that is, a "subject of the signifier," and so cannot have "access to the symbolic, that is to say, to the law and to whatever is held to be proper to the human" (*ATT* 120). In conformity with this Cartesian tradition, then, in what Derrida calls "the most dogmatically traditional manner," the animal would be capable of *reacting* to stimuli but unable to *respond* to questions (*ATT* 122); it would be able to emit and follow the signs of a code but would be incapable of language (*ATT* 123). The animal would thus have, according to this tradition, "neither unconscious nor language, nor the other" (*ATT* 121).

But, again, the real bite of Derrida's analysis resides not in this contestation of Lacan's claim that the animal does not have these things but in his questioning of Lacan's confidence that humans do. For the very same "logic of the unconscious . . . founded on a logic of repetition," that is, on a conception of repetition that would seem to have much more in common with reaction than response, would seem to raise serious questions about whether the human really does have a language that can be rigorously distinguished from a code, or whether the human really can spontaneously respond in a way that excludes all reaction, or, indeed, whether the human really can be distinguished on the basis of language from either the animal or the machine (*ATT* 125). Other questions would then have to be raised regarding the limits of human freedom and the nature of decision and responsibility, questions that any psychoanalysis worthy of the name would have to confront before drawing the line with such confidence between the human and the animal.[20]

What is said here about Lacan will be repeated, in essence, in Derrida's long analysis of Levinas. Despite Levinas's radical rethinking of Cartesian subjectivity on the basis of an idea of infinity that precedes, constitutes, and calls that subjectivity into question, despite a notion of the face that in its nakedness would seem to disrupt all anthropomorphism, it appears that the animal does not have a face, and so cannot be thought in terms of this idea of infinity. Despite Levinas's radical critique of the subject on the basis of alterity, "this subject of ethics, the face, remains first of all a fraternal and human face," which thus puts the animal "outside of the ethical circuit" (*ATT* 106). Derrida concludes: "in the tradition that we are tracking here, the animal, according to Levinas, seems deprived of all possibility, in fact, of all power of saying 'Here I am' and of responding, hence of all responsibility" (*ATT* 111).

Thinkers as dissimilar as Descartes, Kant, Heidegger, Levinas, and Lacan all belong, argues Derrida, to a single configuration with regard to the question of the animal, forming, as it were, "a single living body" or "a single discursive organization with several tentacles" (*ATT* 91).[21] As an explicit critique of a certain logocentric, philosophical tradition of treating the animal, *The Animal That Therefore I Am* and *The Beast and the Sovereign* thus provide a rather unique and strategic entrée not only into the themes of sovereignty and the animal but into all those—centrisms that Derrida will have been tracking from the late 1950s and early 1960s right up to the end. And it can be read as a further chapter in Derrida's long-running engagement with thinkers such as Levinas, Lacan, and Heidegger.[22] One can read what Derrida says here in the seminar about Levinas's restriction of the category of the face or of *Autrui* to the human and follow a direct line back to Derrida's 1980 essay "At This Very Moment in This Work Here I Am," or even his 1964 essay "Violence and Metaphysics," where many of the premises for this argument are already laid out.

In addition to the temporal frame that embraces the "Greco-Judeo-Christiano-Islamic tradition" (*ATT* 55) and the one within the history of Western philosophy that runs from Descartes to the present, Derrida argues throughout *The Animal That Therefore I Am* that an even more dramatic shift or mutation has taken place since about the nineteenth century and that a new "epoch" with regard to the animal must be acknowledged and analyzed. Derrida's hypothesis is that

> for about two centuries, intensely and by means of an alarming rate of acceleration . . . we who call ourselves men or humans, we who recognize ourselves in that name, have been involved in an unprecedented transformation. This mutation affects the experience of what we continue to call imperturbably, as if there were nothing to it, the animal and/or animals. (*ATT* 24)

Hence, Derrida at once points back to "the animal sacrifices of the Bible or of ancient Greece," to millennial traditions of hunting, domesticating, and exploiting animals, *and* claims that "in the course of the last two centuries these traditional forms of treatment of the animal have been turned upside down by the joint developments of zoological, ethological, biological, and genetic forms of *knowledge*," by means of everything from farming on a demographic scale that could not even be dreamed of in the past, to genetic experimentation and artificial insemination, to "the industrialization of what can be called the production for consumption of animal meat," and all of this, says Derrida, "in the service of a certain being and putative human well-being of man" (*ATT* 25). Again, Derrida wants to think together in a single configuration mankind's unprecedented technological progress over the past couple of centuries and the violence with which human's have treated animals during this same period.[23] But then there is the supplementary claim that this violence has become so extreme, that the human subjection of animals has reached such "*unprecedented proportions*" (*ATT* 25), that it is today reaching a critical phase—so critical that it has become more and more difficult to deny or repress it.

As we saw Derrida argue earlier, the dominant philosophical tradition consists of those who have not taken philosophical or theoretical account of the gaze of the animal, of being looked at by the animal. Such a tradition has not developed, however—despite the appearances—because all these philosophers have never actually experienced the gaze of an animal. Indeed all these philosophers, Derrida believes, will have *in fact* experienced such a gaze, though none will have taken it "into account in the philosophical or theoretical architecture of their discourse," that is, none will have taken it into account *in principle* (*ATT* 14). While it may thus appear "*as if* the men representing this configuration had seen without being seen, seen the animal without being seen by it," Derrida ultimately argues that we must look for another cause and so develop another symptomology (*ATT* 14; my emphasis of *as if*). Even the philosophical tendency to group all kinds of animals from the protozoon to the elephant under the general singular name "the animal" has to be considered not just mistaken but "symptomatic" (*ATT* 41). What Derrida thus diagnoses here is not negligence, ignorance, or lack of experience but a systematic *disavowal* or *denegation* whose symptoms can and must be deciphered and analyzed. In other words, the effects of this animal gaze will have left traces in these traditional discourses such that "the symptom of this disavowal remains to be deciphered," indeed must be deciphered (*ATT* 14; see 113). For this human disavowal of the animal is not "just one disavowal among others" but the very one that "institutes what is proper to man, the relation to itself of a humanity that is above all anxious about, and jealous of, what is proper to it" (*ATT* 14). Derrida is speculating here that man's attribution of all those aforementioned capacities to himself and his denial of them to the animal might well have its origin both in man's narcissistic confidence in himself and his categories and in his deeply rooted anxiety with regard to the animal, his suspicion, which is always repressed, that such attributes are not just human but animal, that, for example, the animal *can* indeed die and not just perish or that the animal *does* indeed suffer. Philosophy itself, then, or at least the dominant strain of philosophy that Derrida is reading in *The Animal That Therefore I Am* and *The Beast and the Sovereign*, the one that runs from Plato and Aristotle through Descartes and up to Heidegger, would thus be born out of both this narcissistic attribution of *logos* to the human and its concomitant denial to the animal.

To make a case for such denegation or repression, Derrida evokes here the second of what Freud calls humanity's three traumatisms, not the Copernican trauma, which displaced the centrality of man's planet in the universe, or the Freudian trauma, which displaced the centrality of consciousness in human life, but the Darwinian trauma, which replaced man's exceptional status as a created being in the world with a continuity and evolution between animals and the human (*ATT* 136). Philosophy would be suffering most acutely—indeed, it will have already suffered well before the writings of Darwin—from this Darwinian trauma, that is, from the anxiety provoked by man losing his privileged place in the kingdom of living beings and recognizing that the singular and indivisible line between the human and all other animals can no longer be maintained or justified. It is the denial or disavowal of this trauma that thus appears to be reaching a critical phase along with the unprecedented violence against animals that such disavowal is supposed to conceal.

The language of repression, denegation, or disavowal runs throughout *The Animal That Therefore I Am*, and it is juxtaposed throughout with a series of claims about what cannot be denied or can no longer be denied. Derrida argues, for example, that "no one can deny [*nier*] the suffering, fear, or panic, the terror or fright that can seize certain animals and that we humans can witness. . . . No doubt either, then, of there being within us the possibility of giving vent to a surge of compassion, even if it is then misunderstood, repressed, or denied [*dénié*], held at bay" (*ATT* 28). The contradiction here is only apparent, or rather, it actually bears witness to a logic of denegation: because we cannot deny the suffering of animals, because we cannot deny our compassion for their suffering, all we can do is deny or repress it. Adding denial upon denial, the contemporary scope and urgency of the situation makes the denial at once more and less obvious, at once easier and harder to hide from or to hide from oneself.

> No one can deny seriously any more, or for very long, that men do all they can in order to dissimulate this cruelty or to hide it from themselves; in order to organize on a global scale the forgetting or misunderstanding of this violence, which some would compare to the worst cases of genocide. . . . One should neither abuse the figure of genocide nor too quickly consider it explained away. (*ATT* 26)

Along with this recognition of our long-standing denial and dissimulation of the suffering of animals might thus come, Derrida argues, a new surge in this "surge of compassion," this "fundamental compassion" that is probably behind what Derrida considers to be the admirable and yet "problematic" notion of animal rights. It is, in any case, what arouses protest within us and promises "to awaken us to our responsibilities and our obligations vis-à-vis the living in general" and, on the basis of this, "to change even the very cornerstone . . . of the philosophical problematic of the animal" (*ATT* 26–27).

The Animal That Therefore I Am and the first year of *The Beast and the Sovereign* are thus, as one can no doubt hear, at once a sustained argument and an impassioned plea, at once a series of claims and call for change, both an analysis of the philosophical tradition with regard to the animal and an unmistakable intervention within that tradition. While Derrida thus always argues throughout these works *as a philosopher*, while his aim is always, as I have tried to show, to contest not just certain supposed facts about animals but the principles that are used to frame and interpret those facts for the benefit of the human, his language is often strident and emphatic and not without pathos. For Derrida clearly wants not just to challenge our thinking and recast our distinctions but arouse and motivate our passions. Hence, Derrida, weighing his words, will speak of a "veritable war of the species" (*ATT* 31), a war that is "probably ageless" but that, he hypothesizes, is "passing through a critical phase" (*ATT* 29). The end or goal of this war would be, he claims, to bring about nothing less than "a world without animals," that is, a world "without any animal worthy of the name and living for something other than to become a means for man: livestock, tool, meat, body, or experimental life form" (*ATT* 102; see 79–80). The aim of this "war of the species" would be to transform the animal into a pure means bereft of any value beyond its value for man, bereft of any claim to life beyond its ability to sustain or prolong human life. What remains to be thought, then—and we will return to this in the final chapter—is the relationship between this war and the originary violence that will have made it possible, the relationship between the sovereignty of the human and the sovereignty beyond sovereignty to which even the human must yield.

As we have seen, Derrida's analyses seek to question both the human denial of certain capacities to the animal and the human attribution of these same capacities to the human. His aim is always to rethink the line between the animal and the human, to take up the animal within the human, and to do so for the sake of both animals and the human. Derrida's call to take up the question of the animal thus aims both to question man's confidence and assurance in himself, to analyze the traces of a certain denegation, denial, or repression that is perhaps at the origin of this confidence, and then—by working through or thinking through this trauma—to question, clarify, and multiply the lines separating the human from the animal so as to intervene in this veritable war of the species. That is the ethical motivation, so to speak, behind *The Animal That Therefore I Am* and *The Beast and the Sovereign* and the contemporary urgency that presses Derrida to speak in these works with such passion and, yes, sometimes, with such flair.

2

"If you could take just two books . . ."

Derrida at the Ends of the World with
Heidegger and Robinson Crusoe

It began, no doubt, as an exercise in wistful speculation, an entertaining thought experiment, what they call in French *une hypothèse d'école*, and at some point it became a popular parlor game and a good final-round question for all the dating games of the world: "If you were going to be stranded on a desert island and you could take just *two books* with you, what two books would you take?"[1] During the academic year 2002–2003, in the course of what would turn out to be his final seminar, the second year of *The Beast and the Sovereign*, Jacques Derrida essentially poses himself this question and then answers it in a rather surprising way. His two books, the two books with which he would seclude or isolate himself for the entirely of his final seminar, would be Heidegger's 1929–30 seminar *The Fundamental Concepts of Metaphysics: World, Finitude, Solitude* and Daniel Defoe's *Robinson Crusoe*. Derrida thus did not choose the Bible (which was in effect Robinson Crusoe's unintended choice), or Rousseau's *Confessions* or Proust's *Recherche* (Derrida's first language was, after all, French) or *Finnegans Wake* (which Joyce said it would take the critics generations to understand), but *Robinson Crusoe*. And he did not choose the collected works of Aristotle (which Heidegger said every philosopher should study for fifteen years before doing anything else—but who has time for that?— and so a shipwreck would be a welcome opportunity), or Hegel's *Phenomenology*, or even Heidegger's own *Being and Time* (a twentieth-century classic by any reckoning), but a much lesser-known lecture course given by Heidegger two years after *Being and Time*.[2]

Though this playful question regarding the books one would take to a desert island usually aims simply to clarify personal penchants, orientations, and commitments, to provide a glimpse into someone's personality or character, it is almost always enveloped in a sort of apocalyptic haze: What two books would you take with you to the ends of the world, what historical artifacts would you preserve at the end of history, what works would you save at the end of the world. In this chapter I would like to follow just a single thread of this final seminar of Derrida, which ran from December 2002 to March 2003, as an emphasis on "world, finitude, and solitude"—the three explicit themes of Heidegger's seminar—ultimately gives rise or gives way to the question of the end of history or, indeed, the end of the world. Concentrating on just three passages on this theme of the world or the end of the world, one from the first of the seminar's ten sessions, one from the middle of the seminar, and one from the tenth and final session, I would like to try to explain, without explaining away, what initially appears to be a series of confusing if not contradictory claims about the world. We will see, I think, that while Derrida will remain consistent in his understanding of the world from the beginning to the end of the seminar, consistent, that is, in a series of equivocations with regard to the end of a world, the end of *my* world, for example, as the end of the *world itself*, the pathos shifts dramatically from the beginning to the end of the seminar as a series of events, some of them what we call world events and some much more personal and yet no less world-shattering, come to mark the seminar in its themes, its orientation, and its tone.

In December 2002, then, Derrida begins his seminar—what will turn out to be, let me say it one final time in this chapter, his final seminar—by announcing to his audience, to his students at the École des Hautes Études in Paris, that while his plan is to continue with the previous year's theme of *The Beast and the Sovereign*, his approach in this second year will be quite different. Rather than follow the trope of the sovereign as beast, the sovereign as above or before the law like a beast, the theme of the sovereign as exception or as the one who decides on the exception, in thinkers as diverse as Plato, Aristotle, Hobbes, Machiavelli, Bodin, and Schmidt, to name just a few, he will concentrate in this second year on just two figures, indeed on just two works, a novel of 1719 that many claim to be the first English novel, and a Heidegger seminar of 1929–30—dates to which, let me suggest in passing, Derrida would not have been indifferent. While several other figures will make cameo appearances in the seminar, from Rousseau, Marx, Joyce, and Virginia Woolf to Levinas, Lacan, and Deleuze, most of them because of what they had to say about *Robinson Crusoe*, Derrida will keep his promise of concentrating essentially on these two books, going back and forth between the two, using the one to read and illuminate the other.[3]

If so many writers and philosophers—excluding, interestingly, Heidegger—will have written about *Robinson Crusoe*, if this novel will have exercised for nearly three centuries now an unparalleled "fascination" on the world (*BS 2* 24/51), it is in large part because *Robinson Crusoe* is a novel that essentially creates or recreates the world itself, a novel whose central character resembles either the first man, abandoned to his solitude while being granted dominion over all the creatures of his world, or the very last man at the ends of history or at the end of the world (*BS 2* 21/47).[4] It is this theme of the origin and end of the world that will thus come to dominate Derrida's seminar and provide the most poignant points of convergence between Defoe's novel and Heidegger's seminar.

Derrida's initial pretext for speaking about the world, his principal reason for asking about the sense and unity of the world, is Heidegger's interrogation of the concept of world in his 1929–30 seminar and the use Heidegger makes of it to define the stone, the animal, and man. For it was in that seminar, beautifully translated by Nick Walker and my colleague at DePaul, Will McNeill, that Heidegger famously argued that the stone is worldless, the animal poor in world, and the human world-building or world-forming, three theses that Derrida began to question almost as soon as he came across them, that is, not long after their first publication in German in 1983. (I will return to Derrida's long engagement with this seminar and with these three theses in Chapter 7.)

We would seem to be back on fairly familiar territory at the beginning of this second year of *The Beast and the Sovereign*. As anyone who has read the first year of the seminar or Derrida's *Of Spirit* or *The Animal That Therefore I Am* would be able to predict, Derrida will go on to contest this opposition between the human and the animal based on this presumed access to world. His critique will focus essentially on what is, to his eyes, Heidegger's unjustified confidence regarding the distinction between human Dasein and the animal, a distinction that falls in line, as we saw in the previous chapter, with an entire history of Western philosophy that attempts to draw a single, indivisible line between the human and all other animals. Derrida will go on to attribute to Heidegger, as he had attributed to other thinkers the previous year, the *bêtise*, the common philosophical silliness of stupidity, involved in grouping together under the general name of "the animal"—*la bête* or *l'animal*—creatures as diverse as the ant, the snake, the cat, the dog, the horse, the chimpanzee, the sperm whale, and so on. It is a great *bêtise*, Derrida will argue, to draw a single line between the human, on the one hand, and all these other extremely diverse animals on the other, which would then have "no other supposed unity than a negative one, or one supposed to be negative: namely that of not being a human being" (*BS 2* 8/30). All this is perfectly in keeping with Derrida's earlier analyses of the human/animal distinction in texts ranging from *Of Spirit* and the *Geschlecht* essays to *The Animal That Therefore I Am* and the first year of *The Beast and the Sovereign*.

But as the seminar proceeds, something seems to happen to Derrida's interest and attention, something that will turn a seminar whose objective was initially, it seems, to question the different relations of humans and animals to the world into a seminar about the unity of the world itself. It is as if Derrida's attention shifts from the distinctions themselves to that which forms the basis for them. As Derrida comes to argue, Heidegger's three theses seem less intent "to say something about the stone, the animal, or man, than to say something essential about differences *as to the world*" (*BS 2* 57/96).[5] It will be less Heidegger's hierarchical ordering of stone, animal, and man and much more the question of the world itself that will come to preoccupy Derrida in this second year of *The Beast and the Sovereign* seminar.

It is, it should be noted, Heidegger's own renewal of the Kantian question of world that leads Derrida in this direction, his renewal of this question but also his initial hesitation or circumspection with regard to it.[6] For Heidegger was himself well aware that this question of world, not unlike the question of Being, cannot simply be asked from an already presupposed horizon of the world and so cannot be just one question among others *within* the world.[7] Indeed, he is not even clear that there is or could be a single *approach* to this question of the world. In the final chapter of *The Animal That Therefore I Am*, a transcription of some improvised remarks made by Derrida at the 1997 Cerisy-la-Salle conference devoted to his work, Derrida recalls that in his 1929–30 seminar Heidegger had not only posed the question of world but laid out three very different ways of approaching it. In addition to a historiographical approach that looks at the history of the word and concept of *world* (something Heidegger undertakes in "On the Essence of Ground") and a phenomenological approach of the kind we find in *Being and Time*, that is, an analysis of the phenomenon of world and of Dasein's being-in-the-world, there is, in the 1929–30 seminar, a third, comparative approach, that is, a "comparative examination" of world based on the stone's lack of world, the animal's poorness in world, and man's capacity for world-building (*ATT* 152–153).

Derrida thus seems to follow—to understand and even to sympathize with—Heidegger's initial hesitation with regard to the question of how to approach the question of the world. But it is Heidegger's eventual *decision* with regard to this question, a decision that Derrida will characterize as unjustified or unthematized, that will preoccupy Derrida most in the second year of the seminar. For after having been disoriented or after having at least feigned disorientation with regard to this question of the world, Heidegger suddenly decides to follow the "closest path," the most proximate path, the same one—and there is no coincidence here—that he had followed in *Being and Time* in order to pose the question of the meaning of Being, namely, the path that is man or Dasein. It will be Dasein's having of a world (along with its concomitant possession of *logos*, solitude, and melancholy—a capacity for nostalgia and thus for a certain *loss* of the world) that will set Dasein apart from the stone and, most important here, from the animal, which is characterized as being encircled or benumbed by the world, incapable of a relation to beings *as such* and so incapable of having a world or of *not* having it in the way that Dasein does. We are still very close, therefore, to the central question of the first volume of *The Beast and the Sovereign*, the question of why Dasein rather than the animal, or rather than the animal within Dasein, if one can speak that way, is chosen as the path to question the nature of world. But this time it is much more the question of the world—and the possibility of having or *not* having a world—that holds Derrida's attention.[8]

It is with Heidegger's three theses of 1929–30 concerning the stone, the animal, and man in the background that Derrida in the very first session of this second year of *The Beast and the Sovereign* seminar puts forth what appear to be his own three *countertheses* on the human and the animal in relation, precisely, to their respective relations to the world. While Derrida is usually not wont to present *theses* in this way, while he is no doubt simply trying to counter, by way of provocation, Heidegger's theses, it is necessary to try at least to understand these theses and reconcile them with one another and with Derrida's other claims about and analyses of world both here and in other texts.[9] Here, then, are the first two of these three theses regarding "the community or otherwise of the world," two theses that Derrida calls "incontestable" even though they appear to be, as Derrida himself admits, "incompatible" if not downright contradictory: "1. Incontestably, animals and humans inhabit the same world, the same objective world even if they do not have the same experience of the objectivity of the object. 2. Incontestably, animals and humans do not inhabit the same world, for the human world will never be purely and simply identical to the world of animals" (*BS 2* 8/30–31).

There is much to be said about Derrida's argumentative strategy here, about his posing of a thesis and then a counterthesis or antithesis that, as we will see, will find no resolution or synthesis in what follows. What both theses have in common, however, is the attribution of world or a world to the animal, an argumentative strategy that we saw Derrida deploying throughout *The Animal That Therefore I Am* and the first volume of *The Beast and the Sovereign*. Here, as there, Derrida begins in effect by suggesting that we extend to certain animals a capacity or attribute that has been traditionally denied them, an access to world here, a capacity for language, technology, mourning, or death elsewhere. In short, animals too have a world, despite what Heidegger says, a world that is the same as the world of humans in the first thesis, and one that is different in the second thesis.

But rather than develop this claim any further, rather than continue to contest the animal's privation of a world, Derrida quickly turns, just as he did in these earlier works, to the more principled claim regarding the *human's* supposed possession of a world. If the second thesis, the thesis that "animals and humans do not inhabit the same world," contests the human's access to *all* worlds by depriving him of the world of animals, the third thesis will contest any individual human being's access to any world other than his or her own, a thesis that will come to ruin, as we will see, the very meaning of the word *world*. After thus suggesting that animals might *in fact* possess a world, either the world they possess with humans or their own, Derrida questions the *principle* by which humans are granted access to a world at all. Here is Derrida's third thesis, which is a good bit longer and more lyrical than the first two:

3. In spite of this identity and this difference, neither animals of different species, nor humans of different cultures, nor any animal or human individual inhabit the same world as another, however close and similar these living individuals may be (be they humans or animals), and the difference between one world and another will remain always unbridgeable, because the community of the world is always constructed, simulated by a set of stabilizing apparatuses, more or less stable, then, and never natural, language in the broad sense, codes of traces being designed, among all living beings, to construct a unity of the world that is always deconstructible, nowhere and never given in nature. . . . Between my world and any other world there is first the space and the time of an infinite difference, an interruption that is incommensurable with all attempts to make a passage, a bridge, an isthmus, all attempts at communication, translation, trope, and transfer that the desire for a world or the want of a world, the being wanting a world will try to pose, impose, propose, stabilize. (*BS 2* 8–9/31)

And then comes the dramatic conclusion that Derrida seems to have been sailing toward from the beginning of the passage, a conclusion that is largely motivated by the reading of *Robinson Crusoe* that is to come but that cannot simply be reduced to that reading: "There is no world, there are only islands" (*BS 2* 9/31).

Derrida moves in the space of just a few lines from the question of the animal being deprived of world to the question of whether humans and animals share a world to the question of whether any two animals or humans can share a world to, finally, the question of the unity and existence of the world itself. What we get is thus a deepening and generalization of the second thesis, a hyperbolization or even infinitization of that second thesis that situates nothing less than an abyss or absence of common world between not just humans and animals in general but between and among individual animals and humans, a thesis that then calls into question the very unity and existence of the world as a shared horizon. From a single world shared by animals and humans in thesis one, to two separate worlds, a world of animals and a world of humans, in thesis two, to an endless multiplication of worlds in thesis three, what ends up getting called into question is the very horizon and meaning of the word *world*. Every man, woman, and animal is thus an island before the world; each is situated before any shared horizon, just before the dawn or already at the twilight of what is called "the world."

Insofar as Heidegger distinguishes the human from the animal based on their respective relations to world, the claim that there is no world, only islands, removes almost all common ground between Heidegger's analysis and Derrida's. But the implications of Derrida's claims go far beyond a reading of Heidegger; indeed they go to the very heart of what it is, for Derrida, to have a world and a community within the world. If, according to Derrida's first thesis, the human does indeed share a world with animals, this common world or this "community of the world" is always constructed, never natural (*BS 2* 8/31). It can be presupposed only insofar as it is *imposed* by a set of "stabilizing apparatuses" designed to assure us that we live in the same world. And, in the end, *that* would be the real *end* of the world, that is, the real goal or aim, the *telos*, of what we call "world," a stabilizing mechanism designed to convince us that there is a common foundation beneath our feet or a common history above our heads. No matter how extreme the differences or how great the distances between us, the world would be there to assure us that passages can always be constructed in time and space between one island and another, allowing us to believe that we live in the same world and share a common history.

Derrida's dramatic counterthesis, "there is no world, there are only islands," suggests a very different relationship to world, finitude, and solitude—the three "fundamental concepts of metaphysics" that form the subtitle of Heidegger's 1929–30 seminar.[10] No matter how dramatic or stark this counterthesis may be, it is also not incompatible, it might be argued, with many of Derrida's other texts, including his earliest works on Husserl, where access to the other or to the alter ego is possible only through analogical appresentation rather than direct perception since there is no common world or common horizon of perception to give us such access. Derrida's analyses in *Voice and Phenomenon* and elsewhere of the separation or isolation of egos in Husserl could well have led him to conclude that "between my world and any other world there is first the space and time of an infinite difference" (*BS 2* 9/31), an infinite difference that would constitute or define my very finitude insofar as I cannot transcend or overcome that difference so as to experience what is happening in the other or "on the other side," on the side of the other or on that "other island." As Derrida remarked again in those improvised remarks published in *The Animal That Therefore I Am*, "of course, the animal doesn't eat like us, but neither does any one person eat in the same way; there are structural differences, even when one eats from the same plate!" (*ATT* 159) Once again, Derrida's tendency is not to extend a capacity for world or, here, the ability to eat (as opposed to feed) to the animal but to multiply the differences, first between animals and humans but then and especially between individual human beings.

"There is no world, there are only islands": it is very tempting to think that Derrida has fallen prey here, late in life, or perhaps already from the beginning and we are only now fully noticing it, to that cardinal sin of metaphysicians known as *solipsism*. The sin would be all the more unforgivable inasmuch as the one committing it would have tried to argue in these very same early works that identity is always constituted through the other, that the identity of an ego is only always an *effect* of a series of differing and deferred relations to the other. Derrida will have thus let himself be unduly moved, it might be thought, by this Crusoean rhetoric of separated islands and this pathos of the end of the world so as to argue that individual egos are as isolated from one another as separate islands or separate worlds. To help support this charge of solipsism, one might cite a passage like the following from some improvised remarks made by Derrida a few years before the seminar:

What I think in my head, in my inner sanctum, will, for infinite structural reasons, never be accessible to you; you will never know what's going on on the other side [*de l'autre côté*]. . . . Everything that exceeds the order of originary perception or of proof presents itself as miraculous: the alterity of the other, what the other has in his head, in his intention or in his consciousness, is inaccessible to an intuition or to a proof . . . ("AANJ" 76)

Insofar as the other, the alter ego, remains inaccessible to me and me to it, we live, as it were, in two different worlds, as if on two different islands, with no bridge or means of communication between them. Solipsism would indeed seem to be the name for this situation.

To begin to answer this charge of solipsism, let me turn briefly to my second passage on world near the middle of the seminar, a brief passage on which so much hinges or, as we will see, *turns*. In the midst of a rather extraordinary analysis of Robinson Crusoe's reinvention of the wheel, Derrida argues in effect that all identity, that every *ipse* or *ipseity*—and thus every supposedly *solus-ipse*—is constituted through a relationship to a world that is irreducible and that would seem to resemble that single and shared world of thesis one. Derrida writes—and we will return to this passage in much greater detail in Chapter 4:

> The question, then, is indeed that of the world. The wheel is not only a technical machine, it is in the world, it is outside the conscious interiority of the *ipse,* and . . . there is no ipseity without this pros-theticity in the world, with all the chances and all the threats that it constitutes for ipseity, which can in this way be constructed but also, and by the same token, indissociably, be destroyed. (*BS 2* 88/137–138)

If we are to continue to take seriously the thesis that there is an infiniti-zation of worlds, or rather, that there is no world, only islands, then what Derrida means by islands obviously cannot be individual or individuated egos or identities, since these will have been constituted only through this prosthesis or detour of the world, which may in fact consist in a series of stabilizing mechanisms or may even be, as we will see, the *phantasm* of a shared world. Moreover, these islands will have been constituted in their finitude through a relation both to the world and to what is radically other than the world, to the irreparable loss of presence to which these islands are from the start exposed. The infinitization of worlds would thus have to be thought in terms not of an archipelago of isolated, identifiable worlds, an archipelago of different ipseities or identities, but in terms of an archi-pelago of *singularities* whose finitude is marked by an opening to the world—a certain experience of the trace—and by what might be called an origin or end of the world. From this perspective, there are no islands, there is only the world—a world made up of a multiplicity of finite singularities that are themselves marked by an interruption or absence of world, an end of the world that often goes by the name of *death*.

Such a thinking of the death of a singular being as nothing less than the end of the world had in fact been a constant theme in Derrida's work of the last twenty years. In *Aporias* (1992), for example—and again in relation to Heidegger—Derrida described death in this way: "the impossibility that is possible for *Dasein* is, indeed, that there not be or that there no longer be *Dasein*: that precisely what is possible become impossible. . . . It is nothing less than the end of the world" (*AP* 75).[11] In the years leading up to his final seminar, such references to an end of the world would become even more recurrent. As more and more of his mentors, colleagues, friends, and family members passed away, Derrida was forced to bear witness more and more frequently to this always singular and absolute and yet nonetheless repeated end of the world. In many of the memorial essays gathered in *The Work of Mourning*, for example, Derrida speaks repeatedly of the death of a friend as not just the end of *a* world within the world but as the end of *the* world itself. Derrida even chose to entitle the French edition of that collection *Chaque fois unique, la fin du monde*, that is, "each time unique or uniquely, the end of the world." As he puts it elsewhere, "each time, and each time singularly, each time irreplaceably, each time infinitely, death is nothing less than the end of the world" (*SQ* 140).

While such references become, as I said, ever more frequent in these later texts, the premises for them go much further back. Already back in 1965 in one of the early sections of *Of Grammatology*, Derrida related the trace—which is to say, a certain structure of difference and deferral—to the origin of the world and thus, implicitly, to its effacement as the end of the world. Derrida there argued:

> The instituted trace cannot be thought without thinking the retention of difference within a structure of reference where difference appears *as such* and thus permits a certain liberty of variations among the full terms. The absence of *another* here-and-now, of another transcendental present, of *another* origin of the world appearing as such, presenting itself as irreducible absence within the presence of the trace, is not a metaphysical formula substituted for a scientific concept of writing. (*OG* 46–47/68)

Some twenty years later, in "No Apocalypse, Not Now" (1984), Derrida makes a similar claim, though in an even more shocking way, when he confesses at one point that "there is no common measure able to persuade me that a personal mourning is less grave than a nuclear war" ("NA" 403). While Derrida was surely not suggesting that a personal mourning and a nuclear war are the same or should be considered the same, he seemed to believe that insofar as every individual death is not just a death *within* the world but a death or end *of* the world itself, there is no *common measure*, no common world of measure, no common world against which to measure, the death tolls on the two sides, so as to declare a single, individual death "less grave" than a nuclear war that kills millions.

Each death is thus a catastrophe, *the* end of *the* world, a catastrophe that is repeated in a singular fashion with the death of each singular, irreplaceable other.[12] What is irreplaceable about the other, and what then helps Derrida avoid the charge of solipsism, is thus not the other's identity or ipseity, the constitution of the other's own little island or *solus ipse*—for these are indeed always determined by a passage or circuit through a common world—but the other's unique and irreplaceable opening to or "experience" of the world. What is unique, what I have no access to, is ultimately a certain relation to time, to an unrepeatable, unique time and thus a relation to an unforeseeable future. What is unique is a blind, elementary faith in the world that cannot be reduced to any knowledge, an irreplaceable experience of or testimony to the world that has no place in the world and finds no confirmation *within* it.[13] Let me reread the passage I cited a moment ago that seemed to push Derrida in the direction of a certain solipsism, but this time I will include the lines that immediately precede and follow it:

> the primary miracle, the most ordinary of miracles, is precisely "believe me!" When one says to someone, "believe me!," the appeal to proof is itself not provable. What I think in my head, in my inner sanctum, will, for infinite structural reasons, never be accessible to you; you will never know what's going on on the other side [*de l'autre côté*]. You can simply "believe" . . . Everything that exceeds the order of originary perception or of proof presents itself as miraculous: the alterity of the other, what the other has in his head, in his intention or in his consciousness, is inaccessible to an intuition or to a proof; the "believe me" is permanently inhabited by the miracle. ("AANJ" 76)

What is inaccessible is not some other identity or ipseity but precisely the alterity of an appeal that says to me "believe me," believe me when I say or when I express without explicitly saying that this is what I feel, experience, and so on of the world. What is on the other side is not some identifiable world from which I am barred but the opening to the world—a certain relation to the future, a finitude, precisely, from which I am separated by "the space and time of an infinite distance." This separation or isolation, this distance or difference, does not spell the end of every social relation, the dissolution of every solution bond, but is in fact what first *constitutes* it. As Derrida put it in another set of improvised remarks, this time from March 2003, that is, at exactly the same time as the second year of *The Beast and the Sovereign*: "I have never believed that it is possible to synthesize the existence of any individual, in any case not my own, and therefore I believe that dissociation is inescapable. The social relationship is made of interruption. To relate to the other, as other, is not simply to be linked to the other; it is also to respect the interruption. . . . To relate to the other presupposes faith" (*IW* 66).

Derrida's use of the words *faith* and *miracle* in the preceding passages suggests that everything in the world can perhaps be accounted for by the laws of nature or causality *except* this appeal, which opens up the world like a miracle and can only be affirmed through a kind of elementary faith. If what opens up in this appeal or through this testimony is nothing less than the origin of the world, then the end of that appeal or that testimony is nothing less than the end of the world—an end that is no longer necessarily tied to the ego or to consciousness and so is not necessarily restricted to the human and perhaps not even to the animal.[14] If we can conceive of the trace as a kind of testimony, as the possibility of testimony, then wherever there is a trace there is this origin or end of the world. What makes every other every bit other is thus the fact that there is "within" each other this "other side," an opening to the world or to the future that remains forever inaccessible to me. In an interview from 1993, Derrida explicitly links both the birth and death of the other—the unique and irreplaceable experience of the other and his or her unique relationship to time—to this origin and end of the world:

> With the birth of a child—the first figure of the absolute arrivant—one can analyze the causalities, the genealogical, genetic, and symbolic premises. . . . But even if such an analysis could ever be completed, one could never reduce the element of chance [*aléa*], the place of the taking-place; there will be someone who speaks, someone irreplaceable, an absolute initiative, another origin of the world. . . . What is absolutely new is not this, rather than that; it is the fact that it arrives only once. It is what is marked by a date (a unique moment and place), and it is always a birth or death that a date dates. . . . What resists analysis is birth and death: always the origin and the end of a world. (*N* 104)

Each death, then, is nothing less than the end of the world, and it occasions a mourning not just for some ipseity within the world but for the loss of the world itself through that ipseity. But insofar as mourning for the other begins, as Derrida argues throughout *The Work of Mourning*, well before the death of the other, before the so-called *actual* death of the other, insofar as it begins already from the inception of one's relation to the other, then this end of the world will have taken place in some sense already from the beginning. If the death of the other—the death of an always singular, irreplaceable other—signals not just *an* end of the world but *the* end of the world, and if this end will have already happened in some sense from the outset, then the question becomes what we *must* do, and do every day, how we must live, in the face of this implacable truth, what obligation we must bear as soon as we recognize the strange truth that already from the beginning "there is no world, there are only islands."

Well, in the tenth and final session of *The Beast and the Sovereign* seminar, Derrida at once underscores the seriousness and irremediability of this loss of the world and suggests two possible responses to it. It is at this point that the change in tone or pathos I noted at the outset of this chapter becomes palpable in the seminar, a change that Derrida himself cannot help but notice and comment on. It is *as if* a certain end of the world—which cannot now be rigorously distinguished from the end of the world itself—had come to be registered, marked, inscribed in the time and space of the seminar itself, transforming it into something like a singular event on the event that would be the end of the world.

The tenth and final session of the seminar takes place on March 26, 2003.[15] It's just over three months since the beginning of the seminar and a lot has happened in the meantime that has found its way into the seminar, the death of Maurice Blanchot in February 2003, and then just a couple of weeks later, less than a week before this final session, on March 20, 2003, the beginning of the American-led coalition's invasion of Iraq, in short, yet another "world war" (*BS 2* 259/359). With this as the context, Derrida begins this final session with a long meditation on a line of poetry from Paul Celan that he had treated earlier in the seminar and that he had taken up in several other texts written around the same time, from *Rams* to the introduction to *Chaque fois unique, la fin du monde*. That line—which immediately begins to resonate, as we will see in Chapter 4, with the line of Novalis with which Heidegger begins *his* seminar and, of course, with all of Derrida's prior claims and comments about the world—is "*Die Welt ist fort, ich muss dich tragen*" "the world is far away, I must carry or bear you" (*BS 2* 258/357).[16]

Derrida's reading of this line from Celan at the beginning of this final session of the seminar sets the tone for what is to follow, and particularly for his return to his initial theses regarding the world, his return, as I suggested at the outset, in a different key or with a different pathos. Derrida goes on to interpret this notion of the world being far away, the world being gone, in terms of both the death and birth of the other whom I must bear.[17] The end or absence of the world can thus be occasioned by the death of an other, by the loss of the unique opening to the world that the other is, or else by the coming into being of a unique origin of the world to which I myself have no access, another origin that shall remain forever absent to me. In every birth and every death, then, the world is far away, gone, and that is where responsibility begins.

Each individual death is indeed the end of the world, but with a new world war having broken out around him, with the spectacle of shock and awe in the name of an infinite justice flickering across all the TV screens of the world, with smart bombs raining down upon Baghdad, the seminar takes on a different tone and the interpretation of "the world is far away, I must carry you," a very different valence. Derrida writes—and I cite at length:

> There is no longer any local or national war. Supposing there ever was. And in every war, at stake from now on is an end of the world . . . in the sense that what is threatened is not only this always infinite death of each and every one (for example of a given soldier or a given singular civilian), that individual death I've often said was each time *the* end of *the* world, *the* end, the whole end of *the* world (*Die Welt ist fort*) . . . but the end of the world in general, the absolute end of the world . . . the destruction of the world, of any possible world, or of what is supposed to make of the world a *cosmos,* an arrangement, an order, an order of ends, a juridical, moral, political order, an international order resistant to the non-world of death and barbarity. (*BS 2* 259–260/359)

There is thus the end of the world in every death, but then there is the possibility of the end of the world in general—the destruction of any possible world: the "absolute disaster" (*BS 2* 260/360). Here, it seems, are the two senses of world I tried to highlight in the first two passages we looked at: the world as relation or as opening to the world, and the world as the prosthetic detour that makes any world possible or gives meaning to any world, the world through which any *autos,* any *ipse*—even if it is but a phantasm—must pass in order to gain a sense of itself, in order to become itself. The world war that had just begun with the US invasion of Iraq threatens both of these senses of world, the world that ends with each individual death and the possibility of a world in general, the end, then, of every possible end of the world.

Derrida says to his students at this point that they have reached a crucial point in the seminar before "a long halt" (*BS 2* 261/361), that is, before the summer break and the recommencement of the seminar the following year. For Derrida believed—or he at least allowed himself to project, to hope—that there would indeed be another year (see *BS 2* 264 n. 9/364 n. 2). He mentions a text of Heidegger's that they will read "next year" and he recalls the path they have taken thus far in the seminar, the landscape they will have traversed. It was the question of the beast and the sovereign, he reminds them, that brought them together in the first place. But do the beast and the sovereign, do the animal and man, have "in common," he goes on to ask, "something that one can still call 'world,' *a* world, one and the same world, the 'world'" (*BS 2* 262/363)? It is at this point that Derrida returns, here in this final session, to the three possibilities or theses with regard to animals, humans, and the world that we saw him sketch out in the very first session. He begins by reiterating what is in essence his first thesis—though, interestingly, plants will have suddenly taken root in that common world of humans and animals:

> No one will seriously deny the animal the possibility of inhabiting the world (even if Heidegger claims that the animal does not inhabit as man alone inhabits it), no one will deny that these living beings, that we call the beast *and* the sovereign, inhabit a world, what one calls the world, and in a certain sense, the *same* world. There is a habitat of the animal as there is a habitat of plants, as there is a habitat for every living being. The word "world" has at least as a minimal sense the designation of *that within which* all these living beings are carried (in a belly or in an egg), they are born, they live, they inhabit and they die . . . (*BS 2* 264–265/365–366)[18]

But what is this "world" *within which* these beings live? If it is not simply the earth *on which* they all live, if it is not what it was for, say, Robinson Crusoe, namely, the totality of created beings, the whole of God's creation (*BS 2* 48/83), if it is not, as it was for Heidegger, "the manifestation of beings as such in their entirety," a manifestation to which only human Dasein would have full access, then what is it and what assures its unity? This is where Derrida turns to his second and third theses, which he begins developing more or less as he did in the very first session but which soon take on a force and a pathos they did not have earlier and perhaps could not have had before the start just a few days before of another world war. He begins:

> Of course, one can always question the supposed unity or identity of the world, not only between animal and human, but already from one living being to another. No one will ever be able to demonstrate, what is called *demonstrate* in all rigor, that two human beings, you and I for example, inhabit the same world, that the world is one and the same thing for both of us. (*BS 2* 265/366)

Though there must be "a certain *presumed, anticipated* unity of the world even in order discursively to sustain within it multiplicity," a certain semantic unity that would allow one even to speak of "the dissemination of possible worlds," this unity of the world, this unity of the word *world*, is precisely *semantic*. In other words, the *world* is but

> an artificial effect, a cobbled-together verbal and terminological construction, destined to mask our panic (that of a baby who would be born without coming into the world), destined then to protect us against the infantile but infinite anxiety of the fact that *there is not the world*, that nothing is less certain than the world itself . . . and that radical dissemination, i.e., the absence of a common world, the irremediable solitude without salvation of the living being, depends first on the absence without recourse of any world, i.e., of any common meaning of the word "world," in sum of any common meaning at all. (*BS 2* 265–266/366)

Derrida is arguing much as he did earlier in the seminar, but the tone seems to have shifted quite palpably—and he himself recognizes the shift. He remarks, "This can, I admit, look like a lot of apocalyptic statements, but it is also the very tissue . . . the ever unsewn and torn tissue of our most constant and quotidian experience." And then he turns to his seminar audience to say, *Je ne dis pas cela pour vous émouvoir ou nous faire de la peine*, that is, "I do not say this just to move you, to upset or disturb you," to "roil you up or depress you," as Geoffrey Bennington translates it, "but because it is what I must think and say according to the most implacable necessity" (*BS 2* 266/367). He then continues, with words that are no less pathos-laden and no less personal:

> at every moment of the day and night, we are overcome with the feeling that between a given other, and sometimes the closest of those close to us . . . those with whom we share everything, starting

and ending with love . . . the worlds in which we live are different to the point of the monstrosity of the unrecognizable. (*BS 2* 266/367)

Between us and those closest to us there is, as it were, an unfathomable distance, and it is precisely because of this distance, on the basis of this lack of foundation, that ethics is born. The reference to the *unrecognizable* and the *monstrous* in the passage above is alone enough to suggest this, for Derrida uses these same terms in the first year of *The Beast and the Sovereign* to argue that ethics, if there is to be any, would have to begin *not* with a scene of recognition between humans but with the unrecognizable and the monstrous, even if this turns out to be what is unrecognizable and monstrous *within the human*. As Derrida put it during the previous year's seminar:

> A principle of ethics or more radically of justice . . . is perhaps the obligation that engages my responsibility with respect to the most dissimilar, the entirely other, precisely, the monstrously other, the unrecognizable other. The "unrecognizable," I shall say in a somewhat elliptical way, is the beginning of ethics, of the Law, and not of the human. So long as there is recognizability and fellow, ethics is dormant. . . . So long as it remains human, among men, ethics remains dogmatic, narcissistic, and not yet thinking. . . . The "unrecognizable" is the awakening. (*BS 1* 108/155)

We all know, says Derrida, that those with whom we live or, as we say, share a world, live in worlds that are monstrously, unrecognizably different. We know this "with an undeniable and stubborn, i.e., permanently denied, knowledge," that is, we know this, in conformity with the logic of denegation we followed in the previous chapter, with an undeniable knowledge that can thus only be denied. Between us and those closest to us there is—and we can almost predict the words that are going to follow—an "abyss between the islands of the archipelago" (*BS 2* 266/367). Again, there is no world, no common world, only islands, with no bridges or means of translation between them. In the end, the world would be not just "a convenient and reassuring bit of chatter, the name of a life insurance policy for living beings losing their world" (*BS 2* 267/367–368), but nothing more—or really nothing less, because it is so powerful—than a *phantasm*. The world is but a phantasm, which means that the world *is not*—and *that* is precisely the source of its power:

> it seems to be *as if* we were behaving *as if* we were inhabiting the same world and speaking of the same thing and speaking the same language, when in fact we well know—at the point where the phantasm

precisely comes up against its limit—that this is not true at all. (*BS 2* 268/369)

The world is thus not quite some regulative idea, an *as if* designed to organize our knowledge of nature and encourage us to seek its universal laws, but a fiction or a phantasm in the precise sense that Derrida will have given to these terms since at least *Glas*. It is the status of the world as a phantasm— a no doubt necessary phantasm—that will help explain not simply and not even primarily its mode of existence or nonexistence, but more important its *hold* on or *power* over us. The world is the effect of an *as if*, the result of a projection of the world from out of the abyss of world, a phantasm whose power is undone—as we will see in the final chapter—only by means of a more catastrophic *Walten*. As always in Derrida, the phantasm marks the conflation of two distinct registers, culture and nature, for example, or the prescriptive and the descriptive, what ought to be and what is, a performative *as if*, a *comme si*, and a constative *like that*, a *comme ça*. *Comme si, comme ça*: even if it's only as if, we believe it's like that—and *that* is the "logic" of the phantasm, the logic of every phantasm regarding the unity and being of the world, and the logic of every phantasm regarding every *end* of history or *end* of the world.[19] When Kojève says, for example, in an infamous footnote to his lectures on Hegel's *Phenomenology of Spirit*, that at the end of history man will become like an animal, will construct his edifices like birds build nests and spiders spin webs and will perform musical concerts like frogs and cicadas, he is perhaps testifying to this same conflation of registers, a conflation of a performative *as if* and a constative *like that*, a conflation of culture and nature, the human and the animal, the sovereign and the beast.[20]

We thus pretend that there is a world, make *as if* there is a world, *as if* we share a single and same world. It is, then, *as if* there were a performative *as if* lodged within all our constative assertions and reassuring statements about the world, a *comme si* at the heart of every claim that the world is *comme ça*. Derrida speaks earlier, in fact, of the call to responsibility, the "*ich muss dich tragen*," the "I must bear or carry you," as the performative pearl "lodged" within the constative oyster that is "*die Welt is fort*," "the world is far away" (*BS 2* 259/358–359).[21] The *as if* would here provide both the performative force of the phantasm and the place of its greatest vulnerability and potential undoing. For when this *as if* is shown for what it is, for the performative that it is, then the world appears for the first time *as* a phantasm, as the *effect* of an *as if*. It is not that there is, according to a philosophical tradition that begins already with Plato, another world, a world more real than this world, a world in the light of which this world would appear as a mere phantasm. No, there is no other world, and, worse, even *this* one, the supposed unity and stability of this one, is but a phantasm. Hence, the unity of the world is indeed always an imposed unity, not an imposition upon the world but the imposition of a world, the presupposition, always more or less denied, more or less repressed, that the world is the result of a performative fiction or a pacifying phantasm. As Derrida suggests, we all know—even if this knowledge is always denied—that the world is in the end a construction, a fiction or a phantasm, the human's way of reacting, precisely, to an original loss of world by positing the existence of a world that would be shared. While the notion of a shared world is always there to pacify our anxieties or calm our fears of an originary homelessness or worldlessness, certain moments, like the death—though also the birth—of another, threaten always to pull aside the veil of this illusion, casting us out into the void where there is no world.

At once armed with this "knowledge" of the phantasm of the world and yet necessarily dispossessed by it, since this obviously cannot be just another form of knowledge of or within the world, Derrida in this final session suggests two different possible reactions or responses to this unsettling knowledge. Assuming we do not simply give ourselves over to the power and affect of the phantasm, assuming we do not simply and naively assume a world by repressing or denying the "knowledge" that the world *is not*, there are, it seems, two distinct possibilities for living with this knowledge, two distinct postures. The first, he suggests, would be "to carry the other out of the world, where we share at least this knowledge *without phantasm* that there is no longer a world, a common world: I carry you then in the void . . . [there where] nothing will happen to us nor welcome us ever on any island or any shore" (*BS 2* 268/369; my emphasis). This first possibility would thus involve recognizing that there is no world, only islands, and that all one can do, all one should do with and for the other, is bear him or her into this void, without expectation or event.

But it is the second possibility that is most interesting to me, and it is the one on which Derrida, I believe, continued to place his hope. This second possibility, which might resemble but would have to be carefully distinguished from the naïve assumption of the world as a phantasm, would be to recognize that there is no world and then to make *as if* there were, to make or remake the world—and Derrida clearly chooses his word carefully here—"poetically."[22] This second possibility would thus be, Derrida continues,

> that where there is no world, where the world is not here or there, but *fort,* infinitely distant over there, that what I must do, with you

and carrying you, is make it that there be precisely a world, just a world, if not a just world, or to do things so as to make *as if* there were just a world, and to make the world come [in] to the world . . . as though there ought to be a world where presently there is none, to make the gift or present of this *as if* come up poetically, which is the only thing that—during the finite time of such an impossible voyage between two non-shores where nothing happens—the only thing that can make it possible that I can live and have or let you live, enjoy or have or let you enjoy, to carry you for a few moments without anything happening and leaving a trace in the world . . . (*BS 2* 268/369–370)[23]

To make the gift or present of this *as if* poetically would mean, it seems, to live and act without the assumption that there *is* a world, without passing off a performative for a constative in order to sustain the phantasm of the world and our blind confidence in it. It would be to make the world performatively—teleopoietically, perhaps—from out of the void, or, rather, to allow the world to be made, since this *poiesis* obviously could not be a performance or activity like any other.[24] Aware of its own powerlessness, undone by its own ability, this *poiesis* would be a making *as if* that leaves within the world a trace of the end or loss of the world. It would be a *poiesis* that reveals the performative foundation, the foundationless foundation, of the phantasm, a *poiesis* that then allows a world to emerge poetically— Derrida could have perhaps also said *miraculously*—from out of that abyssal foundation, a world made *ex nihilo*, as it were, in the knowledge now that the world is and will remain far away.[25]

It is with this difference that Derrida leaves us in his analysis of the phantasm of the world in *The Beast and the Sovereign*, with this almost imperceptible difference of an *as if*, the difference between living a world *as if* it were like that, as if it were what it is said to be, and making the world *as if*, leaving a trace of the end of the world within the world by means of this performative. That, I would like to argue, is what happened, what will have happened, in this final seminar of Jacques Derrida, a seminar that not only came to treat, as we have seen, the theme of the end of the world but that itself came to be marked by it, a seminar that will have been shaken by this end of the world and so has now come to bear the traces of it.

Let me conclude this chapter by recalling that Más Afuera—a Spanish phrase that means "farther away"—is the original name of the island off the coast of Chile on which the Scottish adventurer, Alexander Selkirk,

Defoe's model for Robinson Crusoe, was stranded back in the beginning of the eighteenth century.[26] Derrida does not mention this fact in *The Beast and the Sovereign* seminar. There is a good chance he did not know it. He certainly would have been amused by it if he had. But he would have no doubt gone on to suggest that there is an *afuera*—an outside or a far away—that is farther away than any end or ends of the world, a farther away that would nonetheless come to mark our most everyday, mundane experience, a farther away whose traces—whose singular footprint—might be found in all those with whom we have been stranded, or else, if you happened to be the sole survivor, in those two books you decided to take with you to that desert island.

3

To Die a Living Death

Phantasms of Burial and Cremation

"Do not read until after my death," "To be opened only after I am gone": such messages have no doubt been with us in some form or other since the very beginning of writing. Attached to good-bye notes or last wills and testaments of various kinds, they bear witness in a striking and undeniably powerful way to the absence of the author from what he or she has written. But as Jacques Derrida will have taught us from the very beginning of his work, *all* writing is testamentary in precisely this way, not just those writings explicitly labeled "last will and testament." As Derrida argued more or less everywhere, writing is in its essence and not just accidentally, from the beginning and not just eventually, separated from its author. It is in the very structure of writing or of the trace to be readable in the absence of the author, that is, in principle if not in fact, after his or her demise. As Derrida put it in a particularly poignant way in his very last interview in the summer of 2004, *Learning to Live Finally*:

> I leave a piece of paper behind, I go away, I die: it is impossible to escape this structure, it is the unchanging form of my life. Each time I let something go, each time some trace leaves me, "proceeds" from me, unable to be reappropriated, I live my death in writing. It's the ultimate test: one expropriates oneself without knowing exactly who is being entrusted with what is left behind. Who is going to inherit, and how? Will there even be any heirs? (*LLF* 32–33)

All writing thus speaks in the absence of the writer; all writing is in essence testamentary, and so says, in effect, do not open until after my death, open only after I am gone. But while writing is and has always been testamentary in just this way, it has taken us some time to realize this in full. Thanks in large part to recent advances in technology, the power and scope of these very special speech acts called "last will and testament" have been extended and multiplied to such a degree that it is becoming more and more obvious, and thus harder and harder to deny, that all writing is indeed testamentary in its essence. Let me cite just two among a thousand possible signs of this transformation in our understanding of this testamentary structure of writing, one somewhat personal from almost three decades ago, the other not so personal from just yesterday.

The first example or anecdote dates back to 1985, to a time when to watch TV in the United States still meant to be tuned in with a good percentage of the nation to one of the three major networks. I was thus watching a popular TV show one evening with millions of other viewers when suddenly, during a commercial break, a black screen appeared with the following written across it: "Yul Brynner, 1920–1985," and then a voiceover that said "Ladies and Gentleman, the late Yul Brynner." We then saw the face and heard the voice of the famous movie actor whose death had been widely reported just a few weeks before.

> I really wanted to make a commercial when I discovered that I was that sick and my time was so limited. I wanted to make a commercial that says simply, "Now that I'm gone, I tell you, don't smoke. Whatever you do, just don't smoke." If I could take back that smoking, we wouldn't be talking about any cancer. I'm convinced of it.

It was a powerful and extremely unsettling TV moment, an uncanny and unexpected "public service announcement." This was hardly the first time, of course, I had seen someone speaking on television who had subsequently died, someone who appeared very much alive there on the screen even though they had just recently died or had long been dead. But never had I seen someone speaking of his death in quite this way. Never had I seen someone speaking of their own death as what *will have already* taken place, that is, speaking for this public service announcement for the American Cancer Society at a time when death was imminent but had not yet supervened, about a time when the speaker would already be dead, no longer able to speak or do anything else and yet still present enough to speak from out of his death in this way.[1] Though I could not have formulated this thought at the time in the terms that Derrida would go on to develop in *The Beast and the Sovereign*, it was as if Yul Brynner had been given over to the experience of "dying a living death," seeing himself already dead while still alive and still alive and able to speak after death.

My second example is much more recent and demonstrates just how far this ability to speak from beyond the grave through a public medium has come in just three decades. For there is today, in addition to forums like Facebook or YouTube, where one does not need to be the star of *The King and I* to post a message announcing one's imminent death, the specially dedicated website DeadSocial.com, which "allows anyone to create scheduled messages" that are then "distributed across their social networks after their death." It is a service that, as DeadSocial's website puts it, "explores the notion of digital legacy and allows us all to extend our digital life through technology and the social web," thereby allowing "final goodbyes to be told and for people to continue to communicate once they have passed away."[2] Such services are thus taking social networking to a whole new level, indeed, all the way into the afterlife. One can now style not only one's life but also one's death, the very reception of one's death, and continue to update one's profile long after death. Not only occupation, relationship status, and so on, but also life status: alive, dead, still dead, dead a decade and going strong, and so on. One can thus today imagine entire communities in ruin, communities whose inhabitants have long ago deceased, living on through their social networks, computers and mobile devices continuing to send messages to one another in the absence of all their owners or programmers, all their human senders and recipients.

What these two examples suggest—and they could have been supplemented by a thousand more—is that we have today entered what appears to be a new epoch in survival or a new epoch in the *phantasms* of survival. It is from this perspective, then, that I would like to follow in this chapter the themes of dying a living death, survival, and the phantasms of survival, in *The Beast and the Sovereign* in order to ask, along with Derrida, just what is unique today about these phantasms of survival and what, as a result, calls for a new, *comparative* analysis of the rituals of death and mourning in the West and beyond.

As we have already seen, the second year of *The Beast and the Sovereign* seminar is full of surprises and unexpected turns, beginning with the number and choice of texts to be studied, just two works this second year rather than the many of the previous year, Heidegger's seminar of 1929–30, a seminar Derrida had already treated in some detail elsewhere, and then *Robinson Crusoe*, an eighteenth century English novel that one is more apt to read in a US high school than in an advanced philosophy seminar at the École des Hautes Études in Paris. But among all the unexpected elements and moments of the seminar, none is more surprising, I would like to argue, than the emergence of the question of the relative advantages and disadvantages of being buried or cremated and Derrida's subsequent treatment of this supposed *choice* on the part of a large and growing number of people in the world. From two books, then, to two means of disposing of the corpse in the West: it is this odd and unexpected theme that I would like to follow in this chapter, from its unanticipated emergence in the third of the seminar's ten sessions to its repeated deferral in the subsequent two sessions to its explicit treatment in the Sixth Session and its eventual disappearance in the penultimate session. It is an odd theme that, as we will see, interrupts, scans, and is ultimately buried here on one of the margins of Derrida's rather extraordinary archive.

It's January 22, 2003, the Third Session of the seminar. We are about a third of the way through a seminar that has continued to circle around Heidegger on world, solitude, and finitude, and around *Robinson Crusoe* on everything from sovereignty to prayer to, especially, Robinson Crusoe's obsession with being buried alive by an earthquake or swallowed alive by wild beasts or cannibals, his constant fear not just of death but of "dying a living death." As Derrida argues early on in this Third Session:

> He is afraid of dying a living death [*mourir vivant*] by being swallowed or devoured into the deep belly of the earth or the sea or some living creature, some living animal. That is the great phantasm, the fundamental phantasm or the phantasm of the fundamental: he can think only of being eaten and drunk by the other, he thinks of it as a threat but with such compulsion that one wonders if the threat is not also nurtured like a promise, and therefore a desire. (*BS 2* 77/122–123)

Having thus raised the question of dying a living death and of the *phantasms* associated with it in *Robinson Crusoe*, Derrida begins to ask at the very end of the Third Session not just about Robinson Crusoe's speculations regarding death but about *our own*, a turn to the present or to the personal that is surely not unprecedented in Derrida but that emerges in a rather unanticipated way. This theme will come to haunt the rest of the seminar, as Derrida at the end of the session and then in just about every session thereafter asks and sometimes considers at some length the question of what it means for a growing number of people in the Western or developed world to be given the *choice*, to be allowed or made to choose, to have to *decide*, between *two* ways of having their corpses disposed of: burial or cremation.

There is much to say about this aspect of the seminar, about the *phantasmatic* nature of these speculations concerning death, about the concepts of sovereignty and decision that Derrida thinks he can approach in an exemplary way through this question, about the apparently binary nature of this decision, even though other options are today and were already then available, and, finally, about the fact that this decision appears to coincide with a certain moment in European modernity. I will try to address all of these questions here, but let us look first at how Derrida introduces the question of this alternative between inhumation and cremation, internment and pyrification, at the very end of this Third Session. Derrida continues just after having evoked Robinson Crusoe's fears of dying a living death:

> We shall also come back to everything that is at stake, as to the island, in these terrified desires or desiring terrors of being swallowed alive or buried alive—in their relation to insularity, of course, but also to the maternal womb, and also to the alternative of mournings and phantasms of mourning: between inhumation and cremation. (*BS 2* 92/143)

The theme thus surely does not come completely out of nowhere; it is obviously related to Robinson Crusoe's fear of being buried alive, to the themes of the phantasm, death, mourning, solitude, and the end of the world that Derrida will have been following throughout the seminar. But the *alternative* per se—and the question of an alternative—is rather surprising and unexpected. Without addressing the psychological or even biographical reasons for the emergence of this theme in January of 2003, we need to ask how this alternative fits into the logic of the seminar and into the rest of Derrida's work. One obvious sign that the question of the alternative between inhumation and cremation was nourished by questions or concerns that are only tangentially related to a reading of Heidegger and *Robinson Crusoe* is that this alternative is really only *ours*; it was not exactly Robinson Crusoe's and I assume it was not really Heidegger's, though it had certainly become an alternative for many in 2003 and it is an alternative for even more of us today.

Derrida raises this alternative between inhumation and cremation at the end of the Third Session and we expect him to return to it in greater detail in the next session. But that is not exactly what happens. He begins the Fourth Session by evoking once again Robinson Crusoe's fear—his fantasy or desire—of being buried alive, of dying a living death (*BS 2* 93–94/146). But instead of then turning to the question of the alternative between inhumation and cremation, Derrida addresses the more general question of the *phantasm* associated with imagining one's own death, of imagining oneself as dead-alive, imagining what happens to one after death, the phantasm of surviving one's own death, therefore, of *living one's death* or *dying a living death* (*BS 2* 117/176). He writes—and I cite at some length:

> This suffices all the less to distinguish clearly between death as such and life as such because all our thoughts of death, our death—even before all the help that religious imagery can bring us—our thoughts of our death are always, structurally, thoughts of survival. To see oneself or to think oneself dead is to see oneself surviving, present at one's death, present or represented *in absentia* at one's death even in all the signs, traces, images, memories, even the body, the corpse or the ashes, literal or metaphorical, that we leave behind, in more or less organized and deliberate fashion, to the survivors, the other survivors, the others as survivors delegated to our own survival.
>
> All of which is banal and well known. . . . But the logic of this banality of survival that begins even before our death is that of a survival of the remainder, the remains, that does not even wait for death to make life and death indissociable, and thus the *unheimlich* and fantasmatic experience of the spectrality of the living dead. Life and death as such are not separable as such. . . . (*BS 2* 117/176)

Life and death as such are not separable as such: one could spend an entire seminar—indeed more than one—trying to think through the meaning and implications of this claim. As Derrida suggests, any *thought* of my death is always a kind of phantasm, always already bound up in life and in images of a living death. But it is here that things begin getting personal, as Derrida switches from the third person singular—"one's death"—to the first, "my dead body," "my corpse," "my death." After speaking yet again of Robinson Crusoe's fear of dying a living death, he continues:

> What will one do, what will the *other,* the other *alone,* do with me as living dead, given that I can only *think* my dead body, or rather *imagine* my corpse, if anything else is to happen to it, as living dead in the hands of the other? The other alone. I have just said *think* my death or rather *imagine* my corpse. Well, perhaps the supposed difference between thinking and imagining finds here its ultimate root, and perhaps thinking death as such, in the sense Heidegger wants to give it, is still only imagination. *Fantasia,* fantastic phantasmatics.
>
> Whence, on the basis of this phantasmatics, the immense variety, among all living beings, human or not, of the cultures of the corpse, the gestures or rites of burial or cremation, etc. (*BS 2* 117/176)

Derrida thus ends the session by speaking once again, very briefly, of what he believes to be the noteworthy *hesitation* in our culture between wanting to be buried or cremated. Actually, he ends the session by evoking what seems to be a hesitation of his own:

> I was hoping, and I had promised you, I had promised myself to talk today about this and in the direction of this phantasmatics of dying alive or dying dead, of what happens when people among us, in the West, as they say, still hesitate, more and more, or else decide between burial and cremation, whereas in other cultures they have opted, in massive and stable, still broadly durable fashion, for one or the other. I was hoping, I had promised myself to return too, in the wake of *Walten,* to the origin of the difference of Being and beings, which organizes, as you have seen, this whole problematic. I did not have time; I hope and promise that I'll do it next time, at the very start of the session. (*BS 2* 117–118/177)

For a second time, then, Derrida raises at the end of a session but then defers to later a discussion that appears to be motivating much of the seminar but that seems to want to remain just below the surface.

In the Fifth Session, Derrida returns yet again, after a brief detour through Heidegger's *Das Ding* and the question of whether a cadaver is a thing, to the question of the choice, the seemingly *sovereign* choice, of how our bodies are to be treated after our death, that is, for many of us in the West, whether we are to be buried or cremated. It is at this point, however, that Derrida suggests that this supposedly sovereign choice is perhaps *not* ours after all but always the *other's*, always the other's decision and responsibility.

> What is the other—or what are the others—at the moment when it is a matter of responding to the necessity of making *something of me* [faire quelque chose de moi], of making of me some thing or their thing from the moment I will be, as people say, *departed,* i.e., deceased, passed, passed away . . . when I will be, to all appearances, absolutely without defense, disarmed, in their hands, i.e., as they say, so to speak, dead? (*BS 2* 126/187–188)

Derrida had been speaking throughout of a decision, a choice, but now the emphasis shifts from the self to the other, from the self as sovereign decider to the self divested of self and, thus, of decision, from the self that takes things into its own hands to the corpse that finds itself in the hands of others. The famous or infamous other (whether *autre* or *Autrui*) of contemporary French philosophy would thus have to be entirely rethought in light of this passage. No longer simply the one for whom I have an infinite responsibility, the one who makes claims on me, the other would be first and foremost the one into whose hands I will be delivered at death. Derrida continues:

> And however little I know about what the alterity of the other or the others means, I have to have presupposed that the other, the others, are precisely those who always might die after me, survive me, and have at their disposal what remains of me, my remains. . . . The other appears to me as the other as such, *qua* he, she, or they who might survive me, survive my decease and then proceed as they wish, sovereignly, and sovereignly have at their disposal the future of my remains, if there are any. That's what is meant, has always been meant, by "other." (*BS 2* 126–127/188–189)

This passage is not in contradiction with but certainly does put a different face on a certain philosophical understanding of death, mourning, and the other. For dying now means not essentially being-toward-death, not confronting a death that is in each case my own, but being given over to the hands of the other, delivered over to the other—unable to respond, without defense, as Derrida says referencing Levinas. As for this other, he or she is the one—they are the ones—who must *faire quelque chose de moi*, who must do something with me, make something of me, dispose of me in some way. The other is thus not first of all the one who appeals to me to feed or clothe him but the one who will in principle if not in fact survive me, and so the one who will be left to mourn and to bury me *in one way or another*.

Derrida thus displaces the site of decision, of responsibility, and of sovereignty when he defines the other as the one who will have to decide what to do with my body, my corpse and my corpus. As he had already phrased it in *Adieu*, "could it not be argued [that] . . . decision and responsibility are always of the other? They always come back or come down to the other, from the other, even if it is the other in me?" (*AEL* 23).[3] The other is the one who will survive me, and I can only then *imagine* what this other will do with my remains, since the moment I begin to predict or envision any future or propose any hypothesis as to how the other will respond, I already begin to take the place of the other and so am already in the realm of the phantasm.

In the middle of this Fifth Session, Derrida raises yet again the question of the supposed *choice* that a growing number of people living today in Western or Westernized societies now have, or think they have, between inhumation and cremation, and he explicitly links this choice to the "modernity of a Greco-Abrahamic Europe." We thus move in this session from a seemingly *universal* question of the other and a general definition of the other to the question of death and burial in *our time* and for *our culture.*

> One must be able to wonder what is happening today to a culture like ours, I mean in the present modernity of a Greco-Abrahamic Europe, wonder what is happening to us that is very specific, very acute and unique in the procedural organization of death as survivance, as treatment, by the family and/or the State, of the so-called dead body. (*BS 2* 132/195–196)

These references to Europe and to the state suggest that Derrida is engaged in his own comparative analysis of death, mourning, and funerary culture. Having argued that *Robinson Crusoe* is itself, in addition to everything else, a kind of "comparative anthropology" or ethnography, one that betrays a certain ethnocentrism and Eurocentrism (*BS 2* 134–135/197–199), Derrida seems to be attempting his own "comparative analysis of the two ways of managing the corpse that are available to us in the West at this precise moment in the history of burial" (*BS 2* 144/210), a comparative analysis of burial and cremation and an at least virtual comparison between European modernity and other epochs of funerary culture in Europe and beyond. For if bodies have been burned, buried, mummified, and so on, for millennia, Derrida will argue that ours is the first age in which so many people have been given or are now being faced with the *choice* or *decision* of having their corpses either inhumed or cremated.

The first thing to note, argues Derrida, about this contemporary choice, this apparent choice, is that "the alternative remains very strict: *inhume* or *cremate,* following procedures that can be monitored by civil society, by the state or its police, by professional corporations registered by the state, etc." (*BS 2* 145/211) In other words, the choice or apparent choice for the individual is always determined and restricted in advance by certain state or societal structures and institutions. Because "the departed must on no account disappear without leaving a trace," the state or the family through the state must manage these remains (*BS 2* 145/211). "We have long known," writes Derrida, "that the *polis,* the city, the law of the city, politics, are never constituted . . . without a central administration of funerals" (*BS 2* 145/211).[4] There is thus a politics of mourning, to be sure, but there would also be no politics at all, it seems, before or without this management or administration of mourning. As Derrida argued in *Aporias* some ten years before:

> In an economic, elliptic, hence dogmatic way, I would say that there is no politics without an organization of the time and space of mourn-

ing, without a topolitology of the sepulcher, without an anamnesic and thematic relation to the spirit as ghost, without an open hospitality to the guest as *ghost*, whom one holds, just as he holds us, hostage. (*AP* 10)

In short, funeral rites aim always to ensure or assure us. They are "designed by the survivors, our people, the family, society, the state, to ensure that the dead one really is dead, and will not return" (*BS 2* 145/212), and they are meant to assure the living that the death of the citizen has some meaning, that he or she will have died, for example, for the state or for the polis, that he or she rests in peace in the name of a polis that is then actually constituted or reconstituted around those who have died for it—its forefathers, its martyrs, its fallen heroes.

All this helps explain, no doubt, why the worst kind of destruction for Robinson Crusoe, the kind he feared more than anything else, was being "devoured" by beasts or, worse still, savages or cannibals (*BS 2* 139/204).[5] Robinson Crusoe is afraid of dying like a beast, without a proper funeral, without any of the assurances of family, society, or state (*BS 2* 145/211–212). But Derrida is clearly suggesting here that this fear is not just Robinson Crusoe's but our own, that our own funerary culture aims in the end to assuage these same fears, and that "behind or in the unconscious of funerary culture . . . the savagery of the unconscious . . . continue[s] to operate with the cruelty that Robinson seems to fear when he is afraid of dying a living death like a beast" (*BS 2* 145/212).

It is thus a question of fear and of sovereignty, not just the sovereignty of the state over the individual but also the individual's sovereignty over him or herself. Derrida continues, still in this Fifth Session: "I am now finally coming to the two autoimmune double binds that constitute the only two choices left to us today to respond to the fantasy of dying alive: inhumation and cremation. This is first, and again, a problem of sovereignty" (*BS 2* 143/209). What interests Derrida is indeed, as I noted in the introduction, the question of sovereignty and of the seemingly sovereign decision, open to more and more of us in the West, between inhumation and cremation: "whereas in other cultures people have opted massively and in a stable, still largely durable fashion, for one *or* the other, for one to the intransigent exclusion of the other" (*BS 2* 132–133/196), the West has introduced—indeed the West might even be defined by—the necessity of choosing between these two alternatives. As Derrida affirms, this is "a recent thing," "rare on the surface and in the history of the human earth" (*BS 2* 132/196). What seems to characterize Greco-Abrahamic modernity is this apparent freedom to decide between *two* possibilities, a binary alternative (see *BS 2* 139/204), "the great and ultimate question of the choice between cremation and inhumation, at the hands of the other" (*BS 2* 140/205).

As in so much of Derrida's works of the last couple of decades, it is a question of sovereignty, and first of all a question of the sovereignty or authority one would exercise, or seem to exercise, over one's own body. Derrida develops this point here by evoking, expanding, and transforming the juridical notion of *habeas corpus*. A Latin phrase meaning "you shall have the body," a writ of *habeas corpus*, as we know, orders those holding a prisoner to produce the body, that is, the prisoner, before a judge or court so that it can be determined whether he or she has been illegally detained. Derrida here recasts and broadens this notion of *habeas corpus* to suggest "a sort of proprietorial sovereignty over one's own living body": *habeas corpus* would mean, in essence, you shall have your body, your own body, the body that is yours—a philosophical conception of sovereignty over one's body that would in fact be at the origin, Derrida seems to be suggesting, of the juridical notion (*BS 2* 143/209). Leaving aside all the contemporary questions regarding this supposed sovereignty over one's body when it is put to the test by new technologies of conception and of birth, by organ transplants, DNA research, autopsies, and so on, Derrida says he wishes to focus on "the decision, the choice, the alternative between *bury* and *cremate,* and its relation to the fantasy of the living dead" (*BS 2* 143/209).

Questions of life, death, sovereignty, self and other, the phantasm, fears of being buried alive: all these seem to come together for Derrida in the question of the decision, the seemingly *sovereign* decision to be buried or burned, inhumed or incinerated, entombed or cremated, buried in the ground or reduced to ash. It is a decision that, obviously, can be made only before one's death but that can be carried out, just as obviously, only after one's death, that is, only after the death of the one who decided. While it may thus seem that one has sovereign control over one's own body, that one may leave behind a last will and testament to instruct the survivors on how to proceed with one's corpse, Derrida reminds us that "this testament will have force of law only if a third party, the State or a force of institutional coercion, guarantees it and can oblige the inheritors to obey its instructions" (*BS 2* 143/210). In order, therefore, for one's putatively sovereign decision to be *carried out*, in order for one to *exercise* one's own sovereignty, one must yield to the sovereignty of the other, that is, give up one's sovereignty by giving oneself over to the other. Hence, Derrida speaks of "the autoimmune contradiction or aporia in which this last will is fatally caught, at the moment it is trying to choose sovereignly, and to dictate sovereignly, dictatorially, their conduct to survivors who for their part become the real sovereigns" (*BS 2* 144/210).

It is here that sovereignty is reestablished—or established in the first place—only by means of an appeal to the phantasm, that is, only in *imagination*, since, as we all know, "a dead person is one who cannot him or herself put into operation any decision concerning the future of his or her corpse" (*BS 2* 144/210). In other words, "the dead person no longer has the corpse at his or her disposal, there is no longer any *habeas corpus*"—"supposing," adds Derrida, "there ever were such a thing." It is with this little addition that Derrida suggests that what seems to be an exception to one's sovereignty over oneself is in fact the structural condition for it or for any phantasm with regard to it. Just as the very specific speech act of the last will and testament reveals the testamentary structure of all writing, so the threat to the sovereignty of the self that happens at death reveals the originary lack of such sovereignty. What this decision with regard to the end reveals is that we will have been delivered over to the hands of the other from the very beginning—not just at our deaths but already from the day we are born. From ashes to ashes, to be sure, but also from the hands of others into the hands of others. As Leopold Bloom succinctly puts this law of the other in *Ulysses*, "Washing child, washing corpse."[6] Our lives would be but the interval between two washings at the hands of the other.

All this suggests that *habeas corpus*, the sovereign control over one's own body, will have been, like all other kinds of sovereignty, a sort of phantasm. Despite all appearances, we will have *never* had a sovereign power over our own body. Hence, Derrida can argue that, in essence, "this *habeas corpus* never existed and its legal emergence, however important it may be, designates merely a way of taking into account or managing the effects of heteronomy and an irreducible *non habeas corpus*" (*BS 2* 144/210). *Habeas corpus*—"you shall have the body," "you shall have your body"—would thus be but a *reactive* formation, a reaction to a more originary *non–habeas corpus*. Despite the appearance of choice and an entire legal apparatus that aims to protect it, the alternative between cremation and inhumation will have never simply been ours.

Finally, then, at the end of the Fifth Session, Derrida turns—or at least that's what it seems—to the question of the advantages and disadvantages, the pros and cons, so to speak, of being buried or burned. He begins with inhumation, which is statistically the most frequent choice in the West (*BS 2* 146/212). With a view to what, he asks, would one choose inhumation over cremation? In other words, what kinds of phantasies or phantasms are involved in this seemingly sovereign choice? But just after beginning to go down this path, Derrida ends the session by deferring *yet again* a full discussion of the perceived or imagined advantages or disadvantages, that is, the phantasmatic advantages or disadvantages, of being buried or burned. Having briefly sketched out "the form of the question [he] would like now to articulate, both for inhumation and for cremation," Derrida declares that, much to his own relief, there is not enough time in the session to carry out the analysis:

> There is no point telling you, to our common relief, that these questions are always questions one can keep waiting. As long as possible.
> But at least until next week. (*BS 2* 146/213)

Alas, the next week, the sixth of the seminar's ten sessions, comes soon enough, and Derrida can no longer put off the discussion he has been deferring for the previous three sessions, a discussion, finally, of the apparent reasons one might have for choosing to be inhumed rather than cremated, or vice versa. It's February 12, 2003, and Derrida begins the session with a single French word: "*Courage*"—a word that oscillates here between a noun and an imperative—"Courage," "Bravery," but also "Have courage," "Be brave": one must have courage or be brave, Derrida would seem to be suggesting, to think a living death, to think death while living, even if any thinking of death will always entail a certain *phantasm* of death, the *phantasm* of being present at one's own death and so surviving oneself in death (*BS 2* 148/215). It is at this point that Derrida gives us one of the best definitions of the phantasm in all of his work:

> What I called "phantasm" in this context is indeed the inconceivable, the contradictory, the unthinkable, the impossible. But I insisted on the zone in which the impossible is named, desired, apprehended. Where it affects us. I did this for methodological reasons, namely in order clearly to delimit the field we were going to explore in wondering why *today*, in *our* European cultural area—and thus in its law, its language, its civil and political organization—a decision must be taken by the still living mortal or the still living dying person, or by his or her still living relatives, by the survivors, as to the ritual of burial or cremation. (*BS 2* 148/217)[7]

The phantasm is indeed this inconceivable, contradictory, impossible, unthinkable thing—a natural law, an immaculate conception, a living death. That the phantasm is impossible does not mean, however, that it cannot be named or desired; that the phantasm *is not* does not mean that it has no power. On the contrary, argues Derrida, a phantasmatic content can overcome or disarm the distinction between the real and the imaginary. As we all know, what happens in imagination, what happens virtually or in literature, can have the *effect* of what has actually happened (*BS 2* 128–129/191).[8]

Dying a living death can thus only be a fiction or a phantasm. Indeed, it gives us perhaps the paradigm of the phantasm through a life that coincides with and so goes beyond death, through a conflation of life and death that would go beyond life and death: "This power of almightiness belongs to a beyond of the opposition between being or not being, life and death, reality and fiction or fantasmatic virtuality" (*BS 2* 130/193). Derrida thus goes on to relate this phantasm to the "as if," for with the phantasm it is always "as if" something could still happen to the dead, "as if," "perhaps," "something could still happen to the survivors *on behalf of the dead one,* as cremated or buried body, or on behalf of what remains or does not remain of it, which is sometimes called the Spirit, the specter, or the soul" (*BS 2* 149/217).

Uncertain, he says, to what degree his sense of *phantasm* coincides with a philosophical or psychoanalytic understanding of it, Derrida justifies here his choice of terms. While everything suggests to us that with death comes the radical and irreversible interruption of "that power to be affected that is called life," we are unable to accept the "invincible authority" of this evidence and so resort to the phantasm of a living death. It is, says Derrida, "because this certainty is terrifying and literally intolerable, just as unthinkable, just as unpreventable and unrepresentable as the contradiction of the living dead, that what I call with this obscure word 'phantasm' imposed itself upon me" (*BS 2* 149/218). The phantasm is thus the result of an internal aporia or contradiction that both masks and signals an intolerable situation. The phantasm is unthinkable, unbearable, always in contradiction with itself, even though it is also, it seems, precisely what makes a certain form of life tolerable. It is because death is unthinkable, unrepresentable, that we resort to this contradictory thing called the phantasm. Hence, Derrida cites Freud's claim that our death is unbelievable, that "the relation to our own death is not representable" (*BS 2* 157/227), in order to contest Heidegger's assertion that Dasein, unlike the animal, has a certain access to death as such.[9]

We are alive enough to see ourselves and imagine ourselves dead, and therefore, I would add, buried or swallowed up or cremated alive. This is another way of saying, against Heidegger, that we never have any access to our own death *as such,* that we are incapable of it. Our death is impossible. Whence Freud concludes, and I quote: "Hence the psychoanalytic school could venture the assertion that at bottom no one believes in his own death, or, to put the same thing in another way, that in the unconscious every one of us is convinced of his own immortality." (*BS 2* 157/228)[10]

This theme of the phantasm comes to haunt the entire seminar from the third week on and it calls out to be thought in relation to the question of the phantasm of the world or of the end of the world. As we saw in the previous chapter, Derrida argues in the final session of the seminar that the world is itself a *phantasm*, which means that any thinking of the *end* of the world, any apocalyptic vision of the end of the world or of the end of history, will remain a kind of phantasm of or within that phantasm.

After asking about the nature of this phantasm of death and of the phantasm in general, we come, *finally*, here in the middle of the Sixth Session (*BS 2* 159/231), to the question of the alternative between inhumation and cremation. As if he had been deferring a question that so many of us indefinitely put off—what is to be done with our estate, our possessions, our bodies after our deaths—Derrida begins a long consideration of our shared phantasms and phantasmatic investments with regard to burial and incineration. The speculations Derrida indulges in here are not hard to follow, indeed they are almost commonplace, the sort of speculations many people have these days—and this is precisely the point—either alone or with family members around the kitchen table, as they consider the advantages and disadvantages of these two means of having their bodies disposed of.

Derrida proceeds to consider these two possibilities in relation to both *time* and *space*, that is, the time and space we *imagine* will continue to be attached to our corpse or our cadaver after our death (*BS 2* 160–161/232–233). The phantasm of dying a living death is thus always the phantasm of having more time and more space in which to "live," in which to maneuver, after one's time and space have run out.

The first, temporal advantage of burial or inhumation would thus be that it is not immediate or irreversible. Burial assures the cadaver a bit more time on or in the earth, a bit more time to survive as a body and a bit more time for some miracle to happen to the body. So long as the body is not immediately embalmed, the one who opts for burial can console himself or herself with the thought that, given the uncertainty regarding the medical definition of death, a brief window remains open for a falsely declared death to be revealed (*BS 2* 161–2/234). Burial allows a body that is not really dead but only appears to be so to be revived or resurrected—the only imaginable resurrection for a seemingly secular age.

Of course, on the other side of the ledger, the phantasm accorded by inhumation of having more time in or on the earth can easily turn into the Edgar Allan Poe nightmare of waking up alive in a casket six feet under the ground (*BS 2* 164/237).[11] In addition, the fact that inhumation gives us more time means that we cannot but entertain images of the decaying or decomposing body over time in the tomb, images that cremation will spare us (*BS 2* 166/235).

With regard to space, inhumation also has the advantage of providing a specific site for memory or mourning, a grave or tomb where survivors or loved ones can gather to pray or pay their respects. The cadaver has a reserved space and it continues to take up space, to have a place—its place—in the world.

Of course, the advantage attached to this stability of place can also be seen as a disadvantage (*BS 2* 165/238). While one might be consoled by the thought that one's survivors will be consoled by having a place to visit and pay their respects, one might also be troubled by the thought that one's survivors will be troubled by this choice. For by burying the body in a cemetery or some other site, it is as if the survivors were not simply giving the dead a proper resting place but abandoning or exiling them, placing them *outside* the home and consigning them to some publicly sanctioned and authorized place. The work of mourning for the survivors can then always be accompanied by a sentiment of culpability for having exiled the body in this way, for having excluded it from the home as quickly as possible and relegated it to a cemetery (*BS 2* 165–167/239–240).

These are just some of the things one might take into account, just some of the calculations one might make, regarding the time and space of the inhumed body. Though Derrida is speaking here of a personal calculation, it is clear that he also has other more general, culture stakes in view, as if an individual's phantasmatic attachments might illuminate something of the more general phantasmagory of our culture. Before turning, then, to the concomitant advantages and disadvantages of cremation, Derrida poses—more or less in passing—a theological question with regard to inhumation, which has been up until recently by far the most common way of disposing of the corpse in the Western world. He asks whether Christianity, with its imaginary or phantasmagory of death and resurrection, would have been thinkable if Christ had been cremated rather than entombed (*BS 2* 164/238). Would certain conceptions of resurrection or rapture have ever gotten off the ground, so to speak, would a celebration of the Eucharist have ever really gone down, in a culture where cremation was the norm? Derrida seems to be suggesting that if we want to know about Christianity, perhaps even get to the essence of Christianity, we could do worse than to consider our own phantasmatic attachments to and investments in inhumation as opposed to cremation.

As for cremation, then, it offers advantages and disadvantages that are in many respects the opposite of those afforded by burial, with its promise of temporal continuity and spatial stability (*BS 2* 167/241).[12] Cremation destroys the body almost immediately, ends in a radical way the body's time in the world, removing it from the earth and taking away its stability of place, its taking place in any particular place. In cremation, the deceased is reduced to ashes and so becomes "both everywhere and nowhere" (*BS 2* 169/243). The collection of ashes in a portable urn means that the dead have no proper site beyond the urn, no special site, at least not necessarily, for visitation, prayer, or memory. Purified by the modern-day pyre, the dead no longer have a space of their own, and their time—the time of a slow decay—is immediately cut short by the consuming flames (*BS 2* 169/243).

Yet cremation compensates for the lack of a stable place for memory and mourning by giving mobility to one's remains, allowing them to be scattered or transported from place to place. The memorial urn can be moved and a place of memory established almost anywhere. The ashes can even be spread out in a specific site, in a garden or some location at sea that already has or will take on a special meaning. The disadvantage of not having a particular site thus becomes the advantage of a site that can be almost anywhere—indeed that can be in multiple places, since the ashes can also be divided up, between spouse and children or siblings or friends, all of whom can keep a trace of the deceased close by, even in their home, on their mantelpiece.

In relation to both time and space, cremation presents advantages and disadvantages that counter and sometimes offset those of inhumation. Since cremation is immediate, one cannot indulge in images of a body decomposing in the ground over time. And yet, precisely because cremation is immediate and irreversible, there is no possibility for a body that is not in fact dead to be resuscitated once it has been given over to incineration (*BS 2* 162/235). The survivors avoid through cremation the potential culpability of having abandoned their beloved to some public place, but they might just as well be besieged by the culpability of having reacted so swiftly to dispose of the loved one, of having taken the first occasion not just to exile the body but to reduce it to ashes so as to be done with it once and for all. And to make matters worse, they will have resorted to a technique that, "in the modern and ineffaceable history of humanity, can no longer fail to metonymize, in everyone's consciousness and unconscious, the crematoria of the camps" (*BS 2* 179/255).

All the aporias of mourning that Derrida develops in "*Fors*," *The Work of Mourning*, and elsewhere need to be rethought here: the aporia of a fidelity that can be faithful only by being unfaithful, that mourns only by incorporating the other so as to leave the other's alterity intact, or that leaves the other's alterity intact so as not to abandon them to indifference (*BS 2* 168/242).[13] Questions of mourning and melancholia, of incorporation and introjection, all become particularly acute in relationship to these seemingly everyday speculations concerning the phantasms of burial—a sort of incorporation—or cremation. Derrida devotes several pages to this comparative analysis of burial and cremation, drawing up a rather long list of the pros and cons of each, sorting them out, as it were, into columns on the legal pad of the seminar. But what is essential to underscore here is that these speculations are and must remain *phantasmatic*, images we have of ourselves dead while still living, that is, "as if [*comme si*] . . . we still had to suffer, worry, torment ourselves as to what will happen when we are no longer there to suffer, to worry, to torment ourselves" (*BS 2* 159/231). For it is, says Derrida, who insists on underscoring the obvious, only as a *living* human being that we can choose inhumation or cremation, only as a living human being that we can *imagine* our death in any way at all and, thus, imagine how "our" decision will be carried out by those who will survive us (*BS 2* 160/231–232).

Once again, what is important in Derrida's analysis of the alternative between burial and cremation is that it seems to be, precisely, a *choice*, a *modern* choice for a seemingly sovereign subject (*BS 2* 163/236), a choice that is no doubt influenced by tradition and economy (cremation is usually less expensive than inhumation) but also by these various phantasms of death. Derrida thus speaks of

> a highly significant and unprecedented—and thus strictly "modern"—phenomenon of liberation with respect to religious prescriptions, which demand inhumation in European, Greco-Latin or pre-Christian, but also Abrahamic, Judeo-Christian-Islamic religions, and cremation in certain Eastern, and particularly Indian or Japanese, cultures. If one seeks to identify modernity ("what is it to be modern?" "what is the essential and specific criterion of modernity?" "where is the distinctive sign of modernity?"), well, we have the mark of it first of all here. (*BS 2* 163/236)

Derrida does not really consider the specifically religious prohibition against cremation and what it means for religious faith (whether Christian, Jewish, or Muslim) when a growing number of people consider cremation to be a "viable" possibility. But *The Beast and the Sovereign* certainly calls out for such a "comparative ethnography" or comparative analysis of what is happening today with regard to death, mourning, and survival.[14] Once again, it is the question of political modernity and the theologico-political that Derrida is raising. Rather than having one's choice determined in advance, inhumation for most Abrahamic cultures, cremation for certain cultures of the East, modernity might be defined by an apparent freedom or liberation and thus a seeming *choice* between these two alternatives. To the question "What is modernity?" Derrida thus hazards the answer: "it was the opening of the alternative and the choice left by the state, in European and Greco-Abrahamic cultures, between cremation and inhumation" (*BS 2* 179/255). This is no doubt why Derrida throughout the seminar refers somewhat playfully to the partisans of these two options as *inhumants* and *incinerants*, as if they were, precisely, partisans, two political parties vying for our allegiance, two fraternities, clans, or religious groups (*BS 2* 163/235; see also 174/250 and 232/324). It is as if Western society were today divided up into inhumants and incinerants, buriers and burners, just as it is divided into PC and Mac users, Coke and Pepsi people, McDonalds and Burger King devotees.

All this helps justify, in part, Derrida's own choice of *Robinson Crusoe* for one of the two books of his final seminar. The novel was obviously chosen because of its treatment of some of the central themes of the seminar— the human's relation to the animal, man's supposed sovereignty over the beast, Robinson Crusoe's obsession with being buried or eaten alive, and so on. But *Robinson Crusoe*, first published in 1719, is also often considered the beginning of a certain epoch of modern sovereignty and of the modern, self-reliant individual. To ask about the origins and nature of modernity, one could thus do worse—and Derrida would not have been the first to make such a suggestion—than to reread *Robinson Crusoe*. In the Ninth (and next to last) Session of the seminar, Derrida goes so far as to relate the decision to declare oneself an *inhumant* or *incinerant* to liberal democracy, asking why, in this historical epoch, there are only *two* choices, and what other choices the future has in store that will transform our epoch (*BS 2* 232–233/325). As always, Derrida is interested in asking why or how difference or multiplicity has been reduced to a *binary* alternative. The choice is between inhumation and creation, as Derrida presents it, even though other, less popular options were available in 2002–2003, while others still are available to us today, everything from donating one's body to science to cryogenic preservation to liquefaction (or "resumating"), freeze drying, composting, or what have you. Is there, then, Derrida is asking, another epoch of mourning on the horizon, a future epoch where we are not limited to these two choices? What would that mean for religious culture or for European modernity? What would it change? These are the questions that seem to be motivating Derrida's meditations, questions of the alternative between inhumation and cremation and the possibility of an epoch that would offer other possibilities beyond this alternative—the end or closure, perhaps, of a certain *theologico-political* determination of death, mourning, survival, sovereignty, and their phantasms. As Derrida speculates:

> People would speak of the cremators and the inhumers . . . as oddities that were both *unheimlich* and dated, as archaic curiosities for historians or anthropologists of death. I'll let you dream of a death that would no longer leave us in the hands of these itinerant sects of cremators or inhumers, and would definitively put out of a job these arrogant sects that pass for the religions to which they appeal for their authority, or the secularizing laity to which they lay claim . . . (*BS 2* 233/326)

Let me conclude this look at Derrida's meditations in *The Beast and the Sovereign* regarding this contemporary alternative between inhumation and cremation by recalling his parallel reading, some twenty years earlier, in *Aporias* (1992), of Heidegger's analyses of being-toward-death in *Being and Time* and Philippe Ariès's history of Western funeral practices and attitudes toward death in *Essais sur l'histoire de la mort en Occident du Moyen Age à nos jours*. It is as if Derrida in *The Beast and the Sovereign* were following both Heidegger and Ariès to identify a fundamental shift in our understanding of death and in our *phantasmatic* investment in the fates of our bodies after death.[15]

But the parallel between *Aporias* and *The Beast and the Sovereign* may go even further than that. Derrida suggests in *Aporias* that one can always read the relationship between Ariès's treatise and Heidegger's *Being and Time* in one of two ways. One can read Ariès's work from a Heideggerian perspective as just another example of an ontic treatment of death, an analysis of death from an *existentiel* rather than an existential point of view; one can thus read it as a text that is located squarely *within* Heidegger's treatment in *Being and Time* of the various inauthentic ways that Dasein treats death. But, Derrida says, one might also always read Heidegger's *Being and Time* and its understanding of being-toward-death, conscience, and so on, from Ariès's perspective as one discourse among others in the modern archive and memory of Christian Europe, in which case *it* could be squarely located within Ariès's book, relegated to just a footnote within one of its chapters. In other words, each of these two discourses can be considered bigger than the other; each can be considered to frame or incorporate the other, each can be considered to be buried or encapsulated within the other (*AP* 80–81).

Something similar might be said, I would like to suggest, about Derrida's final seminar *The Beast and the Sovereign*: Derrida's analyses of the phantasms of burial and cremation can always be considered to be the object or theme of this final seminar, and so can always be considered to be within it, to be contained or buried within it. And one can always, of course, try to read *The Beast and the Sovereign* in relation to Derrida's biography and health concerns in the spring of 2003. But because of what Derrida says in this seminar about what it means to be buried alive, about how a trace is always a kind of living death, we might also always consider *The Beast and the Sovereign* to be not just *about* being buried alive, and not just a reflection of the concerns of its author, but something that is itself a *living dead*, its exemplary discourse about dying a living death no longer merely contained but *containing*. In this case, we would have the curious example of a trace that will have posed the question of the trace, a seminar—a sort of corpse or corpus—that will have posed in an *explicit* fashion the very question of what it means to die a living death and what it means to survive one's death, not by being immortal, not by being resurrected from the tomb, but by being deposed—and this will be the subject of Chapter 6—in the archive, where it can remain forever buried and forgotten, or consigned to flames and reduced to ashes, or else, as I would wish to think here, reanimated, studied and recalled, for the time of a reading.

4

Reinventing the Wheel

Of Sovereignty, Autobiography, and Deconstruction

I long, as does every human being, to be at home wherever I find myself.
—**Maya Angelou**

I begin this chapter—this central chapter on the question of sovereignty and autobiography in *The Beast and the Sovereign*—a little closer to home, that is, with a line that comes not from Derrida, Heidegger, or Defoe but from the American poet Maya Angelou.[1] I do so because this brief, elliptical sentence will lead us straight back—though only after a rather long detour— to several of the central themes and concerns of Derrida's seminar.

"I long, as does every human being, to be at home wherever I find my-self": it's a seemingly simple but upon reflection a rather complicated line that brings together longing, a certain understanding if not definition of the human, and the notion of home, which, as we shall see, is at the very center of *The Beast and the Sovereign*, whether under this or other names. For Angelou begins with a personal sentiment or testimony ("I long," she says) that then becomes, without argument or transition, something like a general law for "every human being," one that would even seem to define what it is to be human. According to Angelou, *all* human beings long to be at home wherever they are. She does not tell us whether she considers this longing to be proper to human beings alone, though I assume she does, ei-ther because animals would have no home for which to long or because they are always at home and so cannot be defined by such loss or longing, but this longing to be at home appears to be, for the human animal at least, a defining trait.

All human beings, then, long to be at home, but to be at home *wher-ever they may be*. Angelou is thus clearly not suggesting that all humans long to return to some unique place called home, to the home we presume to be uniquely ours. She is not saying, like Dorothy, that there is no place like home and that it is to that place called home that we all wish to return. No, she is saying that we all long to be or to find ourselves at home wherever we may be. This longing to return home is thus not some local or localizable desire, revolving around some specific place, but a general condition that inevitably results, it would seem, in either great satisfaction or endless frustration, ongoing celebration or perpetual disappointment. For this longing to be at home wherever we find ourselves might presumably be satisfied wherever and whenever we happen to feel ourselves to be at home, and even when we find ourselves far away from what we call home. Much more likely, however, is that this longing will remain, for some or for all of us, perpetually frustrated, an endless exile and longing to be at home even when we find ourselves in that place we call home. For one can surely be home and yet not feel at home at all, be home and yet still long to be home, as if the place we call home no longer corresponds to the home we remember or for which we still long, the home to which we will have longed to return, perhaps, already from the beginning.

I begin this chapter, this central chapter, as I said, with Angelou rather than Derrida, Defoe, or Heidegger because one of the underlying themes of *The Beast and the Sovereign* is the possibility or impossibility of homecoming—and because sometimes, as Joyce puts it in *Ulysses*, "the longest way round is the shortest way home." In this case, I would argue, the shortest way round to what is central to Derrida may just be through the detour of this message or summons from Angelou. And I say message or summons because the name Angelou comes from the Greek noun *angelos*, meaning messenger or envoy, which is no doubt why the singer and poet born in 1928 under the name Marguerite Annie Johnson began writing under the penname Maya Angelou in the first place. *Angelos*, the genitive of which is *angelou*, means envoy or messenger, angel even, a messenger sent from the gods to bear tidings or proclaim some good news, a very telling name indeed for a poet and one that is used by the West's very first poet in the context, precisely, of homecoming. In the *Odyssey*, Homer calls the god Hermes an *angelos*, a messenger, at the very moment he is being sent by Zeus to announce to the nymph Calypso that the gods have decided it is time for Odysseus to return home. Zeus there tells Hermes, the *angelos* of the gods, to tell Calypso, who has kept Odysseus on her island for some seven years and so has delayed his return from Troy, that it is finally time for him to return to his native Ithaca. From one island, then, to another, from an island that is not home and where Odysseus does not feel at home to an island Odysseus calls home and where he will presumably feel at home: The story or odyssey of homecoming will have been from the very beginning, as Derrida suggests in his reading of *Robinson Crusoe* and as we will see in this chapter, bound up in Western literature and mythology with islands: Ithaca, Ogygia (Calypso's island), England, Ireland, Más Afuera . . .

In book 5 of the *Odyssey*, the *angelos* Hermes tells Calypso that the gods now wish for Odysseus's long exile to end. They wish for his return, for his *nostos*, this word *nostos* being, of course, at the root of our word *nostalgia*, meaning a pain or a longing (an *algos*) for return (for a *nostos*) (*Odyssey* 5.29–31). In short, the *angelos* Hermes announces that Odysseus's longing to return home, a longing that has not been satisfied wherever he has found himself, that has not been sated by Calypso, must end.[2] It is time to put an end to Odysseus's long time of exile, his long period of nostalgia or home-ache, that is, of homesickness—of what might be translated into German as *Heimweh*. And fortunately for Odysseus, there is, it seems, the promise of just such a homecoming, a genuine *nostos* that will finally put an end to his *Heimweh* or his nostalgia, a return first to Ithaca and then, as a home within that home, to the bed he shared with Penelope, that famous bed anchored in the ground by a bedpost hewn out of an ancient olive tree whose roots still reach down into the earth, that bedpost that will have oriented all of Odysseus's travels as his axis mundi, his north star, his GPS, the axle around which he will have turned like a wheel or wandered like a planet for some nineteen years.

In this chapter, I would like to argue that just as that island and that bedpost provide the coordinates for Odysseus's epic return, so Odysseus's return, his odyssey, provides us in the West with the coordinates for all subsequent homecomings in the figure of a circuit or a circle that returns, or at least seems to return, to its point of departure, the figure of a detour through the world that ends up returning back to its origin. That is, as we will see, the promise of every homecoming. Every homecoming describes, or seems to describe, a circle, which is thus the figure for every return to home or to the self, indeed, for every relation of self-return or self-identity. It will thus be to this figure of the circle, or of the wheel, more precisely, that I will wish to turn as I take up just a few passages from Session Three of the second year of *The Beast and the Sovereign*.

But I am not there yet, for there was another reason for wanting to begin this chapter with the tidings of Maya Angelou. Whether or not we all do indeed long to be home wherever we find ourselves, Angelou's claim resonates rather uncannily with a line from the eighteenth century German poet Novalis, who once wrote: *"Die Philosophie ist eigentlich Heimweh, Trieb, überall zu Hause zu sein."*[3] That is, "Philosophy is really homesickness, an urge to be at home everywhere." Philosophy, says Novalis, is essentially *Heimweh*, that is, precisely, a homesickness, a *mal du pays*, as one says in French, a longing to be everywhere at home. Philosophy is longing, nostalgia, homesickness, an urge, desire, or drive, a *Trieb*, to return to a home that would not be here or there, in some particular place or other, but wherever we might find ourselves, or else, for this might be something else altogether, everywhere. Philosophy would be the drive, the homesickness drive, the urge to be *everywhere* at home. The longing that Maya Angelou finds in all human beings is thus limited by Novalis to philosophy. In the one case it is just philosophers, in the other it is all human beings, who long to feel at home wherever they may be, and this longing would be, it seems, a sort of inheritance, something passed on from generation to generation, the common lot of all philosophers or all humans.

If I have begun this chapter with a series of detours, that is—like wheels within wheels—with a line from Maya Angelou that recalls Homer and echoes Novalis, it is in part because this same from Novalis is cited at the beginning and then really comes to be at the center of Heidegger's 1929–30 seminar, the one that becomes so central to Derrida's seminar. Near the end of Chapter 2, I suggested that Derrida in *The Beast and the Sovereign* turns round a single line from the poet Paul Celan (*Die Welt ist fort, ich muß dich tragen*) much as Heidegger in his 1929–30 seminar turns round this line from Novalis. It is no coincidence, then, it seems to me, that both lines evoke a certain loss or exile, a loss of world or an exile from home, no coincidence that both implicitly raise the question of how we must live in the face of this originary loss, lack, or exile.

If Derrida thus turns round Heidegger's seminar and *Robinson Crusoe* throughout his final seminar, two works that differ so greatly in terms of time period, language, and genre, if he restricts his gaze to these two texts as if he were himself stranded on a deserted island and had only these two books to read during his yearlong journey or exile in the seminar, it is perhaps because both of these works are concerned with questions of the home and homecoming, with what it means to be away from home and what it means to return, and thus, at least implicitly, with the figure of the circle or the wheel in its relationship to homecoming and return. This figure of the circle or the wheel will eventually come to be, for Derrida, as we will see, the figure not just of every homecoming, from Homer's *Odyssey* to Defoe's *Robinson Crusoe* and Joyce's *Ulysses*, but the figure of all identity or self-identity, that is—or this is at least the fiction or the phantasm—the figure of a self that is able to return to itself, as if returning home, in order to say "I, I am home, I have returned home after my long sojourn through the world." For if every homecoming traces a circular movement of departure and return, if each takes the shape or figure of a circle, of a movement away from a particular point out into the world and then a return back to the point of departure, then perhaps homecoming is not some particular, identifiable moment or movement within the world but the very movement of identity itself. And this might be the case even if this homecoming that is so much desired or longed for is always interrupted or perpetually deferred, not simply because there so many obstacles to returning home but because the home is perhaps never what we thought it to be and so is never that to which we can ever simply return, because it is perhaps from the outset a fiction or a phantasm, in short, to make use of her first name this time, a veil of Maya.

This is my final reason for wanting to begin this chapter with the voice of the American poet Maya Angelou: the fiction or phantasm of home is perhaps always, in the tradition we are following here, the phantasm of an essentially male or masculine protagonist who wishes to return home after a certain detour through the world, the phantasm of a male sojourner who wishes to return home to the woman who will have been waiting there for him at the point of departure (Penelope, Molly, Robinson Crusoe's wife—for he too had a wife, though, as Derrida recalls, he almost never mentions her). Between longing to be at home wherever we may be and longing to return to the home as to an original point of departure, what we see emerging is perhaps not only the question of identity and difference, of the self and of sovereignty, of autobiography, but the question of sexual difference and, however tangential this may at first appear, the question of the difference between the circle and the wheel.

So let me begin again, after all these detours and false departures, by turning to a crucial but very odd moment in this very odd seminar *The Beast and the Sovereign*, the moment when Derrida considers Robinson Crusoe's reinvention of the wheel. As we will see, Derrida will relate Defoe's brief tale of this technological invention or reinvention to nothing less than a rethinking of sovereignty and the sovereign self, a rethinking, therefore, of identity formation and of the possibility of autobiography, a rethinking of the meaning of exile and homecoming, of departure and return, though also, as I will try to tease out, of the very time and future of philosophy or of deconstruction. That's a pretty ambitious trajectory, I realize, but it is one that Derrida traces out in the course of a few very difficult but extraordinarily rewarding pages in the middle of the seminar, pages whose gravitational pull draw almost everything else in the seminar, indeed almost everything else in Derrida's corpus, into their orbit.

It's January 22, 2003, the Third Session of the seminar and the first session in the new calendar year, the first, that is, after the turn of the new year. Derrida returns to questions of solitude and of the speech act with which he began the entire seminar. He recalls having begun the seminar—just like Robinson Crusoe's journal, as we will see in a moment, indeed just like the entire novel *Robinson Crusoe*—with the first-person singular pronoun, I, *je*.[4] He began by saying, as if he were just waking up or coming to after having been shipwrecked on the shores of a seminar, of yet another seminar, *je suis seul(e)*, "I am alone." (Let me note in passing the way in which the parenthetical *e* of *seul* already introduces the question of sexual difference. Just as Derrida begins the first session of the first year of *The Beast and the Sovereign* seminar with the masculine and feminine definite articles, *la . . . le*, so he begins this second year with the masculine/feminine adjective *seul(e)*.) Derrida thus recalls this opening and then returns to the three theses regarding the stone, the animal, and the human from Heidegger's seminar of 1929–30—the theses, to recall, that the stone is worldless, the animal poor in world, and the human world-building. He then goes on to question Heidegger's privileging of the close or the proximate as the proper place or path for beginning his questioning, that is, Heidegger's choice, both in *Being and Time* two years before and in the seminar of 1929–30, of human Dasein as the "exemplary being for the question of Being because it is closest to *us*, as questioning beings" (*BS 2* 63/105). As Heidegger asks and Derrida cites, "What could be closer to us than our own *Selbst*?" (*BS 2* 72/116), that is, Heidegger asks, what could be more proximate to us than our own self, our own *autos*?

Now because this "supposed proximity of oneself to oneself raises . . . the question of orientation" (*BS 2* 73/116–117), Derrida turns next—after a somewhat extended detour through Rousseau on islands and isolation and Heidegger on boredom—to Kant and the question of orientation. And this then leads Derrida to ask, as if he had been circling around it from the very beginning, about how one orients oneself on an island, where every step one takes brings one at once further away from one's point of departure and closer to it, and where there is always the chance—the opportunity or the threat—of encountering one's own footprint or the footprint of another, or one's own as another's, in the circuit or return back round to oneself. (You may recall that one of the central events in Defoe's novel is Robinson Crusoe's discovery of a single, human footprint on the shores of his island, which he had thought to be deserted.) Derrida comments:

> the step that seems farthest from my starting point [*mon point de départ*], on an island where one goes round in circles, like a wheel, like the rotation or rather the wheeling of a wheel, can also be <the one> closest to it. My last footstep always might coincide with my

first. This is the law of the island and the law of the wheel. (*BS 2* 74/118)

It is at this point that Derrida, finally, relates the question of the circularity of islands and the inevitability or impossibility of returning to one's point of departure to Robinson Crusoe's invention of the wheel, or, rather, his *reinvention* of it, as if Crusoe had to return to it precisely like a wheel in order to rediscover or reinvent it (*BS 2* 74–75/118–119).[5] It is this reinvention of the wheel, as we will see, that leads to all of Derrida's speculations concerning not only the significance of the wheel in the history and development of human civilization but its relation to self-reference, ipseity, auto-affection, autoimmunity, and, I will argue in conclusion, deconstruction (*BS 2* 75–76/119–120).

But before turning to Derrida's analysis, let us look briefly at how Defoe himself depicts this moment of reinvention in *Robinson Crusoe*. While Crusoe notes in his journal that he had tried the previous year without success to make a wheelbarrow—"I fancied I could make all," he confesses, "but the wheel" (*RC* 76)—he eventually succeeds with another kind of wheel some months later. Here is how Robinson Crusoe puts it in his journal entry dated April 22—that is, April 22, 1660, seven months after his first journal entry:

> April 22 . . . though I had a grindstone, I could not turn it and grind my tools too; this cost me as much thought as a statesman would have bestowed upon a grand point of politics, or a judge upon the life and death of a man. At length I contrived a wheel with a string, to turn it with my foot, that I might have both my hands at liberty. NOTE: I had never seen such a thing in England, or at least not to take notice how it was done, though since I have observed it is very common there; besides that, my grindstone was very large and heavy. This machine cost me a full week's work to bring it to perfection. (*RC* 85)

Let me make three points with regard to this fascinating passage. First, the date—the *fact* of the date. *Robinson Crusoe* is a novel that contains within it the fiction of an autobiography in the form of a journal, a journal that is punctuated by dates, and whose first entry is dated September 30, 1659, just a little less than a year before the birth of the author, Daniel Defoe, in London. Here is how the journal, which is embedded or incorporated in the novel, begins—and note that it too, like the novel, and like Derrida's seminar, as we just saw, begins with the first person singular pronoun:

September 30, 1659. I, poor, miserable Robinson Crusoe, being shipwrecked, during a dreadful storm in the offing, came on shore on this dismal unfortunate island, which I called the "the Island of Despair," all the rest of the ship's company being drowned, and myself almost dead. (*RC* 72)

Now inasmuch as a journal is dated, it is unlike most novels and certainly unlike most books of philosophy, unless, of course, that book of philosophy happens to be a seminar, written from week to week and then delivered in weekly, dated installments. For a seminar—at least the kind of seminar prepared by Derrida—is itself dated, like a journal, and whether it intends or aims for it or not it ends up reflecting or even documenting the instructor's evolving thoughts over a period of time, with each installment being marked by a date, that is, by a coded sign that marks the place where a singular, unrepeatable event, an event that never happened before and will never happen again, becomes encoded and so iterable, repeatable, as the unique event that it is or was. As Derrida wrote back in 1984 in "Shibboleth:

A date is a specter. . . . The first inscription of a date signifies this possibility: that which cannot come back will come back as such, not only in memory, like all remembrance, but also at the same date, at a date in any case analogous . . . And each time, at the same date, what one commemorates will be the date *of* that which could never come back. This date will have signed or sealed the unique, the unrepeatable, but to do so, it must have given itself to be read in a form sufficiently coded, readable, and decipherable for the indecipherable *to appear* in the analogy of the anniversary ring . . . (*SQ* 18–19)

The second point of interest in this journal entry chronicling Robinson Crusoe's reinvention of the wheel is Crusoe's avowal of his own technical ignorance regarding the wheel, his recognition of the gap between knowing how to use something and knowing how to produce it. As Derrida suggests, "the wheel was [Robinson Crusoe's] cross, if one can thus cross or encircle these two figures together" (*BS 2* 74/119), for if the wheel will save Crusoe much time and energy once invented, it costs him much thought and effort to reinvent it. Because, as he says, he had never taken note in his native England of just how such a turning machine is made, Robinson Crusoe literally had to reinvent the wheel. Hence Derrida recalls in *The Beast and the Sovereign*, just as he did in "Faith and Knowledge" and elsewhere, the great and ever-growing distance between our enormous technological know-how and our ignorance with regard to our own technology, technology being, as we know—though Derrida will have none of this thesis—one of the ways that philosophy has traditionally distinguished the human from the animal (*BS 2* 76/121). We today are all, of course, Robinson Crusoe's umpteen times over, insofar as we use—and often with great skill—everything from computers and iPhones to microwaves, televisions, and airplanes without having the slightest clue how to make any of them or explain how they work.

Third and most important, Derrida's claim, which I will turn to in a moment, that the circular movement of the wheel provides the figure or metaphor of sovereignty itself, along with the notion of identity that is inseparable from it, finds a telling confirmation, if not its original inspiration, in Defoe's own description of Robinson Crusoe's reinvention of the wheel. As we just heard, Robinson Crusoe compares the attention he must give to this reinvention to two moments of sovereignty—one executive or legislative, the other judicial: the statesman's deliberations over a matter of great political importance and the judge's consideration of a capital case. As sovereign over his island and, at this point, over only its nonhuman inhabitants, Robinson Crusoe's reinvention of a quasi-automatic form of labor that puts the feet to work in an effort to free the hands and, by extension, the rest of the sovereign body, beginning with the eyes, ears, and mouth, can only be compared to the reinvention of state sovereignty and the sovereign's authority over others, over all those others *beneath* him.[6]

It is thus in large part because of what he finds already in Defoe that Derrida in *The Beast and the Sovereign* will argue that the wheel is an image, figure, metaphor, or trope of sovereignty and autoaffection, that is, of a self that would return to or affect itself, return to and affect itself as the same or self-same. It is nothing less than the very notion of the self, of the *ipse*, and of what Derrida calls *ipseity*, that is thus reinvented by Robinson Crusoe there on the island over which he is sovereign, even if, as Derrida now goes on to argue, this concept of sovereignty and of the self is, in the end, but a *phantasm*. Derrida continues:

> This mechanizing and automatizing autonomization—both auto- and hetero-affective—is not without relation, at least an analogical relation, with what is called sovereignty, or at least with the power of its phantasm, with the phantasm itself, with power as phantasm, with the force of the phantasm that imposes the same on the other, with an unconditional all-powerful self-determination. The nearest and the farthest, the same and the other, touch each other and come into contact in the circle, on the island, in the return, in the wheel and in the prayer. (*BS 2* 78–79/124)

Hence, Derrida relates the invention or reinvention of the wheel in *Robinson Crusoe* to a certain concept of sovereignty—as well as to prayer, as we will see in the following chapter, prayer as itself a kind of automatic, circular, wheel-like movement.[7] Now to be clear, Derrida is not suggesting any kind of causal relationship between the wheel and sovereignty or ipseity, between the circular motion of the wheel and the notion of a self that travels out and away from itself in order always to return. What he *is* suggesting is that these things all belong to the same structural configuration, so that the task is to try to think together "the technical possibility of the wheel, as a circular, auto-hetero-affective machine, and the possibility of the auto-affective and auto-biographical relation to self in confession, repentance, prayer." The task is to think at once "the reinvention of the wheel and the reinvention of prayer as the reinvention of two automobile and auto-affective machines" (*BS2* 83/131).

It is thus not only sovereignty that is linked to this wheel but the *autos*, the very capacity to say "I" in confession, repentance, prayer, or autobiography. To think the *autos* or the self, Derrida is suggesting, one must think the wheel, a self that returns to itself like a wheel, a self that has a certain ambit, that takes a certain detour or turn through the world but that always returns—or at least that's the phantasm—to its point of departure. The self, the *autos*, though also perhaps, let me suggest in passing, God. Again, it's not that the invention of the wheel is what made possible a certain conception of God. The question is rather whether it is really possible to imagine a monotheistic God, a single, unique God who is self-moving or self-acting, in a world or culture that has yet to invent the wheel.

Indeed, let me ask here parenthetically whether it is possible to imagine a dialogue such as Plato's *Timaeus,* in which the Father-Demiurge creates a spherical cosmos, along with the circular motions of celestial bodies within it, in a world or culture that had not yet invented the wheel? Everything—or almost everything—seems to revolve in that dialogue around two different values of the circle, one that is not in time and space and one that is, an intelligible model of the cosmos that is situated beyond time and space, in a certain eternity, and then the cosmos itself, with its circular movements and its time understood as "the moving image of eternity" (*Timaeus* 37d). Everything—or almost everything—thus seems to revolve around the difference between the one eternal and eternally rediscoverable circle, the one to which the Demiurge looks in creating the cosmos, and the many fashioned, invented, or reinvented wheels that are made on the basis of that circle.[8] Plato's entire ontology—with the notable exception of *chōra*—thus seems to revolve around this difference between the one circle and many wheels or, more simply, between the circle and the wheel.[9] (And is it a coincidence, we would then want to ask parenthetically within this parenthesis, that this relationship between two different values of the circle, between the circle and the wheel, is also marked by sexual difference, that is, by an essentially *male* form of production, a relationship between Father and son, model and copy, the one and the many, being and becoming that is limited and interrupted in the *Timaeus* only by the turn to *chōra*? As the condition of all production, the "place" of trope or of turning that gives rise or gives place to every inscription of the intelligible circle within the sensible realm, to every becoming-wheel of the circle, *chōra* would be the only "thing" that exceeds this paradigm of male production, the only "thing" that exceeds and withdraws from both the intelligible and sensible realms and from the kind of production it—or she—makes possible.) Derrida's thinking would thus seem to be following in some of the well-worn tracks laid down by Plato, Aristotle, and others, even if it is being developed here by means of a curious and unexpected passage through *Robinson Crusoe*, and even if the opposition that merits the most attention for him is perhaps not, I will argue, that between the circle that is outside of time and the wheel that is within it but between the wheel and the point of departure or zero point—another way of thinking *chōra*, as we will see, or else the Good beyond Being— that at once initiates and interrupts the wheel's detour through the world and through history.

It seems to be no coincidence, then, that Robinson Crusoe, there on his island, longing to return home, longing to return to his point of departure, Robinson Crusoe as Odysseus or as the prototype of the bourgeois individual, has to invent or reinvent the wheel, and, through this, the very notion of a sovereign self. And it is probably no coincidence that the phantasm is, again, the phantasm of coincidence. The wheel is the model, figure, or metaphor of sovereignty, but this sovereignty is also— and this is the very source of its power—a phantasm, the phantasm of sameness, of a wheel that in fact returns to its point of departure, a wheel that thus promises the fusion or coincidence of spontaneity and automaticity, of nature and technology, *physis* and *technē* or *physis* and *nomos*, indeed of the circle and the wheel. But because, as Derrida argues, the wheel does *not* in fact return to itself in a movement that is without space and time, because it returns in a time that is always different, because it must pass through the circuit of history or of the world, the affirmation of any self-identity, the self-immunizing gesture through which one tries to reaffirm oneself through this return, inevitably yields to what Derrida calls autoimmunity. Derrida more or less begins his comments on the wheel as a figure of sovereignty and ipseity by speaking of this very autoimmunity:

The *metaphora* of this extraordinary apparatus is a figure, the turn of a trope that constructs and instructs in the relation to self, in the autonomy of ipseity, the possibility for unheard-of chances and threats, of automobility, but also, by the same token, of that threatening auto-affection that is called autoimmunity in general. What I call iterability, which repeats the same while displacing or altering it, is all at once a resource, a decisive power, and a catastrophe of repetition or reproduction. (*BS 2* 75/120)[10]

Several pages later, Derrida returns to the wheel in its relationship to autoaffection, confession, biography, prayer, and, especially, autoimmunity in relation to all these notions (*BS 2* 83/131):

This is the motif of self-destruction that I also call, generalizing and formalizing its use, autoimmune, autoimmunity consisting for a living body in itself destroying, in enigmatic fashion, its own immunitary defenses, in auto-affecting itself, then, in an irrepressibly mechanical and apparently spontaneous, automatic, fashion, with an ill which comes to destroy what is supposed to protect against ill and safeguard immunity. Well, Robinson is often invaded by the feeling that a self-destructive power is mechanically, automatically, of itself, at work within him. (*BS 2* 83–84/131)

Derrida will thus go on to argue that "a sort of logic of automatic self-destruction organizes the whole of Robinson's discourse" (*BS 2* 84/132). This autoimmunity is manifest in Robinson Crusoe's (unconscious) compulsion to self-destruction, a death drive of sorts that ruins every plan he has to save himself, that constantly makes him, as he says, his *own destroyer*, the destroyer in effect of his own return or *nostos* (*BS 2* 84/131–33). His deepest longing, his most hidden desire, appears to be precisely *not* to be everywhere at home; it is in fact not to return home at all, not to return to his point of departure, and to destroy every prospect of ever returning home. His longing is, we could say, simply to continue to long; his desire a desire to desire—as if such longing or desire, even if autoimmune, because autoimmune, were coextensive with life or survival itself.

This autoimmunity is at work, Derrida argues, not simply in those acts where Robinson Crusoe seems, more or less consciously or unconsciously, to subvert his own attempts to return home but, precisely—especially—in every attempt actually to return home, every attempt of his to reappropriate himself through language or the trace more generally. Autoimmunity thus appears to be another name for what Derrida calls exappropriation, and it can be seen in every act of self-naming or auto-appellation whereby a supposedly living voice or living present must pass by way of something outside itself—by way of the world, in short—in order to return to itself. The most striking example of this occurs when Robinson Crusoe's parrot Poll one day repeats Robinson Crusoe's name—"Robin Crusoe," he says—just as he had heard it or had been taught to say it by Robinson Crusoe himself. Robinson Crusoe thus hears his own name, a human name, spoken by what sounds like a human voice but issuing forth from a living creature that hardly resembles a human, out of an animal that speaks like a human but resembles a sort of automaton, message machine, or talking toy. Hence, Derrida goes on to relate the automatic, autoimmune self-return of the wheel to "the mechanical and automatic hetero-appellation come from Poll the parrot" (*BS 2* 85/134).[11] What we have here, then, is an auto-appellation, Robinson naming himself, by means of the hetero-appellation of Poll, a sort of originary Poly-semy or Poly-graphy that expropriates right from the start what we might believe to be a live, spontaneous, self-naming voice (*BS 2* 86/136). That is why Poll's repeating of Robinson Crusoe's name is not a simple repetition in which Robinson recognizes himself but an event that utterly startles him. His own name surprises him, having been iterated and thus altered, coming from the outside—a bit like Narcissus's phrases returning to him from Echo as something other than a mere echo.[12]

It is thus not only the wheel that turns on its own and turns away from its point of departure, thereby becoming inscribed in the world, but every trace—whether this be Poll the parrot or, indeed, the book called *Robinson Crusoe*—which also now names Robinson Crusoe in his absence. This is precisely what Derrida calls survival or *survivance*—a survival that would always be, it seems, away from or in excess of what we call life and what we mean by home, a survival that is always caught up in the movement of some wheel. Derrida says much later in the seminar:

> And the machination of this machine, the origin of all *tekhnē* . . . is that each time we trace a trace, each time a trace, however singular, is left behind, and even before we trace it actively or deliberately, a gestural, verbal, written, or other trace, well, this machinality virtually entrusts the trace to the survival in which the opposition of the living and the dead loses and must lose all pertinence, all its edge. The book lives its beautiful death. (*BS2* 130/193)

Every trace is thus a sort of machine, a self-speaking trace, like Poll the parrot, like the book *Robinson Crusoe*, which itself now speaks all by itself the name "Robinson Crusoe." This ability of the book to speak of itself can thus be generalized well beyond *Robinson Crusoe* to the structure of autobiography in general, as if every autobiography were the crafting or re-invention of a wheel that might now turn all by itself and speak of itself in the absence of its author, a wheel or a disc, a gramophone or phonograph, a prosthesis that now names the author in a space and time he or she could not have predicted and from which he or she will have been, in principle if not in fact, forever separated or exiled. It is worth recalling in this regard that the 1997 conference at Cerisy-la-Salle that was devoted to Derrida's work and that was to be the basis for many of the questions posed in *The Beast and the Sovereign* was organized under the title "The Autobiographical Animal," an obvious provocation to any tradition that would restrict the capacity for autobiography to the human. Derrida thus writes, and I will return to this passage in much greater detail in Chapter 6 on the archive:

> One could say of every autobiography, every autobiographical fiction, and even every written confession through which the author calls and names himself, that it presents itself through this linguistic and prosthetic apparatus—a book—or a piece of writing or a trace in general, for example the book entitled *Robinson Crusoe*, which speaks of him without him, according to a trick that constructs and leaves in the world an artifact that speaks all alone and all alone calls the author by his name, renames him in his renown without the author himself needing to do anything else, not even be alive. (*BS 2* 86–87/136)

As we can see, once Derrida gets going, once the wheels start turning, more and more themes and questions get drawn into the orbit of the analysis: we thus move from the wheel to the machine, from the machine to prayer, from prayer to the parrot, from the parrot to autobiography, from autobiography to the book, from the book to the trace in general, and from the trace in general back to the wheel and the *autos*: it's a real round robin round Robin Crusoe's reinvention of the wheel. For all these things turn or work all by themselves—and all of them, I would suggest, disrupt anything like a world that would function as a shared horizon, or anything like a home understood as a sort of originary place or point of departure that would exist before the exile brought on by culture, time, the other, or the world. Derrida continues just a page later—and it was this passage, I should confess, that was at the origin of all these reflections in this chapter, this passage that first got me thinking, that first got my own wheels turning:

> Beyond these relations of causality or induction, I am thinking, rather, of a structural configuration, both historical and genetic, in

which all these possibilities are not separated, and in which everything that can happen to the *autos* is indissociable from what happens *in the world* through the prosthetization of an ipseity which at once divides that ipseity, dislocates it, and inscribes it outside itself *in the world*, the world being precisely what cannot be reduced here, any more than one can reduce *tekhnē* or reduce it to a pure *physis*. The question, then, is indeed that of the world. The wheel is not only a technical machine, it is in the world, it is outside the conscious interiority of the *ipse,* and . . . there is no ipseity without this prostheticity in the world, with all the chances and all the threats that it constitutes for ipseity, which can in this way be constructed but also, and by the same token, indissociably, be destroyed. (*BS 2* 88/138)

Every *autos* must thus pass through the circuit of the "world"—through an original prostheticity that is in or of the world, even if, as Derrida suggests, the notion of world—the world as a shared horizon—is itself but a construction if not an illusion, a philosophical fiction or phantasm. It thus appears from this passage that identities are *not* isolated from one another like individual islands or egos but that they are only first constituted through the world, through "this prostheticity in the world"—a notion of world that seems worlds apart from the world as shared horizon, the kind of world that, in Heidegger, would account for Dasein's privileged access to beings and distinguish the being of Dasein from that of all other animals. Only through the detour of the world do we come to have any ipseity, any identity, at all, and, thus, any phantasms of identity. The home is thus not that from which one leaves in order to return, since it is actually first constituted through the return, or rather, through the longing for return or the phantasm of it.

Ipseity is always inscribed *in the world*, in a world that is thus *irreducible*, that is, before and beyond the phantasm of an ipseity without circuit and without magnitude, without time and space, and thus without world. It is this irreducible relation to a world that makes each turn, each return to one's island or oneself, different. It might thus be said that by returning to itself, by passing as it must through the world, the sovereignty of the self opens itself up not only to detour but, as Derrida will suggest later in the seminar, to the originary violence or *Walten* that makes all repetition possible and so establishes but also undermines all sovereignty. And this would happen at that point, that point of departure, that place of absolute initiative, which itself is not *of* or *in* the world but is at the origin—and thus already at the end—of the world and its history.

To say that the wheel is in the world, that ipseity is inscribed in the world, means that the ipseity that is characterized as returning to itself like a wheel requires always a circuit or passage through the technologies and terminologies, the culture and language, of one's own time and place. The world is not a common place or shared horizon in which we live but the material prosthesis for an ipseity or identity that is always already, from the beginning, *in the world*. There is thus no solipsism that needs to be overcome by putting worlds together or by demonstrating that we in fact belong from the beginning to a shared or common world. It is, as it were, only through the circuit or *detour* of the world—only through the self's detour through the world as originary prosthesis—that the self, that any ipseity or identity, is first constituted, including, of course, that of the world, the world as shared horizon; it is only through a circular return to self that the self—like a wheel—comes to have any identity at all. What all this means, of course, is that there is no self or no world before the world, and that it is through a return to the same that the self runs the risk—an irremediable, unavoidable risk—of getting lost or of losing itself in the world.[13] It is, then, only by means of another *point of departure*, by means of another absolute initiative, that the self is able to return to itself, giving rise at once to the phantasm of return and to the inevitability of loss, exappropriation, and perpetual exile.

Now, I have been emphasizing *point of departure* here because in "Cogito and the History of Madness," for example, Derrida speaks of the point or the instant that at once opens up and interrupts history as just such a point of departure. He there argues that "the hyperbolic audacity of the Cartesian Cogito, its mad audacity," "would consist in the return to an original point which no longer belongs to either *determined* reason or a *determined* unreason, no longer belongs to them as opposition or alternative." "Invulnerable to all determined opposition between reason and unreason," he goes on to argue, this point, this zero point, as Derrida calls it in this essay of 1963, is "the point starting from which [*le point à partir duquel*] the history of the determined forms of this opposition . . . can appear as such and be stated. . . . It is the point at which the project of thinking this totality by escaping it is embedded." ("CHM 56") Derrida will then go on to compare this point, this point of departure, along with "the project of exceeding the totality of the world, as the totality of what I can think in general," to "the light of a hidden sun which is *epekeina tes ousias*," that is, to the Good beyond Being whose image would be, precisely, the sun, both round in itself and in its circuit through the cosmos—the sun, we could say, as yet another circle or yet another wheel that is fashioned in the image of the Good, that is, in the image, if we can think this, of what is before or beyond not only all becoming but all being, not only all wheels but the one circle, that source point or point of departure that itself has no being, that itself is not, but that gives or provides the place—a bit *like chōra*—for all these initiatives ("CHM" 56–57).

I have thus emphasized *point of departure* here but also *detour*—another name, it seems to me, for the *prosthesis*—because Derrida speaks throughout *The Beast and the Sovereign* of having to take detours, but also because it was through this notion of a *detour* that Derrida in a few early texts defined the very movement of *différance*.[14] Back in the 1968 essay "Différance," for example, Derrida spoke of différance as an "economic detour" that at once always defers a full presence that is desired *and* remains open to the absolutely other in the form of an "irreparable loss of presence," that is, in the form of what might be called an *absolute detour*, or else, though the term was not available to him then—and that is the whole point of a detour through the world—in the form of *autoimmunity*. Derrida there asks:

> How are we to think *simultaneously*, on the one hand, *différance* as the economic detour which, in the element of the same, always aims at coming back to the pleasure or the presence that have been deferred by (conscious or unconscious) calculation, and, on the other hand, *différance* as the relation to an impossible presence, as expenditure without reserve, as the irreparable loss of presence, the irreversible usage of energy, that is, as the death instinct, and as the entirely other relationship that apparently interrupts every economy? It is evident—and this is the evident itself—that the economical and the noneconomical, the same and the entirely other, etc., cannot be thought *together*? ("D" 19)

It should be clear that from the "Différance" essay or the "Cogito" essay right up through *The Beast and the Sovereign*, Derrida kept on returning to himself, to familiar thoughts, thoughts that were always familiar in their shared relationship to distance, difference, irreparable loss, and exappropriation. In the passage from *The Beast and the Sovereign* that we have been reading here, Derrida turns round Robinson Crusoe's reinvention of the wheel, thinking it in relationship to developments in human civilization and technology but also in relationship to sovereignty, the possibility of the trace, the *autos*, and autobiography. Derrida turns round these new texts, these new elements of or in the world, that is, Heidegger's seminar and especially the novel *Robinson Crusoe*, all the while subjecting these elements to a recognizable turn. We should thus not be surprised to find this same thematic configuration of sovereignty, identity, and circularity at the center of other texts, for example *Rogues*, which Derrida would have completed just months before his final seminar for the Cerisy-la-Salle conference devoted to his work in the summer of 2002.

In *Rogues*, one will recall, sovereignty again has to do with a kind of auto-affective return to self that occludes or effaces—or at least gives the illusion of doing so—the necessary passage through the other, through the world or through history. And the image of this sovereignty is there, once again, that of a circle without magnitude, without time in its passage through the world. To rethink this notion of sovereignty and of a sovereign self that coincides with itself, to rethink the circle, in short, Derrida thus tries once again in *Rogues* to rethink or reinvent the wheel as a figure of what returns to its point of departure always altered. Should we be surprised, then, to find Derrida returning to *himself* in *Rogues* in a somewhat altered form, in the guise of another turner of wheels, in the guise, precisely, of a potter working on his wheel? How else are we to explain why Derrida, in the course of a discussion of the turns and the "by turns" of democracy, opens up, rounds off, and then closes up a long parenthesis in which the work of the philosopher is compared to that of a potter throwing a pot? Derrida writes in *Rogues*, a text that—to speak autobiographically just this once—I had a hand in translating, that is, a hand in sculpting, molding, and trying to keep from falling flat in the language of Daniel Defoe:

> ("Ah, the *tour*, the wheel! Let me confide in you here how much I love this image of the potter, his art, the turns of someone who, on his wheel, makes a piece of pottery rise up like a tower by sculpting it, molding it, but without subjecting himself, or herself, to the automatic, rotating movement, by remaining as free as possible with regard to the rotation, putting his or her entire body, feet and hands alike, to work on the machine. . . . For as sculptor or architect, the potter in his turn is by turns poet and musician, rhetorician and political orator, *perhaps even a philosopher . . .*) (*R* 13)[15]

To write an autobiography, then, nothing would be more false or misleading than to speak of oneself as isolated from or independent of the world in which one's *autos* was first formed. It was thus for structural reasons, reasons of necessity, that Derrida would have repeatedly written his autobiography through other figures and other texts, through Freud, Heidegger, Plato, and Socrates, among others, in *The Post Card*, through Augustine in "Circumfession," through Fantin-Latour, Diderot, and scores of others in *Memoirs of the Blind*, and through Heidegger, Robinson Crusoe, and, as we will see, Benjamin in this final seminar. Since there is no *autos*, no self, no *bios*, no life, and no *graphy*, no writing, before the world, autobiography begins always with a detour through the world and through the other, that is, with exappropriation and the intimations of death that come through every act of exappropriation.

The impossibility of returning home or to one's point of departure would have been the constant theme or preoccupation of deconstruction, that to which Derridean deconstruction would have constantly returned. The impossibility of return would have been and would still be both the content and the form, so to speak, of every deconstructive text or reading. Hence, deconstruction will have been from the very beginning a reinvention and deconstruction of the wheel, or, better, of the circle by means of a detour through the wheel, a deconstruction of the one circle that then leads to a new thinking of the wheel, along with the notions of self-identity, exile, and return. It should thus come as no surprise that what is said in Derrida's final seminar about return and about homecoming as perpetual wandering, exile, and exappropriaton should have been marked already earlier and elsewhere. Already back in 1964 in "Violence and Metaphysics," for example, Derrida in an oft-quoted passage questioned the priority of return and of circularity, of homecoming, in short, in Levinas's critique of Western philosophy. In *The Trace of the Other*, for example, Levinas suggested that Homer's *Odyssey*—yes, we are back to Homer's *Odyssey*—already provided the founding narrative for all Western philosophy in the form of a speculative journey into the foreign that is motivated always by the longing or nostalgia—perhaps like Novalis, perhaps like Maya Angelou—to return home. It was to this supposedly Greek model of return that Levinas opposed a Jewish model of perpetual exile: "To the myth of Odysseus returning to Ithaca, we would prefer to oppose the story of Abraham leaving his country forever for an as yet unknown land, and forbidding his servant to take back even his son to the point of departure."[16] But already back in "Violence and Metaphysics"—many moons or cycles of the moon before *The Beast and the Sovereign*—Derrida was skeptical of this opposition between a Greek philosophical nostalgia that finds its prototype in Odysseus's return to Ithaca and that can still be seen in Hegel and Heidegger, on the one hand, and a model of Jewish departure and exile, on the other. Already back then, Derrida questioned—and in *The Beast and the Sovereign* some forty years later he himself recalls having questioned (*BS 2* 95–96/146)—whether this Western model of philosophical speculation was not more self-serving or symptomatic than diagnostic. He thus wrote in "Violence and Metaphysics," essentially defending Heidegger against Levinas's criticism by extending a notion of exile and wandering into Heidegger:

The impossibility of the return doubtless was not overlooked by Heidegger: the original historicity of Being, the originality of difference, and irreducible wandering, all forbid the return to Being *itself* which is nothing. Therefore, Levinas here is in agreement with Heidegger. ("VM" 320 n. 92)[17]

Like Levinas, Derrida sees in the wheel or in the circuit of return a certain model of sovereignty and ipseity. But because, for Derrida as for a certain Heidegger, the circuit of return implied in this model is always frustrated by the originality of difference, because the return home is always interrupted by irreducible wandering, the home is never that to which we can ever really return, or is that to which we can return only in the guise of a phantasm. It would be as if, whenever we return home, we find ourselves always speaking like another, as another, speaking not a mother tongue in our fatherland but always a foreign language in a land that is no longer and in fact never simply was ours.

In the course of his final seminar, *The Beast and the Sovereign*, delivered in Paris just months after the writing of *Rogues*, we see Derrida again returning to his point of departure, rethinking the wheel in order to rethink sovereignty, though also ipseity, the *autos*, a certain conception of autobiography, the trace and the book, as well as the notions of an originary prosthesis or detour, différance, supplementarity, and autoimmunity. But this short list of terms might suggest that there is one final turn of the wheel in this reading of *The Beast and the Sovereign*, one that would read this meditation on the self and autobiography *in* the seminar as a *metaphora* or trope *of* deconstruction itself. For the passage we have been reading on the originary prosthesis of the world seems to describe the very "method" or, better, the very movement or historicity of deconstruction, the reason why *différance*, for example, both is and is not just one word among others, a quasi-synonym, for supplementarity, dissemination, autoimmunity, detour, democracy to come, and so on. It helps explain why no one of these can ever be a master term, and why any one of them—and who knows which one, for that's democracy—can always come to prevail for a time. And it explains, finally, why things can always go so terribly wrong, why one term can always be taken for a master term, why one word—whether *physis*, *différance*, autoimmunity, or *Walten*—can claim a kind of transcendental or transhistorical precedence, lording it over the others for a time while claiming it is for all times. Just as the self can return to itself, understand itself but first of all even become or be itself, only by means of a detour through the world, so any reading—Derrida's or anyone else's—can return to and reflect upon itself only after a detour through other texts, other terms, through other discourses, to be sure, but also through other forces, other times and spaces. That is why, at the heart of deconstruction, there is an ineluctable detour—at once difference and deferral, the need always for another point of departure, another singular point of departure that opens up history but is not itself within history. For if the wheel turns always *within* history, the very turning of the wheel, the turning of the wheel *into* history, does not.

To rethink the home, to rethink the desire to return home, we thus need to rethink the wheel, the *autos*, sovereignty, autobiography, the book, the trace, the archive, life, survival, living on, and who knows what else. It's a lot, it's everything, and it may always look as if the wheels are about to come off, but without this detour through these others we really would be condemned to solipsism, or at least to its phantasm. To rethink the home, we must thus consider not only what the texts of Maya Angelou or Novalis, Defoe or Heidegger, Levinas or Derrida will have said about the home, but also what these texts, as traces of an originary exappropriation, already tell us about their own survival. For all these texts, severed from the outset from the living voice and presence of their speaker, exiled originarily from their author, now turn upon themselves like wheels, exposed to all the chances and dangers of the world, to wandering, errancy, mutation, and destruction, though also to chance encounters and surprise. It is the wheel that makes every homecoming possible and it is the wheel that takes us always away from ourselves and from the home, from a home that is not, we come round to see, what we thought it was and what we might have longed for, since it too will have always been in the world and so will have always already been other than itself, always in another time and space, always off center, uprooted, always in the world.[18]

There is no choice, then, but to risk reinscription, to reappropriate while risking further exappropriation, to long to return home all the while knowing that this longing always risks further exile. As opposed to the phantasm of a return to the same and to the one, Derrida will have spoken from the beginning of his work of a return to the same that always entails iteration, original difference, supplementarity, autoimmunity, and so on—where this *and so on* is, and precisely because of the wheel, not some rhetorical banality but a structural necessity—a sign that, in time and for a time, there is always one more turn of the wheel—and thus one more point of departure—to go.

5

Pray Tell

Derrida's Performative Justice

If the second year of *The Beast and the Sovereign* seminar seems in many ways to pick up where the first year left off, if it returns throughout the year to its explicit and announced theme, the relationship between the animal and the human, the beast and the sovereign, other themes such as autobiography, burial rituals, the phantasm, and, as we are about to see, prayer, mourning, and the archive, begin creeping in so as to give the seminar a very different tone and orientation. These shifts in theme and tone become in fact so pronounced that it is hard not to think that the seminar is itself being transformed into something more or at least something very different than just another seminar *on* a topic such as the beast and the sovereign, something like an autobiography or an extended prayer, a last will and testament or a self-inhumation in the archive. Though no Derrida seminar is quite like any other, this one—this last one—challenges the very genre of the seminar in ways the others did not and perhaps could never have.

In this and the following chapter, I would thus like to show that in this final year of *The Beast and the Sovereign* Derrida does not simply speak of such themes as prayer, mourning, or the archive but actually *performs* them in accordance with a theory of performativity that he will have been developing from at least as early as "Signature Event Context" in 1971. To demonstrate this, I will take some initial guidance from J. Hillis Miller's essay on this question of the performative in a chapter of his *For Derrida* entitled "Derrida's Special Theory of Performativity."[1] I turn here to Miller's work at the outset both because it is so helpful on this question and because, in the spring of 2003, Derrida was himself, it seems, thinking even more than usual about J. Hillis Miller, preparing for a conference on his work that would be held at the University of California, Irvine, on April 18 and 19, 2003. The title Derrida would choose for his presentation on that occasion was, simply, "Justices," an English title that wavers between a plural noun and the third-person singular form of the poetic verb "to justice," as in the "just man"—and Derrida has J. Hillis Miller in his sights here—"justices" ("J" 689). It is a fitting homage to Miller's work, full of insight, humor, and affection. But it is hard not to read this essay today—along with the seminar *The Beast and the Sovereign*, which was being delivered at almost exactly the same time—not just in light of Derrida's death some eighteen months later but also as an example of an even more special form of Derrida's "special theory of performativity" that we might call *testamentary*.

It was in the spring of 2003, then, that Derrida was presumably writing and preparing not only the final sessions of the second year of *The Beast and the Sovereign* but his essay "Justices." We should thus not be surprised to find several points of intersection between these two texts, even though their explicit topics are rather different, the works of J. Hillis Miller, in the one, Heidegger's 1929–30 seminar and Defoe's *Robinson Crusoe*, in the other. In addition to a shared reference to Pascal, as well as an emphasis on solitude and separation, there is, as we will see, the question of the performative, especially the performative of prayer, and, as I said, of the *testamentary*—as if the testamentary were in the end not a special case of the performative utterance but a structural possibility of every speech act, every address to the other.

As Miller reminds us in *For Derrida*, performativity is today a rather ambiguous notion that needs to be, in the lexicon of Wikipedia, "disambiguated," that is, its various senses clearly distinguished.[2] Miller thus sets out at once to clarify these different meanings and to explain precisely how "a certain confusion in the 'academic mind' came about."[3] He proceeds to distinguish the performative theory of John Austin from that of Judith Butler, both of these from the performativity of performance studies and "performativity theory," and then all of these from Derrida's special theory of performativity.[4] Whereas Butler's theory of performativity was no doubt inspired by Derrida's and shares many traits with it, Butler took that theory in directions Derrida could not have predicted, in order to show, for example, as Miller phrases it, that "sex and gender are not natural, biological, innate, and pre-existent but the violent product of iterated discursive formations that sequester as unnatural and 'unreal' sexual and gender minorities in their considerable variation." And whereas Derrida's theory of the performative was itself inspired by Austin, it differs from it in several significant ways. Miller names three. First, iterability—"a fundamental feature of performatives"—means that "the context of a performative can never be 'saturated,' that is, exhaustively identified." As a result, Austin's distinction between the felicitous performative—which requires a complete inventory of the circumstances for any performative—and the infelicitous one breaks down. Second, "iterability means that the parasitical or etiolated performative"—"writing a poem, acting on a stage, uttering a soliloquy"—cannot be definitively excluded, as Austin had wished. There is, writes Miller, "no such thing as a fully 'serious' performative utterance [that] exists as a unique, one-time-only event in the present. The possibility of the abnormal is an intrinsic part of the normal." Finally, and most important, says Miller, "iterability disqualifies the requirement that a felicitous performative must depend on the self-consciousness of the ego and its 'intentions,' the 'I' who says 'I promise' and means to keep that promise."[5]

This is about as clear and straightforward a summary and analysis as one will get of the "special theory of performativity" that Derrida developed in texts such as "Signature Event Context" and *Limited Inc.* and that he would continue to reiterate and refine right up until the end. For instance, Derrida begins "Justices," his essay of 2003 on J. Hillis Miller, by underscoring and then questioning the value of *presence* in this traditional speech act theory:

> Everything in this culture that acts, thinks, and speaks intentionally, everything that does something, and especially with words, in the performative mode, must be signed, implicitly or explicitly, by a responsible *je*, I. Austin stresses the point: the condition of the pure performative, the temporal modality of the felicitous and serious performative, is the *present*. ("J" 689)

Now, as Miller goes on to show, if Derrida initially develops this special theory of performativity through a reading or deconstruction of Austin's or Searle's works on the performative, he also deploys it—thereby using it as well as mentioning it, as it were—in almost *all* of his texts after his explicit reading of Austin and debate with Searle. Miller writes: "The idea of the performative speech act appears in many, perhaps most, of Derrida's many essays, seminars, and interviews after 1977. The performative is an essential aspect of Derrida's ideas about the secret, literature, friendship, hospitality, perjury, decision, sovereignty, politics, responsibility, justice, death, temporality, religion, and so on."[6] Miller's long but hardly exhaustive list—he could have included, for example, prayer, testimony, and the testamentary—could not be more telling. Rather than placing emphasis on what the subject *can* do with his or her words, everything from, in Austin, baptizing a child to marrying a couple to christening a ship, Derrida—in his rethinking of everything from justice, friendship, and hospitality to death and prayer—puts emphasis on the other who makes demands on me and who first of all calls into question any presumption I might have to a *power* or *capacity* to perform what we call a speech *act*.

> The performative is seen as a response to a demand made on me by "the wholly other" (*le tout autre*), a response that, far from depending on preexisting rules, on a preexisting ego, I, or self, or on preexisting circumstances or "context," creates the self, the context, and new rules or laws in the act of its enunciation.[7]

As a result, Miller goes on to argue, "I must say 'yes' to a performative demand issued initially by the wholly other. My 'yes' is a countersigning or the co-performative validating of a performative command that comes from outside me."[8] There is thus a kind of performative *before* every performative, an implicit or elementary performative that conditions not only the performative in the restricted sense of the term but the constative as well, which Austin himself also came to see was really a veiled performative. What Derrida in *Specters of Marx* calls "an originary performativity" would thus be the condition of every speech act and every address to the other, an originary "pray tell" or "I pray you," as we will see, that would precede every request of the other and every response to the other, an "I pray you" that would be the countersignature of the other's silent demand, the "pledge," to cite *Specters of Marx* again, that "responds without delay to the demand of justice."[9]

It is with these remarks by Miller regarding the Derridean performative in mind that I would now like to turn to Derrida's treatment of prayer in *The Beast and the Sovereign*. For a certain understanding of the performative—and, here, the special performative of prayer—will there be a linchpin for calling into question philosophy's distinction between the beast and the sovereign, the animal and man, as well as a certain conception of the sovereign self, subject, or individual. Inasmuch as prayer in its restricted sense introduces a dimension of language that has traditionally been understood to precede truth and falsity and, thus, to precede philosophy in its emphasis on truth or on the question, it will be an ideal lever by which to show a more fundamental, more elementary performativity as the condition of all language—including the question—a dimension of language that conditions even philosophy and so cannot be reduced to it.

The theme of prayer is first introduced in the Second Session of *The Beast and the Sovereign* seminar and is then taken up more fully in the Third Session, before more or less disappearing until its full reemergence in the Eighth and Ninth Sessions in February and March 2003, right around the time, I would like to imagine, that Derrida was considering how best to respond—how to respond most justly—to the invitation to speak at the conference at Irvine devoted to Hillis Miller's work. Between Heidegger's 1929–30 seminar and *Robinson Crusoe*, the two principal texts of this final seminar, there would thus be, I would like to imagine, the essay "Justices," which Derrida would have recently written or would still be writing as he prepared for the Irvine conference.

In the Second Session, then, of *The Beast and the Sovereign* Derrida introduces the theme of prayer by declaring that "the whole of *Robinson Crusoe* can be read as a rhythmic series of attempts to learn how to pray properly, authentically, in the Bible, on the Bible" (*BS 2* 48/83). In the subsequent session, Derrida will follow Robinson Crusoe step by step in this apprenticeship in prayer, beginning with a first, inarticulate, not yet authentically Christian prayer (*BS 2* 77/123). It is, writes Derrida, the "terror of being buried alive that inspires [Robinson Crusoe's] first prayer, in truth a still irreligious prayer, a prayer before prayer, the precursory plaintive breath of a distress call which, during the earthquake that threatens to bury him alive, is not yet truly and religiously addressed to God, to the Other as God" (*BS 2* 77–78/123). Given everything Derrida will argue about prayer later on, one might wonder whether this first prayer, this prayer before prayer, this "still irreligious prayer" in the eyes of Defoe, does not, for Derrida, already bear some of the traits of prayer itself, of authentic prayer even, insofar as it is a prayer addressed not yet to the Christian God and made not yet on the Bible but drawn out of Robinson Crusoe as a kind of non–fully intended and animated, quasi machinelike reaction to a dangerous situation, a spontaneous or automatic call for help. Derrida continues:

> it is a cry that is almost automatic, irrepressible, machinelike, mechanical, like a mainspring calling for help from the depths of panic and absolute terror. God is here, apparently, merely that other who would save the life of the child threatened with being carried off, eaten alive in the deepest entrails of the earth. It would be interesting to follow, through the whole book, the apprenticeship of prayer; and to read the whole of *Robinson Crusoe* as a book of prayer, as an experience of "learning how to pray." (*BS 2* 77–78/123)

Much of the drama of *Robinson Crusoe* would thus come down, we might say, to "learning how to pray finally," though Robinson Crusoe's sense of authentic prayer will no doubt be, as I have suggested, much different than Derrida's. At once mechanical and autoaffective, this still irreligious prayer turns or turns on itself automatically at the same time as it turns, without full intention, toward an unknown other. That is why, as we saw in the previous chapter, Derrida relates this first step in Robinson Crusoe's reinvention of prayer to Crusoe's reinvention of the wheel (*BS 2* 77–78/123). Like a wheel, prayer turns on itself, automatically, auto-affectively, from the depths of a self that is already without self, without a fully self-conscious ego or animating intention behind it. We can thus already see Derrida building in to his analysis of prayer a couple of the features of performativity underscored by Miller, its iterability, the possibility of non-seriousness, and, especially, the lack of any animating intention by a self-conscious I, any respectful attention, only the opening to the other—even, perhaps especially, the opening to an unknown other.

This first prayer on the part of Robinson Crusoe, this still irreligious prayer in the eyes of both Defoe and Crusoe, "this inchoate, mechanical, and not very serious prayer lasts only the time of fear between two forgettings" (*BS 2* 80/126). Crusoe will ultimately recognize that this cry for help was, in the end, "not a real prayer 'attended with Desires or with Hopes,'" but "rather the Voice of meer Fright and Distress" (*BS 2* 80/126). It is only later, then, "after another meditation on his sins, especially on the words of his father who had warned him and announced divine justice," that "he finds the accent of a *true* prayer, the first authentic prayer, worthy of the name: '*Lord be my Help, for I am in great Distress.* / This was the first Prayer, if I may call it so, that I had made for many Years'" (*BS 2* 80/126). This first true prayer will coincide, significantly, with Robinson Crusoe's "resolution to read every morning and every evening from the New Testament" (*BS 2* 80/127). According to *Robinson Crusoe*, then, real, true, or authentic prayer would be prayer with the Lord as its addressee, prayer made on a specific book, the New Testament. Only this book would be a prayer book or a book to pray on, and only it will allow Robinson Crusoe not just to pray for the first time but to "discover for the first time in his life the true meaning of the word 'prayer'" (*BS 2* 81/128), the possibility of "authentic prayer" (*BS 2* 82/128).

Let me pause for a moment on this word *authentic*, which is used by Derrida not just once but a couple of times in these pages.[10] For Robinson Crusoe and, no doubt, for Defoe, authentic prayer would be prayer addressed to "God in the person of his son" (*BS 2* 81/128). For Derrida, on the contrary, it would seem that this so-called real or authentic prayer bears many of the traits of an inauthentic or potentially inauthentic prayer to the extent that it turns toward a particular God and expects an answer from that God. Derrida invites just such an interpretation when he says in an aside during the seminar that prayer "at bottom, is addressed to nobody—one does not know to whom it is addressed" (footnote on *BS 2* 78/124). It is as if, for Derrida, prayer, authentic prayer, is to be addressed not to a known but to an unknown God, an unknown Other, even when it *seems* addressed to some particular Other or some specific God.

Now I risk the words *authentic* and *inauthentic* here, with all their potentially Heideggerian overtones, among others, precisely because Derrida himself takes the risk of using them, and not only here but elsewhere, and not only as a way of glossing what Crusoe or Defoe believes but, it seems, in his own name. In a series of improvised remarks made before a meeting of the American Academy of Religion and the Society of Biblical Literature right around the same time he was presenting this session of the seminar, that is, in remarks made in late November 2002 and subsequently published under the title "Epochē and Faith," Derrida seems to want to distinguish an authentic faith that is able to suspend all certainty with regard to its addressee from an inauthentic one that cannot.

> When I pray, I am thinking about negative theology, about the unnameable, the possibility that I might be totally deceived by my belief, and so on. It is a very skeptical—I don't like this word, "skeptical," but it will have to do—prayer. Instead of "skepticism," I could talk of *epochē*, meaning by that the suspension of certainty, not of belief. This suspension of certainty is part of prayer. I consider that this suspension of certainty, this suspension of knowledge, is a part of an answer to the question, "Who do you expect to answer these prayers?" That suspension must take place in order for a prayer to be authentic. If I knew or were simply expecting an answer, that would be the end of prayer. ("EF" 30–31)

Prayer must thus be skeptical and, in a certain sense, hopeless, beyond all calculation or expectation.[11] After speaking approvingly of negative theology, of "a culture of atheism" and "a critique of idolatry, of all sorts of images in prayer," of a critique of the onto-theological "reappropriation of God in metaphysics," Derrida says, risking yet again—and this time acknowledging the risk—the notion of authenticity: "if you don't go through these in the direction of atheism, the belief in God is naïve, totally inauthentic. In order to be authentic—this is a word I almost never use—the belief in God must be exposed to absolute doubt. . . . 'I pray to someone who doesn't exist in the strict, metaphysical meaning of existence'" ("EF"

46).[12] Derrida goes on to cite Plato's *epekeina tēs ousias* and Heidegger's Being of beings, before then identifying "true believers" with a certain experience of atheism and true belief with the suspension of all belief: "It is in the *epochē*, in the suspension of belief, the suspension of the position of God as a thesis, that faith appears. The only possibility of faith is in the *epochē*" ("EF" 47).

These references to authentic belief and true believers are, to be sure, a little surprising in Derrida. But if there is a prayer that is *authentic*—a word, Derrida is right, he almost never uses—then its authenticity would have to be thought not in relationship to prayer's truth or falsity, its correspondence or not to the truth of some God, or to the genuineness of some intention, but precisely in relation to the suspension of the entire regimen of truth and falsity. In other words, authenticity would have to be thought otherwise, in accordance not with truth and falsity but with the conditions of performativity.

In this Third Session of *The Beast and the Sovereign* seminar, Derrida treats in some detail, as we have seen, Robinson Crusoe's reinvention of or apprenticeship in prayer, the question of authentic prayer, and so on. But the theme of prayer then languishes or goes underground for five weeks, reemerging only in Session Eight, on March 5, 2003, in relationship now to Heidegger. Derrida begins the session by asking about the nature of prayer itself, the possibility of prayer, or, rather, the impossibility of refraining from prayer, the limits of prayer, therefore, when prayer is perhaps present in every address to the other, when it would always say something like—to deform just slightly a line from "Faith and Knowledge"—"believe in me, I pray you, as you would believe in a miracle" (*BS 2* 202–204/285–287; see "FK" 63–64). Derrida begins:

> What is it to pray? How to pray? How not to pray? More precisely, if praying consists in doing something, in a gesture of the body or a movement of the soul, what is one doing when one prays? . . . Is one doing something with words, as in a performative that consists in "doing things with words," doing something with words, without describing, without being constative, without saying what is as it is? Or else can one pray wordlessly? And in that case do something that does not presuppose the *logos,* at least the *logos* as articulated language, or as enunciative proposition? (*BS 2* 202/285–286)

Invoking here the language of speech act theory, Derrida is clearly interested in prayer because, as a kind of performative, it initially seems to set a limit to the constative. But by going on to speak of the *enunciative proposition*, Derrida is already indicating the direction of his analysis, the theme or question of prayer in Heidegger's *Identity and Difference* and, especially, in the 1929–30 seminar *Fundamental Concepts of Metaphysics*.

But before turning to Heidegger, Derrida asks more generally about prayer and about what it means to "pray someone," as when one says, "I pray you." Derrida asks—turning around a French phrase that is as common as it is enigmatic:

> What is one doing when one says to someone "I pray you," "*Je vous en prie*," "I pray you to"? Can one pray without praying *to someone*, i.e. without "addressing" one's prayer to the singularity of a "who"? . . . Can one pray without asking or expecting something in return? Is there a link between the quotidian and trivial "*je vous en prie*" and the orison or chant of religious and sacred prayer that rises and lifts itself above the quotidian . . . and brings with it a sort of ecstasy beyond automatic triviality? (*BS 2* 203/286)

Even "more radically," asks Derrida—and this will be, in short—the angle of attack in his reading and critique of Heidegger:

> can one address oneself to someone or indeed to any living being at all—or even something not living—without some implicit prayer coming to bend, to inflect the discourse, or even the simple silent look which, addressing itself to the other, cannot fail to ask of him or her "listen to me, please [*je t'en prie*], listen, I pray you, look at me looking at you, please, turn toward me, turn your attention toward what I'm saying or doing to you, be present to what is coming from me." . . . One always prays the other to be present to one's own presence. Can, then, this experience of prayer be limited, circumscribed? Or else does it invade the whole field of experience from the moment the other enters into it, i.e. without ever waiting, since the other *is* already, whether I'm expecting it or not, whether I want it or not. (*BS 2* 203/286–287)[13]

Derrida is suggesting here that there is a kind of *originary* or *elementary* performative that is the condition of every speech act and every address to the other, including the constative or the enunciative proposition.[14] One always addresses the other, it might be said, with an "I pray you—pay attention to me, listen to me, look at me; believe me as you would believe in a miracle." And one always invokes or calls on the other with a "pray tell," a "pray, tell," a "pray, tell me, what is it that you hear, see, experience, believe, and so on." "I pray you" or "pray tell"—this would be the implicit injunction or silent prayer behind or before every address to the other.[15] From this perspective, then, even the atheist prays, and prays all the time.

Having thus raised these more general questions about prayer, and having looked in detail, some five weeks earlier, at Robinson Crusoe's apprenticeship in prayer, his rediscovery of authentic prayer, Derrida turns to the second of the two figures at the center of *The Beast and the Sovereign* seminar, namely, Heidegger, who, on at least two occasions, and at an interval of almost thirty years, will have spoken of prayer. Derrida is here resorting to an interpretative practice he will have been honing since at least the *Geschlecht* essays and *Of Spirit* in the mid-1980s, that is, the practice of showing the fundamental consistency in Heidegger's thinking across decades and despite all the apparent shifts, turns, and differences. Derrida will want to show the compatibility of Heidegger's claims about prayer in two very different places and with two very different purposes. He begins with Heidegger's 1957 *Identity and Difference*, where Heidegger says of the God of philosophy, that is, the God of onto-theology, God as the highest, most supreme Being, God as *causa sui* or as the *Ursache*: "Man can neither pray nor sacrifice to this God. Before the *causa sui,* man can neither fall to his knees in awe nor can he play music and dance before this God" (*BS 2* 208/292). What this perhaps means—and I say *perhaps* here because it is not obvious that Heidegger is actually enjoining us to seek out a God to whom we *can* pray and sacrifice—is that if we wish to pray and sacrifice it must be to a God who has withdrawn from onto-theology and so is bereft of the sovereignty that is always attributed to a *causa sui*, supreme principle, or "highest being" (*BS 2* 207/291). It is as if Heidegger were suggesting that in order to pray and sacrifice to God one would need to think a God whose unconditionality is severed from his sovereignty, a God of powerlessness, weakness, or fragility. Derrida ends these speculations:

> The God of the philosophers (Aristotle's *noesis noesos* or pure act, Spinoza's *causa sui,* etc.) is not, in essence, a being who receives prayers and sacrifices and chants and praises and hymns, etc. Does that justify a return to faith or religion? Does that call on us to go beyond all sovereignty, or only onto-theological sovereignty—those are the questions that await us, along with the agency of *Walten,* which I shall attempt to show in a moment is both foreign or heterogeneous, excessive even, with respect to this ontic and therefore theological or theologico-political sovereignty, and that nonetheless, and by that very fact, perhaps constitutes an ontological super-sovereignty, at the source of the ontological difference. (*BS 2* 208/293)

It is at this point that Derrida, having juxtaposed at a distance of some five weeks Robinson Crusoe's reinvention of prayer and Heidegger's evocation of prayer in *Identity and Difference*, goes on to contrast these two discourses in the terms of speech act theory. Whereas Heidegger's discourse about prayer remains, says Derrida, "theoretical or constative," whereas Heidegger speaks throughout *of* prayer and *of* God without actually praying or performing in the strict senses of these terms, Robinson Crusoe "is writing a book which, in itself, and as an autobiography, is a sort of prayer, a sort of prayer in view of prayer" (*BS 2* 209/293). Unlike Heidegger, Robinson Crusoe "insistently quotes prayers, and prayers that are essentially linked to the Christian revelation, as the only prayers worthy of the name. And these are prayers that he learns, that he learns to relearn, and that he quotes as though he were reiterating them in his very writing" (*BS 2* 209/293–294). Derrida himself does not take the insight or the regress any further back, though we are surely invited to—and the previous chapter on the question of autobiography should help justify such a move: the character Robinson Crusoe quotes prayers from the New Testament that are taken up and incorporated in the novel entitled *Robinson Crusoe*, and these prayers are then taken up, quoted, and incorporated by Derrida in *The Beast and the Sovereign*. What, then, are we to make of the fact that it is right here, in his reading of Heidegger's claims about prayer in *Identity and Difference*, that Derrida, after evoking Heidegger's understanding—his critique, really—of the God of the philosophers, interrupts his reading of Heidegger to quote at some length a rather particular prayer of Pascal's? I will return to this question—and to this prayer of Pascal's—in a moment, but let me simply note here this curious gesture of interrupting the reading of Heidegger on prayer with a prayer—a posthumous prayer, as we will see—from Pascal.

Following his long detour through Pascal and the question of prayer, Derrida returns to Heidegger, who, unlike Pascal and unlike Robinson Crusoe, does not pray and does not even quote prayers, who speaks of the God of onto-theology in the third person and who then makes in the following section of *Identity and Difference* what Derrida calls "a very serious remark,"

> namely that thought without God (*das gott-lose Denken*), and thus atheistic or a-theological thinking under the regime of onto-theology, and thus the thinking of those who, as philosophers, declare themselves to be atheists . . . is perhaps closer to the divine God, to the divinity of God, more open to it than the thinking of a theism, or of a philosophical belief in the God of the philosophers and of onto-theology. (*BS 2* 214/300)

In Heidegger's view, says Derrida—who also, as we saw, embraces or endorses a certain experience of atheism—"philosophical atheism would be closer to the divinity of God, more respectful and more open, better pre-pared for a God to whom one would pray and sacrifice, than is onto-theology when it refers to God as supreme Being and *causa sui*, i.e., as sovereign and all-powerful, as origin, cause and ground of all that is, and therefore of the world" (*BS 2* 215/301). This claim of Heidegger's "casts light," Derrida concludes, "on what Heidegger often says about his own atheism and about a philosophy which, as such, is incompatible with be-lief (*Glaube*) in God" (*BS 2* 214–300).

Read in the context of the entire seminar, and with the remarks cited earlier from "Epochē and Faith" in mind, we can begin to sketch out some preliminary hypotheses. By suggesting that the divinity of God thought by philosophical atheism is, precisely, "foreign to the attributes of power and of sovereignty, of height and of causal and fundamental principal-ity," Heidegger could be read as suggesting exactly the kind of severing of unconditionality from sovereignty—the kind of deconstruction of sovereignty—that Derrida speaks of in *Rogues* and elsewhere. He could also be read as trying to think "another sovereignty," one that is "foreign to ontic power, and therefore foreign to political theology and to creation-ism, and to fundamentalism, in all senses of the term, in particular the sense that refers to a founding God" (*BS 2* 215/301). It is precisely this other sovereignty—if not this beyond of sovereignty, this beyond, in any case, of the theologico-political—that Derrida, as we will see in Chapter 7, will seem to find in Heidegger's notion of *Walten* as originary violence, as *physis* or, indeed, as *différance*. In order to approach this other sovereignty or this other of sovereignty, what is required, Heidegger suggests, is a step that "goes backward from metaphysics to the essence of metaphysics," a step backward toward *Walten* or toward "a God who would no longer be the sovereign God of onto-theology" (*BS 2* 215/301–2). But if that step backward leads us beyond the God of onto-theology to whom we can nei-ther sacrifice nor pray, if it leads us to a thinking of *Walten* as originary vio-lence or as *physis* before the ontological difference, then the question imposes itself—and it is with this question that Derrida ends his reading of *Identity and Difference*—"Can one pray to *Walten*?" (*BS 2* 215/300–301)

As always, the difference between Derrida and Heidegger is at once great and almost imperceptible. On the one hand, Derrida seems to share if not endorse the philosophical atheism spoken of by Heidegger. Like Hei-degger, he wishes to submit the god of onto-theology to critique or decon-struction. But Derrida seems to suggest that in his haste to purge thinking of all religion, in his desire to keep his philosophical atheism pure of all religious belief or faith, Heidegger neglects or overlooks the very faith that, in other places, he himself shows to be at the origin of all thought. In his insistence that philosophical thinking remain atheistic, in his fear—one born, perhaps, of a certain Enlightenment tradition—that faith and knowledge might be conflated or might be shown to share a single source, Heidegger would have denied thinking the *Glaube* or elementary faith that, in other places, he will have nonetheless affirmed in the form of an originary *Zusage* or an elementary *Verlässlichkeit* as the condition of all thinking.

After considering Heidegger's critique of onto-theology in his 1957 *Identity and Difference* and after recalling that it is toward the question of *Walten* in Heidegger that he is ultimately headed, the question of whether one can pray or not to this non-onto-theological *Walten*, Derrida now turns to the question of prayer in the 1929–30 seminar that he has been reading throughout *The Beast and the Sovereign*. He hones right in on the place in this seminar where Heidegger, following Aristotle, wishes to distinguish the beast from the sovereign, that is, the animal from man, on the basis of the claim that man has *logos* while the animal does not, that is, that while man is *zōion echon logon* the animal is essentially a *zōion alogon* inasmuch as it does not have access to the as-structure of being (*BS 2* 218/304).[16] To make this claim, however, Heidegger will have to rely upon a distinction between two different kinds of discourse or *logos* that will come to trouble his entire analysis, namely, an apophantic *logos*, the form of *logos* that is *most* proper to man, a logos of the enunciative proposition, and a nonapophantic *logos*, the best example of which, following Aristotle, would be prayer.[17] Without actually using the terms of a speech act theory that had yet to be invented, Heidegger in 1929–30 is essentially reading Aristotle to distinguish the constative from the performative.[18] In contrast to the enunciative *logos*, prayer is precisely not an attempt, as Heidegger says, "to inform the other about something in the sense of increasing his or her knowledge." It is rather "the concrete act," the performative, so to speak, of a "praying another (*einen anderen Bittens*)" (cited at *BS 2* 217/303). What distinguishes the *logos apophantikos*, the enunciative *logos*, from the nonapophantic *logos* of prayer, what distinguishes, Heidegger might have said, the constative from the performative, is thus this dimension of making known, of truth and falsity, the possibility of telling the truth or lying. As Derrida parses it:

> Prayer, for its part, a human thing, is a *logos semantikos* but not *apophantikos*, it speaks but could neither lie nor tell the truth. A prayer says nothing that could mislead. It cannot and could not be shown to be false. . . . The *logos apophantikos*, for its part, is also human discourse, but one that can always mislead and lie. The *logos apophantikos* can speak the truth and make the truth only by withdrawing

from deceit, lying and retreat, or even from error as such. (*BS 2* 230/320–321)

This is a gesture that Derrida clearly admires in Heidegger. By distinguishing so "lucidly," as Derrida says, the nonapophantic from the apophantic enunciation on the basis of truth and falsity—even if Heidegger will go on to suggest that traditional notions of truth and falsity need to be questioned—Heidegger has effectively isolated the performative dimension of language. Derrida could not but admire as well the way in which, for Heidegger, lying is an essential *possibility* for speaking the truth and the apophantic *logos* can be true only by withdrawing from deception, claims that in their form and content are not unlike Derrida's assertion, as we saw earlier, that a felicitous speech act always depends upon the possibility of an infelicitous one.

What Derrida contests, then, what he finds unjustified in Heidegger, is not the distinction between the apophantic and the nonapophantic or the withdrawal of prayer from the realm of truth and falsity but Heidegger's next move, which is, says Derrida, to "brutally exclude from his discussion" the "non-enunciative aspect of *logos* represented by prayer, on the pretext that it belongs to rhetoric or poetics" (*BS 2* 216/302). However pertinent the distinction between apophantic and nonapophantic *logos* may be, the exclusion of the latter from the former would be, it seems, yet another sign or symptom of Heidegger's desire to keep philosophical language at arm's length from any hint of faith, in this case, from any prayer. It is also symptomatic, according to Derrida, of Heidegger's desire to follow Aristotle in distinguishing man and what is proper to man from the animal. By going on to deprive the animal not just of the apophantic *logos* but of every kind of *logos semantikos*, Heidegger in effect deprives the animal—the animal in general—not just of the ability to make known or to make propositions but of the ability to pray, to trust, or to have faith. And the exclusion is just as serious, it might be said, on the side of man, for whom the nonapophantic and the apophantic aspects of *logos* have been not only, so to speak, disambiguated but completed separated.[19]

By questioning Heidegger's unjustified and seemingly symptomatic exclusion of the nonapophantic *logos* from his analysis, Derrida can go on to suggest that there is perhaps a kind of nonapophantic *logos* at the origin of every apophantic *logos*. Not only may there be a form of animal prayer, just as there is, as Derrida suggests in "Epochē and Faith," a form of animal faith, but that which was in effect the proper of the proper of man, that which was truly proper within the general category of the *logos semantikos*, namely, the *apophantic logos*, may itself be conditioned by a nonapophantic *logos*, a performative, if you will, that conditions every truth claim and every *as such*.[20] We are back to Derrida's strategy, as we analyzed it in Chapter 1, with regard to the animal-human distinction. Instead of simply suggesting that a capacity that has traditionally been attributed to the human but denied the animal should be granted to the animal as well, Derrida suggests that we first of all question the purity of that attribution to man.

Hence Derrida follows Heidegger's initial isolation of the performative, this dimension of "praying another" before it is ever a question of truth and falsity, a distinction that runs parallel to Austin's initial distinction between the performative and the constative. But Derrida then wonders, just as he did when he was reading Austin some thirty years earlier, "how [the performative] can be circumscribed in all rigor, how its domain and its frontiers can be drawn in the *logos* in general"; for "is there not," he asks, "some implicit prayer in every address to the other? And is there not an implicit address to the other in every statement . . . even if it be an *Aussagesatz,* an enunciative proposition or proposition destined to make known?" (*BS 2* 217/304). Derrida thus finds it all the more surprising that Heidegger would here exclude any "supplementary reflection on prayer (*eukhē, Bitten*) on the pretext, which," says Derrida, "looks scarcely credible, that it has to do merely with poetics or rhetoric and not with the proper task of this seminar," namely, to elucidate the enunciative *logos.* Heidegger seems to have forgotten, says Derrida in an aside, that "even the enunciative proposition, insofar as it is addressed to someone, indicates some prayer, a 'listen to me, I say to you'" (*BS 2* 217/304). Hence, Derrida can suggest contra Heidegger, or contra *this* Heidegger, that a certain prayer, a certain performative of prayer, is at the origin of all discourse, constative as well as performative. And all this, recall, will have been motivated in large part by Heidegger's attempt to distinguish the beast from the sovereign, to show that "the animal is *alogon* . . . it can neither speak, nor pray, nor lie" (*BS 2* 229/320).

We are now up to the Ninth Session of the seminar, which took place on March 12, 2003. It begins yet again with what Derrida calls "the immense and undelimitable question of prayer." Derrida asks:

> Can one in fact talk of a "question of prayer?" . . . Every question presupposes a prayer, but prayer as such does not ask a question, it remains foreign to the question properly speaking. When one prays, one may ask or desire, but one is not posing a question. (*BS 2* 231/323)

With this question of the question of prayer, we are surely being invited to return to everything Derrida said on this same subject in, for example, *Of*

Spirit, which bears the subtitle "Heidegger and the Question." We are invited above all to reconsider Derrida's long and infamous footnote in that text, added in part because of a question, precisely, from Françoise Dastur, about the dimension of the *gage* or the engagement, the *Zusage*, in Heidegger's thinking, a question that Derrida will have then pursued in so many subsequent texts on Heidegger, from "Faith and Knowledge" right up to this final seminar (*OS* 129–136). Prayer is significant because it is a dimension of language that would seem to precede truth and falsity, because it seems more primary than the question, more originary than the ability, capacity, or power to pose questions. Derrida thus asks at the beginning of this penultimate session about the power of prayer, or really, about the power or ability to pray—the question being, I take it, whether a rethinking of the performative that withdraws power and ability from the one praying will not at the same time make prayer, properly speaking, *impossible*, that is, beyond the capacity or possibilities of any living I (*BS 2* 234–235/328).

The Beast and the Sovereign is thus a seminar not only about prayer but—and we now see that this could not be otherwise—also a seminar *of* prayer, a seminar that includes prayer and a seminar that has become prayer. I alluded earlier to the fact that in the Eighth Session of the seminar, on March 5, 2003, Derrida interrupts his reading of Heidegger with a rather peculiar prayer from Pascal. But why Pascal? First, no doubt, because Pascal can be related in certain ways both to *Robinson Crusoe* and to Heidegger, to the former insofar as Pascal, born in 1623, was more or less contemporaneous with the fictional Robinson Crusoe, who was born in 1632, and to the latter insofar as Pascal, like Heidegger, criticizes, albeit in a different way and with different intentions, the very same God of the philosophers and onto-theology. But beyond these connections, this prayer of Pascal's will raise all kinds of questions with regard to some of the central assumptions of traditional Austinian speech act theory, as we heard J. Hillis Miller develop them earlier, namely, that it be in the first person by someone living, someone speaking out of good faith and not mechanically or automatically repeating, and so on. As a result, it will raise, as we will see, serious questions regarding traditional ways of thinking writing, the trace, the archive, and the testament.

While I will not look in any detail at this prayer itself, which is cited in its entirety but not commented on at any length in *The Beast and the Sovereign*, I would like to underscore the way it was found and, thus, the way it now finds itself in the middle of this Eighth Session. This is the famous prayer that Pascal had sewn into his garment several years before his death and that was found on his person, on his corpse or in his clothes, upon his death in 1662. Derrida cites at some length an account of the discovery of the prayer:

> "A few days after the death of Monsieur Pascal," said Father Guerrier, "a servant of the house noticed by chance an area in the lining of the doublet of the illustrious deceased that appeared thicker than the rest, and having removed the stitching at this place to see what it was, he found there a little folded parchment written in the hand of Monsieur Pascal, and in the parchment a paper written in the same hand: the one was a faithful copy of the other. These two pieces were immediately put into the hands of Madame Périer who showed them to several of her particular friends. All agreed there was no doubt that this parchment, written with so much care and with such remarkable characters, was a type of *memorial* that he kept very carefully to preserve the memory of a thing that he wanted to have always present to his eyes and to his mind, since for eight years he had taken care to stitch it and unstitch it from his clothes, as his wardrobe changed." (*BS 2* 212/297)

Derrida then quotes with just a minimum of commentary the entire prayer, which begins, just after the date, "The year of grace 1654. Monday, 23 November," and then several references to the Christian calendar, with the single word "*Feu*," that is, "Fire."[21] It is just after this word "*Feu*" that Pascal famously addresses the prayer *not* to the God "of philosophers and savants" but to the "God of Abraham, God of Isaac, God of Jacob," an address that is itself a quotation from Exodus and from Matthew.

Now, in "Justices," the essay written, recall, for J. Hillis Miller in spring 2003, Derrida again turns to Pascal's prayer and to the unique performative gesture that consists in quoting a prayer—emphasizing, this time, another biblical quotation and another aspect of such quotation. Derrida writes: "In his famous *Mémorial*, the little paper found after his death that had been sewn into his garment eight year earlier, Pascal quotes from John's Gospel, when the latter cites the words and prayers of Jesus (we thus have the chain of transmitted words in J: Just [God], Jesus [his son], John [the evangelizing disciple]) . . . 'O righteous Father, the world hath not known thee: but I have known thee, and these have known that thou has sent me' (John 17:25)" ("J" 694).

Quotes within quotes, papers within parchments, texts within texts, prayers within prayers, prayers within texts within garments within texts: Derrida seems to be deploying a very special kind of performativity here in "Justices" and, especially, in the second volume of *The Beast and the Sovereign*. While almost any Derrida seminar could, of course, be read or taken in this way, something unique seems to have been set to work, buried, in truth, here in the middle of the Eighth Session of *The Beast and the Sovereign*—though also, as if the one text spilled over into or was sewn into the other, in "Justices." Apart from a brief return in the tenth and final session to Robinson Crusoe's "apprenticeship of Christian prayer," Derrida more or less abandons his reflections on prayer in the Ninth Session, turning instead to questions of originary violence, Heideggerian *Walten*, and the question of the end of the world or the world as a *phantasm*.

In "Justices," however, delivered just about a month after the final session of the seminar, all these themes return, beginning with the performative, and particularly the performative of prayer, but also the archive, poetry, singularity, even a reference to Heidegger's *Identity and Difference* and the God of onto-theology to whom we neither pray nor sacrifice.[22] But what returns especially—and this is not unrelated to prayer, to an "excess, in prayer, over onto-theology" ("J" 703)—is an emphasis on the separation and isolation of singularities, of singular beings, the separation of not only different species from one another but, just as we saw in Chapter 2, of different individuals of the same species from one another, individuals that would be irremediably separated because of a *selftaste*—a notion Miller takes from Gerard Manley Hopkins—that can never be shared.[23] Derrida writes, for example, in "Justices": "The isolation, the insularity of whoever is 'selved'—and one should say severed, separated, cut off, removed—is the experience of a 'selfbeing,' a 'selfhood,' a 'self-awareness' that, long before *thinking itself*, long before the *cogito*, senses the taste of self" ("J" 698). Selftaste, then, would come before the cogito and before any knowledge to be shared—before any performative carried out by a fully intentional, present I. Still reading Miller, Derrida relates this "radical solitude," this isolation or insularity, "to the tradition of the *ultima solitudo* of Duns Scotus." As Derrida puts it, "at the deepest center of selfhood a man is alone" ("J" 701). Derrida's very powerful and moving words in *The Beast and the Sovereign* about the difference or infinite distance between individuals, indeed, between worlds or islands, a difference or distance that is often most palpable between us and those closest to us, those we most love, are echoed as well in "Justices," as Derrida claims that "love and friendship are born in the experience of this unspeakable selftaste: an unshareable experience and nevertheless shared, the agreement of two renunciations to say the impossible" ("J" 699). Even if there is compassion, says Derrida in words that could have come right out of *The Beast and the Sovereign*, this "compassion cannot cross the abyss of solitudes. On the contrary, it only makes the abyss deeper" ("J" 702).[24] Between the I and the other, then, it cannot be a question of knowledge or community, but of a friendship born of solitude, separation, and interruption and, I would like to think, a certain "pray tell." Between friends, there would always be a silent "correspondence" of or between prayers—though these prayers would always be, like Pascal's prayer, testamentary and posthumous.

I would thus like to conclude this chapter by suggesting that this strange gesture of preserving a prayer is now not only Pascal's but also Derrida's, who has in effect sewn this prayer, among so much else, into this final seminar, and thus into his corpus—into a seminar that he could not have *known* would be published but that he could have certainly predicted would be found on or near him, at the IMEC archives in Normandy or at Irvine, sometime after his death. For even if the seminar had *in fact* been lost or become irrecoverable, even if, by some improbable set of circumstances, all copies of it had been burned and the memories of those who heard it erased, it would have remained structurally and from the beginning testamentary—like all writing. Indeed, that is exactly what Derrida says as he introduces this very unique prayer of Pascal's. It is, he says, a "*posthumous* piece of writing," at which point he opens a parenthesis that brings us right back to the very origins of deconstruction in texts such as "Signature Event Context" and "Plato's Pharmacy," origins that he would thus continue to recall and reiterate right up until the end:

> As you well know, it is in a *posthumous* piece of writing (now of course, all writings are posthumous, each in its own way, even those that are known and published during the author's lifetime, but within this generality of the posthumous, within the trace as structurally and essentially and by destinal vocation posthumous or testamentary, there is a stricter enclave of the posthumous, namely what is only discovered and published after the death of the author or the signatory). Pascal's writing on the God of Abraham was strictly posthumous in this latter sense, even though we're not sure that Pascal wanted it to be published. It was posthumous in this very strict sense since it was found written on a piece of paper found in Pascal's clothing after his death. (*BS 2* 209/294)

All writing is posthumous, testamentary, and, as Derrida will have shown in those early texts to which I just referred, all traces—including spoken ones—participate to some degree in writing. Prayer too, then, even spoken prayer, must be understood as written, as posthumous and testamentary, the moment there is no animating intention, no sovereign subject, no fully living I, behind it. Pascal's unique, posthumous prayer simply reveals better than most the testamentary character of all prayer, indeed of every trace, including, now, Derrida's own seminar, which is not just any seminar insofar as it too will have essentially been an apprenticeship in prayer and insofar as it will have posed in an explicit fashion—and so will have at once described and performed—the very "special theory or performativity" of which the seminar speaks.

Derrida goes on to say of Pascal's prayer:

> There can be little doubt that this little piece of paper was destined, if not for someone, then at least to remain, to survive the moment of its inscription, to remain legible in the exteriority of a trace, of a document, even if it were readable only for Pascal himself, later, in the generation of repetitions to come. This is indeed what has been called a *memorial*, to use the word of a witness, Father Guerrier. (*BS* 212/297)

There is something exemplary about this prayer of Pascal's—and now this seminar of Derrida's—in relation to the testament and to the archive. It is posthumous, like all writing, and yet it is also a prayer, like every trace. Recall Derrida's question cited earlier of whether one can "address oneself to someone or indeed to any living being at all—or even something not living—without some implicit prayer coming to bend, to inflect the discourse, or even the simple silent look which, addressing itself to the other, cannot fail to ask of him or her 'listen to me, please [*je t'en prie*], listen, I pray you'" (*BS 2* 203/286–287). It would always be in relation to some "Pray tell," I would like to suggest, that we write and that we respond, that we *must* respond.[25] The archive is thus perhaps—as we will see more fully in the following chapter—not simply the place where past prayers are recorded and stored but the place, the only place, where they "take place," beyond any animating intention, beyond any self or I. The archive would then be like a polyphonic "pray tell" or "I pray you" addressed always to the other—to an other who is always unknown, who may not even be born, and into whose hands will pass my corpse and my corpus. It would be like a series of prayer wheels where simply spinning the wheel—what we call reading—has the effect of an "animated" recitation, the only kind of resurrection possible for philosophical atheism. Derrida's *The Beast and the Sovereign* will have not only treated the question of prayer, the question of prayer as what comes before the question, but will have itself turned round prayer like a wheel, turned round prayer in the second and third sessions and then in the third and second from the last. *The Beast and the Sovereign* will have thus not only analyzed prayer in Heidegger and for Robinson Crusoe but will have given us the law of prayer itself. For if all prayers, even those that are spoken aloud or silently pronounced, are to some extent written, that is, mechanical, autonomous, bereft of any fully animating intention, then the posthumous prayer will have been the very vocation of prayer itself. Every text would thus say not only, in the words of Derrida's beloved Augustine, "pick up and read," but "pray tell," "pray and then tell," "pray as you tell," so that someone—a reader, say—may someday come along who can tell it's a prayer.

6

Derrida's Preoccupation with the Archive

"*L'archive* pré-occupe *l'avenir*," says Derrida in an interview published in the *Cahiers du Cinéma* in 2001, "the archive *pre-occupies* the future."[1] In this one brief phrase, buried in a relatively obscure corner of the Derridean corpus, we find the already divided essence of Derrida's thinking in *The Beast and the Sovereign* and elsewhere about the archive, about what might be called the two sources or two *archai* of the archive, that is, the archive as both threat and promise, turned toward both the past and the future, at once commencement and commandment.

The archive preoccupies the future and so preoccupies—cannot but preoccupy—us: that is to say, the archive concerns us, matters to us, the archive is our concern, but also, the archive occupies us in advance, determines all our preoccupations through a process of identification, selection, and repression that invests or occupies the terrain ahead of time so as to anticipate and predetermine what is worthy to be preserved and what not. When it comes to the archive, then, we cannot but be preoccupied, preoccupied by what at once opens up the future and forecloses it.[2] Whether we like it or not, Derrida seems to suggest, the archive preoccupies the future and so preoccupies us.

While it might seem that the archive was a relatively late and local or localizable—even marginal—theme in Derrida's work, a closer look suggests that it was in fact a constant preoccupation.[3] One thinks immediately of the title *Archive Fever*, of course, but there is also *Geneses, Genealogies, Genres, & Genius*, which bears the subtitle, *The Secrets of the Archive*, as well as the posthumously published *Copy, Archive, Signature,* and then *Typewriter Ribbon,* the first section of which is titled "The Next to Last Word: Archives of the Confession." But then, quite apart from titles, there are texts such as *A Taste for the Secret, Above All, No Journalists, Echographies,* and "No Apocalypse, Not Now," where the concept of the archive or of archivization is absolutely central. And then there are texts—too numerous to list—where the notion of the archive or of archivization is at work under other, related names. For example, Derrida's entire thinking of the trace in *Of Grammatology* or "Freud and the Scene of Writing" was in essence a rethinking of the archive, or at least of the possibility of the archive, a rethinking of the temporality and spatiality, the iterability and futurity, of what remains. His entire thinking of spectrality or hauntology in *Specters of Marx* or *Ulysses Gramophone* was nothing other than a rethinking of the archive or at least of what makes the archive possible, a rethinking, precisely, of the way in which voices from the past always come to anticipate or occupy our own, calling into question, for example, the distinction between so-called live, present speech and its inscription, recording, repetition, and preservation in the archive.

From the very beginning of his work right up to the very end, Derrida was thus preoccupied in a particularly acute way by the archive, sensitive from the very beginning to the way in which past discourses, past archives, come to occupy the terrain in advance, sensitive, therefore, to the impossibility of ever escaping the archive, though also to the *undesirability* of ever wishing to do so. For if the archive preoccupies and invests us in advance, it also contains, according to Derrida, places or moments where it opens onto what exceeds it, places where an archive oriented by the past is turned toward the future and what remains to come.

Unable to trace here Derrida's long itinerary in his thinking of the archive and, thus, of the trace, writing, spectrality, and so on, I look in this chapter at the role played by this theme or question in this final year of *The Beast and the Sovereign* seminar, since the archive is clearly not just one question among others for Derrida in the seminar but, in some sense, the central question, even, as I will argue in conclusion, the central question of philosophy itself.

I begin, however, not with *The Beast and the Sovereign* but with a seemingly trivial or banal example of archivization from *Archive Fever,* since it will help us establish the terms in which the archive is to be thought, the divided essence, as I called it, of the archive. This banal, everyday example is to be found in Derrida's description of trying to save a text on his home computer—the one he would have written *The Beast and the Sovereign* on, for example—trying to save or archive a text that has for the moment only appeared on his computer screen.[4] Derrida writes:

> I asked myself what is the moment *proper* to the archive, if there is such a thing, the instant of archivization strictly speaking, which is not . . . so-called live or spontaneous memory (*mnēmē or anamnēsis*), but rather a certain hypomnesis and prosthetic experience of the technical substrate. Was it not at this very instant that, having written something or other on the screen, the letters remaining as if suspended and floating yet at the surface of a liquid element, I pushed a certain key to "save" a text undamaged, in a hard and lasting way, to protect marks from being erased, so as to ensure in this way salvation and *indemnity*, to stock, to accumulate, and, in what is at once the same thing and something else, to make the sentence available in this way for printing and for reprinting, for reproduction? (*AF* 25–26)

Now these references to spontaneous memory and hypomnesis recall Derrida's analyses more than a quarter of a century earlier of writing and the Platonic critique of writing in "Plato's Pharmacy" and elsewhere, while the references to salvation and *indemnification* recall Derrida's analysis of "the two sources of 'religion'" in "Faith and Knowledge," written just a couple of months before *Archive Fever*. Derrida's own analysis of this trivial little example of archiving thus draws upon—in some sense is already preoccupied by—his own already immense corpus or archive on these questions of the trace, memory, supplementarity, indemnification, and so on.

There are, it would seem, *two sources* of the archive, just as in "Faith and Knowledge" there are two sources of religion. The first would be rooted in an attempt to protect, save, or indemnify a unique text, a singular event, the text Derrida has just written on his computer screen. This first moment of the archive would thus be oriented toward the protection, safeguarding, and indemnification of this unique past or experience of the past, this irreplaceable and unrepeatable work. As Derrida argues in *Archive Fever*: "each time in its original uniqueness, an archive ought to be idiomatic, and thus at once offered and unavailable for translation, open to and shielded from technical iteration and reproduction" (*AF* 90).

But in order for this unique and irreplaceable text to be saved, protected, or indemnified, it must be inscribed in a medium that will make it readable in the future. In other words, the text must become legible, readable, repeatable not only for the one who has written it, the one who thus becomes another to his own text the moment he has written it, but for others who will come to read it, in principle if not in fact, long after he or

she is gone. It must offer itself, as the unique text that it is, to future iterations, future readings. The second source of the archive would thus have
to do with an *affirmative* relation to that past or that text in the form of a
promise or performative repetition that enlists the deracinating powers of
some technoscientific supplement (whether tablet or papyrus or paper or
hard drive or, today, "tablet" again). It is this supplement that then makes
possible not only the repetition of what has already happened and could
have already been predicted but also that which will have not yet arrived,
novelty and surprise, displacement and deformation, in short, *events* of
reading.

To put it in other terms, terms that run more or less parallel to Derrida's reading elsewhere of the relationship between revelation and revealability, there is the archived event, the event that is archived, and then
there is the archiving event, the event of archiving; the event that is saved
and the saving event; a saved event that always risks predetermining and
thus annulling the saving event and the saving or archiving event that always risks undermining or destroying the event that is saved.[5] It is thus
hardly a leap to want to claim, reading Derrida on the archive in the light
of other texts from around the same time, that the archive is *autoimmune*
and that it is this autoimmunity that both threatens the archive and allows
it to live on. By protecting or safeguarding itself, the archive opens itself up
to iterations that may either distort or destroy it, reveal hidden possibilities concealed within it or allow us to lend an ear to what is and must remain unthought within it.[6]

The archive is thus as much about the future as the past; it is turned as
much toward the performative affirmation of a unique event as toward
that past event. Derrida writes again in *Archive Fever*: "The affirmation of
the future *to come*: this is not a positive thesis. It is nothing other than the
affirmation itself, the 'yes,' insofar as it is the condition of all promises or
of all hope, of all awaiting, of all performativity, of all opening toward the
future, whatever it may be, for science or for religion" (*AF* 68).[7] In the end,
the archive is founded upon a *promise*—Derrida could have said a *faith*, an
elementary or elemental *faith*—that precedes and must be thought before
all *knowledge*. The archive would therefore be that which preoccupies us
only by opening our concern to what exceeds it, to what is anarchival in
the archive, to that moment or decision, which can itself never be archived, when we affirm or promise a text for the future by clicking "save,"
or sometimes, for this too is a structuring moment of the archive, "delete,"
or sometimes even—though one should always think twice before doing
this—"yes I am sure I want to delete all the contents of this folder."

But while the archive, like religion, has two sources, while it too is, in a sense, autoimmune, while it is repeatable, like any trace, what distinguishes the archive from the trace in general is a certain relationship to power and, especially, political power. As Derrida recalls at the beginning of *Archive Fever*, *archē* "names at once the *commencement* and the *commandment*" (*AF* 1). The archive would thus coordinate and name, he goes on to write

> two principles in one: the principle according to nature or history, *there* where things *commence*—physical, historical, or ontological principle—but also the principle according to the law, *there* where men and gods *command*, *there* where authority, social order are exercised, *in this place* from which *order* is given—nomological principle. (*AF* 1)

In a word, the archive always plays for keeps; it keeps what is given by nature or by history only by then keeping what is thereby given in line, in order, in check. And this is what distinguishes the trace from the archive. As Derrida would affirm in a series of remarks about the archive from June 2002, that is, just a few months before the beginning of *The Beast and the Sovereign* seminar, "There are no archives without a power of capitalization or of monopoly, of quasi-monopoly, of a gathering of statutory traces that are recognized as traces. In other words, there are no archives without political power" ("TA" 23).

To speak of the archive is thus, for Derrida, to speak of everything from time, space, finitude, and the event, to performativity, repetition, the promise, the trace, and, of course, the relationship or difference between the animal and man, since the animal too, according to Derrida, leaves traces. To speak of the archive is thus to speak of time, of the trace, of the performative, but also, inasmuch as it involves power, of the sovereign or of sovereignty. It is thus hardly surprising, then, that a preoccupation with the archive would pervade the entirely of the second year of *The Beast and the Sovereign* seminar, even if this is not evident at first glance. *The Beast and the Sovereign* is quite obviously and explicitly concerned, as we have seen, with Heidegger's seminar of 1929–30 on the themes of world, finitude, and solitude, as well as on originary violence—as we will see in the following chapter. It is obviously concerned with questions of the animal, technology, and death in *Robinson Crusoe*. But it is also—and from start to finish—concerned with the question of the archive, whether under this or other names. There is, for example, this rather playful moment late in the seminar where Derrida characterizes himself as a kind of archival animal (a library rat or, better, a squirrel in "the sublime") who has been sniffing around Heidegger's archive for the past nine sessions and who has just found buried within the 1929–30 seminar a sort of avowal of something he, Heidegger, will have neglected in *Being and Time*: "Could he foresee that in the posterity of the probable improbable archive, the day would come when a French animal, in turn conducting a seminar on this seminar and every Wednesday sniffing out the footprints or the track of an improbable Friday, would come to worry away at these . . . traceless traces of an avowal without avowal on the subject of a fault without fault" (*BS 2* 240–241/335).[8]

This is just one of many references, whether explicit or implicit, to the archive. Derrida even introduces several of the central themes of the seminar, including the relationship between the human, the animal, and the stone, as well as the respective relationships to world, solitude, and finitude, by means of an opening fiction that brings us right into the question of the archive. Derrida imagines coming across a stone (a bit like Robinson Crusoe coming across a human footprint) with a phrase written across it, without context or explanation, as if he had just stumbled upon it in the archive: "animals are not alone." It is through this fiction that Derrida will go on to ask a series of questions about the context for such a phrase, the possible author of it, and so on—precisely the kinds of questions one might ask of an unidentified document discovered in the archive.

The question of the archive also becomes for Derrida, as one might imagine on the basis of what we saw in Chapters 3 and 4, a very *personal* question. In the Fifth Session, for example, Derrida recounts the somewhat amusing anecdote of an American archivist or librarian who wants to ask him what will happen to his "papers," his "archive," after his death, though instead of saying "'on your death' or 'after your death,'" he or she says politely, modestly, courteously, like they do in funeral homes . . . 'after your lifetime'" (*BS 2* 140/205). The story is amusing but also poignant, for this *after your lifetime*, which resonates with everything in the seminar about death, finitude, solitude, and the end of the world, is also, in some sense, the very watchword of the archive itself, so long, that is, as we understand that this *after* will have supervened upon life from its very inception.

Everything, then, about this final seminar seems to be haunted by thoughts of the archive. The theme is always lurking in the background and it emerges in an explicit way in some of the most personal, lyrical, and provocative passages in the seminar. It surfaces, for instance, in the Second Session, as Derrida turns, quite unexpectedly in the middle of a reading of *Robinson Crusoe*, to a line from John Donne's *Holy Sonnets*. In the midst of a long and almost breathless improvisation on Donne's "I run to Death and Death meets me as fast / And all my Pleasures are like Yesterday," Derrida speaks of death as "always anterior, in its very futurity, like what remains to come, affecting itself in advance from the nostalgia of its own archive," and he ends the passage by affirming that "everything begins with the archive or with archive fever" (*BS 2* 51/88).[9]

But it is the narrative *Robinson Crusoe* that provokes Derrida's most sustained meditations about the archive. As we saw in Chapter 4, Derrida reads or interprets Robinson Crusoe's parrot Poll as a sort of prosthetic memory or, indeed, a kind of archive, a living machine that in effect records Robinson Crusoe's voice and sends it back to him (*BS 2* 85/134).[10] After thus looking in some detail at the passage in which Poll repeats— like a machine, like a living archive—Robinson Crusoe's first name, Derrida embarks on a long analysis of the relationship between the personage Robinson Crusoe and the book named *Robinson Crusoe*, before then generalizing this self-naming trace to every autobiography and then every trace in the archive. He writes:

> One could say of every autobiography, every autobiographical fiction, and even every written confession through which the author calls and names himself, that it presents itself through this linguistic and prosthetic apparatus—a book—or a piece of writing or a trace in general, for example the book entitled *Robinson Crusoe*, which speaks of him without him, according to a trick that constructs and leaves in the world an artifact that speaks all alone [*tout seul*] and all alone calls the author by his name, renames him in his renown without the author himself needing to do anything else, not even be alive. (*BS 2* 86–87/136)

With this introduction of a prosthetic memory that passes by way of the book, a selected and organized configuration of traces, we are getting closer to that divided essence of the archive with which I began. Some fifty or so pages later, Derrida returns to this theme in his analysis of Robinson Crusoe's obsessive fear of being buried or eaten alive, his fear of "dying a living death." It is at this point in the seminar that Derrida stages a strange hypothetical conversation between himself and his audience, or between himself and an imaginary interlocutor, whom he will try to convince that "Robinson Crusoe" was indeed buried alive, since "Robinson Crusoe" is the name not only of a character in the novel but also of the novel itself, one that has indeed been swallowed up by the archive and so now survives like a "living dead" within it (*BS 2* 127–130/189–192). It is here, then, that the themes of the corpse and the corpus come together, the body and the archive, the question of different ways of disposing of the dead body and different means of preserving—or not—the traces of the deceased. But because the extraordinary fate of *Robinson Crusoe* is, of course, shared by other books, all other books, including Derrida's, it is also at this point that Derrida's writing *about* the archive starts to become conflated with the archive or the possibility of the archive that his writing, that his seminar, *is*. He thus *writes*—knowing that his writing would no doubt be preserved, reproduced, translated, as it has been *here*:

> Now this survival, thanks to which the book bearing this title has come down to us, has been read and will be read, interpreted, taught, saved, translated, reprinted, illustrated, filmed, kept alive by millions of inheritors—this survival is indeed that of the living dead. As is indeed any trace, in the sense I give this word and concept, a book is living dead, buried alive and swallowed up alive. (*BS 2* 130/193)

What is said here about *Robinson Crusoe* can thus be said of any trace, so that the archive now appears to be but a skein of traces that have been consigned to this *living death*—to a mode of living on that contests the simple opposition between life and death. Every trace is a living death, a *sur-vivance*—a Gradiva of sorts—with all the threats and promises, all the fictions and phantasms of life, that this may entail.

Being buried alive is thus another way for Derrida to speak of *survivance*—a surviving, a living-on that would be without superiority or sovereignty, that is structurally possible from the outset and yet, as we saw in Chapter 4, always dependent on the world in which the trace is inscribed, dependent on the repetition and preservation of the sign, on its burial in the archive, on its salvation, therefore, and its provisional and always finite resuscitation or reanimation. Hence Derrida underscores that the *sur-* of this *survivance* signals not some height, altitude, or superiority, certainly not some *sur-vie* in the sense of an afterlife or eternal living on (*BS 2* 131/193–194). Dependent always upon the technoscientific supplement, and upon some kind of support, some kind of *subjectile*, the survival of the archive is always a finite survival, precarious and uncertain. Derrida continues:

> Like every trace, a book, the survivance of a book, from its first moment on, is a living-dead machine, sur-viving, the body of a thing buried in a library, a bookstore, a cellars, urns, drowned in the worldwide waves of a Web, etc., but a dead thing that resuscitates each time a breath of living reading, each time a breath of the other or the other

breath, each time an intentionality intends it and makes it live again by animating it . . . (*BS 2* 131/194)

Derrida's claims here about reanimation and the breath could easily lead one to believe that he now believes in the very thing against which he will have argued from the very beginning of his work, namely, that there is a living breath that animates a work and that what gets left behind after the death of the author, after the animating presence of the author has expired, is but the trace of that presence or that author, the present trace of that once living but now past presence. To disabuse us, then, of such an interpretation, Derrida goes on to locate the moment of the archive not just after but right in the midst of this supposedly live presence:

> This survivance is broached from the moment of the first trace that is supposed to engender the writing of a book. From the first breath, this archive as survivance is at work [*Cette survivance est entamée dès la première trace qui est supposée engender l'écriture d'un livre. Dès le premier souffle, cette archive comme survivance est à l'oeuvre*]. But once again, this is the case not only for books, or for writing, or for the archive in the current sense, but for everything from which the tissue of living experience is woven, through and through. A weave of survival, like death in life or life in death, a weave that does not come along to clothe a more originary existence, a life or a body or a soul that would be supposed to exist naked under this clothing. (*BS 2* 132/195)

From the first breath, says Derrida: from the first living breath, the archive—or at least the *possibility* of archivization, of repetition or iterability, of *survivance*—is already at work. From the very first breath, the archive, or at least the possibility of archivization—and thus its two sources or *archai*—is underway. We here see Derrida extending the very sense of the archive from books or from writing more generally to "everything from which the tissue of living experience is woven." If the archive preoccupies us so greatly, it is perhaps because there seems to be no outside of the archive, no *hors-archive*, or at least no outside of the general text and thus outside the movement of archivization.

Because of the enormous and unprecedented advances over the past couple of centuries in the technical possibilities of archivization, it is becoming today harder and harder not to indulge in the dream of an archive that would become so effective, so performative, that it would be more or less total or absolute. In *Paper Machine*, Derrida confesses that he often dreams of just such "an absolute memory . . . A multimedia band, with phrases, letters, sound, and images: it's everything, and it would keep an impression of everything" (*PM* 65). This dream is today being fed and encouraged by the extraordinary powers of the archive in the digital age, an archive that includes sounds and images and, one day, probably today already, tastes, touches, and smells. And it is nourished by the fact that the virtual archive has been freed of so many of the constraints of time and space, allowing it to be located no longer in the special collections room of a library but in some off-site server or, even more nebulously, in the *cloud*.

But this dream of an absolute memory, an absolute archive, is still, precisely, a dream, for it would spell the end of the archive, destroy any restricted and recognizable concept of the archive, by circumventing or breaking one of the unimpeachable laws of the archive, the law of its *finitude*. An archive that would be total would be no archive at all. For reasons both contingent and necessary, one cannot keep or save everything—even if, as we know, Derrida himself tried his best to keep as much as possible. In a public discussion with Jean-Luc Nancy and Philippe Lacoue-Labarthe that took place in Strasbourg in June 2004, that is, only four months before his death, Derrida reveals just how far he pushed the limits of his own finite archive. After confessing to having once violently destroyed a letter correspondence, he says:

> As for the rest—and here we are speaking of the problem of the archive—I've never lost or destroyed anything. Right down to the little notes that Bourdieu or Balibar would leave on my door when I was a student saying "I'll come by later" . . . Or from Bourdieu: "I'll give you a call," and I still have these things—I have *everything*. The most important things and the most apparently insignificant things. Always hoping, of course, that one day—not thanks to immortality but thanks to longevity—I might be able to reread, to recall, to revisit, and, in some way, to reappropriate all of this for myself. (*FS* 26)

The archive can thus be large and it can include the most seemingly insignificant things, but it can never be infinite. In *The Beast and the Sovereign*, Derrida is clear about the finitude of the archive and its always violent selectivity. In the course of a brief analysis of Freud's notions of the phantasm and of censorship, he writes:

> The number of inscriptions to be inscribed is finite—that's finitude. . . . It is like a topological economy of the archive in which one has to exclude, censor, erase, destroy or displace, virtualize, condense the archive to gain space in the same place, in the same system, to be able

to continue to store, to make space. Finitude is also a sort of law for this economy. (*BS 2* 156/227)

It is the finitude of the archive and the necessity of selection, censorship, and erasure that distinguishes the archive from the trace. Derrida underscores this point with great clarity in a text published under the apt title "Trace and Archive," a transcription of improvised remarks made just months before the beginning of his final seminar, that is, on June 25, 2002, at the Institut National de l'Audiovisuel (INA) in Paris, an institution devoted to radio and television archives that had been established some ten years earlier, in part, as the organizer of the event recalls, because of Derrida's support—in other words, because of Derrida's preoccupation with the archive.[11]

Derrida there begins by affirming that "the concept of the trace is so general" that it is difficult to "see any limit for it" ("TA" 23). Extending "well beyond what is called writing or inscription on some known support," the notion of the trace seems to be coextensive with experience itself, for "there is," says Derrida, "a trace as soon as there is experience, that is, referral to the other, difference, referral to something else, etc. Thus everywhere there is experience, there is trace, and there is no experience without trace." Not only writing but also speaking, even gesturing, is a trace, something that involves "retention and protention, and thus some relation to what is other, to the other, or to another moment, another place" ("TA" 23). No longer limited to the intentional production of traces on paper or some other support, "coextensive with the experience of the living in general," Derrida can thus affirm that "animals trace," indeed that "every living being traces" ("TA" 23). It is thus obviously not only the concept of the trace that needs to be rethought, but also the concepts of experience and of life.

But here is where the difference between trace and archive comes to be marked, and it is where the question of the archive becomes an always *political* question. As Derrida goes on to argue in "Trace and Archive," "there is no archive without trace," but "every trace is not an archive insofar as the archive presupposes . . . that the trace be appropriated, controlled, organized, politically under control" ("TA" 23). The condition of finitude, the fact that one cannot save or select everything, thus becomes in the archive a political condition, as some and not others are given the authority to choose what is to be selected and what not, what kept and what not, how it is to be classified and how not, where the archives are to be located and where not. "The archive begins by selection, and this selection is a violence," writes Derrida ("TA" 23), for every time an authority chooses, and he or she has to choose, that which is not chosen is neglected, consigned to forgetting or destruction, while that which is selected is saved for an always finite and "relative survival."

> The archive thus begins there where the trace is organized, selected, which presupposes that the trace is always finite. . . . Archivization is thus a type of work made for organizing a relative survival, as long as possible, in given political or juridical conditions, of certain deliberatively chosen traces. . . . It is this evaluation of traces, with authority and competence . . . that distinguishes the archive from the trace. ("TA" 24)

Due to this selection, certain things will live on and others will not, and it is up to those who constitute, inherit, and then pass on the archive to take upon themselves the responsibility for this selection, this fidelity to the past and this violence with regard to it. Archivization is thus not simply a process of preservation, conservation, or salvation but one of violence and destruction. The trace becomes archive always under the authority of some power of selection or interpretation, an authority that is sometimes invested in the state but that is at work already in the individual. Indeed, as Derrida affirms, "this archivization takes place already in the unconscious" ("TA" 24). Hence, there is no individual without this archival selection, without an "economy of memory" that keeps some things and not others, represses some things and not others. Derrida will thus go on to say, here in 2002 in relation to the archive, what he said about the registering of the trace back in 1966 in "Freud and the Scene of Writing":

> The archive drive [*pulsion d'archive*] is an irresistible movement not only to keep traces but to master them, interpret them. As soon as I have an experience, I have an experience of the trace. As soon as I have an experience of the trace, I cannot repress the movement to interpret these traces, to select between them, to keep them or not, and thus to constitute the traces in archives. ("TA" 25)

And that is why the archive always involves the future, and why this drive toward the future always entails a certain violence. "I violently select what I think must be repeated, what must be kept, what must be repeated in the future. This is a gesture of great violence" ("TA" 25). The archive drive is thus a destructive drive, determining what is to be kept—kept and kept in control, selected and already interpreted—and what not. Such an archive drive has no doubt often resulted in poor things being retained and good things forgotten, in mediocre works being kept and works of genius destroyed. That's the terrible work of the archive. The duplicity of the archive we spoke of earlier here takes on a new character; turned toward both the past and the future, toward both a unique past and its repetition, the archive is always

> at once beneficial and monstrous, both at once . . . a chance and a threat, and this is the case not only in social and political institutions but in the unconscious, it is what happens in us. . . . To keep, precisely, one destroys, one lets many things be destroyed; that is the condition of a finite psyche, which works . . . by killing just as much as by assuring survival. To assure survival, one must kill. That's the archive, archive fever [*le mal d'archive*]. ("TA" 26).

The archive drive thus betrays an archē-violence that is as ineluctable as it is irrepressible. That the trace is finite means that not all traces can be kept, though also, and perhaps first of all, that no trace is permanent, that every trace is effaceable or erasable. Just as an infinite archive would be no archive at all, so an ineffaceable or unerasable trace would be no trace at all. As Derrida goes on to argue:

> A trace can be effaced. That belongs to its structure. It can be lost. Moreover that is the reason why one wants to keep them, because they can be lost. It is part of the trace that it can be effaced, lost, forgotten, destroyed. That's its finitude. . . . An archive is always finite, always destructible . . . ("TA" 24)

It is this finitude that drives the archive drive—a desperate, autoimmune drive that, instead of putting more and more of what we save or archive in our own hands, puts more and more in the hands of the *other*. This is, again, what Derrida calls exappropriation. In the same public discussion from June 2004 where we heard Derrida speak of wanting to keep or appropriate everything for himself, from the texts he has written to personal notes he has received, Derrida makes it clear that the archive drive is indeed an autoimmune drive and that the more one appropriates for oneself the more one expropriates oneself to the other:

> In the gesture of appropriating something for oneself, and thus of being able to keep in one's name, to mark with one's name, to leave in one's name, as a testament or an inheritance, one must expropriate this thing, separate oneself from it. This is what one does when one writes, when one publishes, when one releases something into the public sphere. One separates oneself from it and it lives, so to speak, without us. And thus in order to be able to claim a work, a book, a work of art, or anything else, a political act, a piece of legislation

or any other initiative, in order to appropriate it for oneself, in order to assign it to someone, one has to lose it, abandon it, expropriate it. That is the condition of this terrible ruse: we have to lose what we want to keep and we can keep only on the condition of losing. (*FS* 24)

This brings me to one final inscription of the theme of the archive in Derrida's *The Beast and the Sovereign*, a place where the archive is thought in relation not just to the book, and so not just to the corpus, but also to the *corpse*. We have looked at this moment in some detail, though with a very different purpose, in Chapter 3. It occurs near the middle of the seminar as Derrida, rather unexpectedly, on the heels of a long meditation on Robinson Crusoe's obsession with being buried alive, speaks of the phantasms we contemporaries have of our own deaths and of what will happen to our bodies after death, our hesitation between the alternatives of inhumation or burial, on the one hand, and incineration or cremation, on the other. This change in theme gives to the seminar, as we have heard, a very different tone and a unique performativity. It is as if—though the fiction is less hypothetical than ever—Derrida were asking here in his seminar what would become of his body, who would decide to bury or incinerate his body, but then also what would become of his archive, his corpus, whether at IMEC or at Irvine or somewhere else. In these very uncanny pages, Derrida gives us if not the answer at least the principle of a response to these questions: as always, it will be the *other* who decides. No matter how much one plans or insists, no matter how much or how clearly one instructs the inheritors through the seemingly sovereign decision of what we call a last will and testament, it will always be the other who decides. By thus linking in this final seminar, this final, very autobiographical, seminar, the question of dying a living death, of being buried alive, to that of testimony, the testament, and the archive, it is *as if* Derrida were attempting to bury himself alive in his own archive, though he knew with all the knowledge in the world that he could not know what would ultimately happen to that archive, whether it would be buried alive—and thus occasionally read, interpreted, discussed, and so on—or, someday, for this can always happen, go unread or else be incinerated and forever lost.

If the theme of the archive will have been, as I have tried to show, central to Derrida's thinking from the very beginning, it begins to take on a very different cast, a palpably different pathos, in this final year of *The Beast and the Sovereign*. Though there is nothing in the seminar that contradicts what is said elsewhere about the trace, about the archive, about survival and the other as survivor, the very survival of this seminar in our archive, its contingent and finite remaining, gives to this text a very different status as a living-dead or as a living machine, as a trace that has been buried alive. For everything said *about* the archive in the seminar now comes to envelop, like the cocoon of a silkworm, the seminar itself, at once the words that are spoken and the one doing the speaking. Listen, then, to how Derrida, in the Fifth Session of the seminar, speaks of survival and survivance, how he implicitly opposes this survival to the Heideggerian notion of being-toward-death, and how, questioning the limits between life and death, he begins to speak, some eighteen months in advance, of a death that will come or that will have already come as survival. Insisting that this survivance "does not add something extra to life," Derrida continues:

> The survivance I am speaking of is something other than life death, but a groundless ground from which are detached, identified, and opposed what we think we can identify under the name of death or dying (*Tod, Sterben*), like death properly so-called as opposed to some life properly so-called. *It* [*Ça*] begins with survival. And that is where there is some other that has me at its disposal; that is where any self is defenseless. That is what the self is, that is what I am, what the *I* is, whether I am there or not [*Voilà ce qu'est le moi, voilà ce que je suis, ce que le je est, que je sois là ou pas*]. (*BS 2* 131/194)

Let me simply note here, before continuing the quotation, that this line already seems to echo Derrida's final words, written on an envelope not long before his death, words that conclude "*d'où que je sois,*" "wherever I may be"—this strange subjunctive coming to mark the first person singular of verb *être*, the very *to be*, in both places, as if the *je*, the I, were already subject to a repetition without the I, as if the I were, as Derrida will go on to suggest, a self-repetition in the absence of self.[12]

Having spoken of the I as what is always at the disposal of the other, Derrida goes on to define this other:

> The other, the others, that is the very thing that survives me, that is called to survive me and that I call the other inasmuch as it is called, in advance, to survive me, structurally my survivor. Not my survivor, but the survivor of me, the *there* beyond my life [*Non pas mon survivant, mais le survivant de moi, le* là *au-delà de ma vie*]. (*BS 2* 131/194)

Life or survivance thus begins "there beyond my life," *là au-delà de ma vie*, "beyond my lifetime," we might say; the references to *Tod* and *Sterben* suggest that Derrida is rethinking here the Heideggerian analysis of being-toward-death and reinscribing the *Da-*, the there, of Dasein. *To be* is indeed to be thrown, outside or beyond oneself, but there is no possibility of self-reappropriation, not even as the possibility of no longer being possible, since in this being-there I am already given over to the other, to the one who is structurally my survivor or, rather, the survivor of me.

This is the experience of the trace, experience as trace, and, within this more general field, of the archive. It is always the other who decides insofar as the trace, and thus the archive, is, by definition, separated from me. Derrida says in "Trace and Archive": "The trace parts from me, that is, it proceeds from me and, proceeding from me, separates itself from me. And that's why it leaves a trace. I can die at any moment, the trace remains there" ("TA" 18).[13] The trace remains, but having separated itself from the origin from its origin it does not remain as the present trace of a past present. Because the separation is immediate, it remains not only "beyond my life" or "beyond my lifetime" but also beyond every present and every ontology rooted in the present.[14] Indeed, the beyond of ontology would be the very condition of the trace and, thus, of the archive in its finitude, contingency, and originary violence.

It should thus be clear that the question of the archive is nothing less, for Derrida, than the question of philosophy itself. For rather than understanding philosophy as a care of the self or as the practice of dying, as a way of caring for the self in this life or as a means of overcoming life in the name of a value or a life greater than life, Derrida will have tried to think—to undergo, to experience, and feverishly so—the archive as that with which and by which we are preoccupied, that over which we must exercise our concern or our care, and that which will remain only provisionally and for a time after our lifetime. No immortality of the soul, therefore, no authentic experience of death or facing up to death as such, only a finite and contingent survival in the archive, a survival—and thus an archivization—that begins with the first trace and that thus takes place always and from the beginning *without me*. Hence, Derrida shifts our gaze from the archive as that which gives us access to the idea of an immortality that goes beyond the archive, and thus the notion of an archive as the mere supplement to speech and to thought, toward a thinking of the archive as finite and precarious, as what anticipates us, invests us, and preoccupies us. As what remains for a time.

Let me conclude this chapter on the archive by citing, once again, some last words, some dying words even, words that of themselves raise all the questions of the trace and the archive, of life, death, and survival, though also of the animal and the human, the beast and the sovereign, that I have been pursuing throughout this work: they are not Derrida's last words, this time, though they echo them rather strangely, nor are they Heidegger's or

Robinson Crusoe's or, as my reference to philosophy and the immortality of the soul might have suggested, Socrates' in the *Phaedo*. They are the last words not of Alexander Selkirk, the Scottish explorer, as we recalled at the end of Chapter 2, whose shipwreck and adventures were the model for Defoe's *Robinson Crusoe*, but those of Alex, the African Grey parrot trained by animal researcher Irene Pepperberg. At the time of his death in 2007, Alex, age thirty-one, was said to be able to speak up to hundred English words. According to Pepperberg, then, Alex's last words to her—his last words *tout court*—were, "You be good, see you tomorrow. I love you."[15]

And, you know, even when written in the archive like this, you can almost hear him saying it: "You be good, see you tomorrow. I love you."

7

"World, Finitude, Solitude"

Derrida's *Walten*

"World, Finitude, Solitude": these are, of course, not Derrida's words but Heidegger's, words Derrida borrows from Heidegger's seminar of 1929–30, *The Fundamental Concepts of Metaphysics: World, Finitude, Solitude,* and then follows throughout the second year of *The Beast and the Sovereign.* The words are Heidegger's and yet Derrida seems to have chosen to make them his own, or at least to make them the focus of an entire year of his seminar, of what would be, to repeat it again, his final seminar. What are we to make of this "choice" or this "decision"—and of the event, the writing event, to which such a "choice" or "decision" will have given rise?

In this chapter, as in the previous ones, I would like to follow just a single path through this ten-week or ten-session seminar that ran from December 2002 to March 2003, just one path where the themes of world, finitude, and solitude are taken up and analyzed but then also supplemented and, ultimately, supplanted by the thought of an originary violence before or at the origin of the world, a shift in themes that might have been anticipated by those who knew Derrida's work and itinerary but that ended up inflecting or even dominating Derrida's seminar in a completely unforeseeable way. My question here in this final chapter will thus be how or in what way a seminar, what is sometimes called in French un *cours magistral,* can become overtaken by events or by an event it could never master, open to a force or a violence that will have always preceded it and to which it must ultimately yield.

"World, Finitude, Solitude": Derrida begins the very first session of this very final seminar with a three-word sentence that sets the tone and introduces all three of these themes: "*Je suis seul(e),*" "I am alone," he begins, and then just a bit later, "*Je suis seul(e), seul(e) au monde,*" I am alone, alone in the world" (*BS 2* 1).[1] We do not yet know where the speaker of this phrase is headed, whether the phrase is a statement, a sigh, or a complaint, a confession, an exaggeration, or a citation, but one already suspects that this second year of *The Beast and the Sovereign* seminar will be quite different from the first. This suspicion is borne out when Derrida goes on to explain that unlike the previous year of the seminar during which he treated a whole host of figures, from Plato and Aristotle to Montaigne, Machiavelli, Hobbes, Rousseau, Schmitt, and Agamben, on the question of the beast and the sovereign, the beast as opposed to the sovereign, the sovereign as a beast, he will in this second year concentrate on just two figures, indeed on just two texts. The first of these is a real surprise, completely unanticipated and, I think, unanticipatable, Daniel Defoe's *Robinson Crusoe*. The second is in some sense less surprising inasmuch as Derrida had treated it previously in a couple of places in some detail, which then makes it in some sense all the more surprising that he would return to it again for the entirety of a seminar, Heidegger's 1929–30 seminar *The Fundamental Concepts of Metaphysics: World, Finitude, Solitude*, where Heidegger famously says that the stone is "worldless," the animal "poor in world," and the human "world-forming" or "world-building," three theses that Derrida began to interrogate almost as soon as he came across them and that he would devote a good deal of *Of Spirit* and *The Animal That Therefore I Am* to discussing. In order to approach the question of how Derrida's seminar of 2002–2003 came to be marked or inflected, as I suggested a moment ago, by a kind of originary violence or power that of necessity exceeded it, I would like to follow Derrida's rereading of this Heidegger seminar, the places where he returns to familiar territory and the places where he heads out into uncharted waters, the places where Heidegger's text appears, from Derrida's point of view, problematic or criticizable and the places where it seems to take over or dominate Derrida's own seminar and, finally, the places where Derrida's text comes in effect to countersign Heidegger's—and right down to its final word. As interesting as Derrida's reading of *Robinson Crusoe* is on questions such as the animal, technology, death, and so on, I will restrict my reading here to Derrida's use and rereading of this 1929–30 seminar of Heidegger, which is clearly not just another Heidegger seminar for Derrida and Heidegger not just another thinker.

Indeed Heidegger appears to occupy a truly singular place in Derrida's work. As an enthusiastic and admiring even if always critical reader of Heidegger, Derrida's engagement—what he often called his *explication* or *Auseinandersetzung*—with Heidegger began in the early 1960s, and it continued right up to the end.[2] As even a cursory glance at texts such as "Violence and Metaphysics," "Différance," "Ousia and Grammē," and *Of Grammatology* makes clear, Heidegger was central to much of Derrida's early work. Just how central he was will no doubt become even clearer with the publication of some of Derrida's earliest seminars, such as his 1964–65 seminar "Heidegger and the Question of Being and History." I cannot possibly rehearse here Derrida's long confrontation or engagement with Heidegger's work, the different strategies Derrida deploys in reading him, sometimes to criticize him outright, sometimes to read him against himself, and sometimes to defend him against the criticisms of others. I also would not be so imprudent as to try to assess or evaluate Derrida's reading *as a reading of Heidegger*.[3] What I would like to do instead, then, is follow the role played by Heidegger's 1929–30 seminar in Derrida's own seminar of 2002–2003. To do this, however, it is necessary to give a brief account of Derrida's prior engagement with this same Heidegger seminar.

Derrida appears to have had a particular fascination for the 1929–30 seminar, drawn to it almost from the start in a powerful and perhaps overdetermined way. As if by a happy coincidence, this seminar was first published in the *Gesamtausgabe* in 1983, the year that marks a new phase in Derrida's work in general and in his engagement with Heidegger in particular. For that is the year Derrida moved from the École Normale Supérieure to the École des Hautes Études en Sciences Sociales. No longer under the constraint of offering courses designed to prepare students for the *agrégation*, Derrida soon began at the EHESS a series of yearly seminars under the general title "Philosophical Nationality and Nationalism." The *Geschlecht* essays and Derrida's entire engagement with Heidegger of the 1980s need to be considered, I think, with this in mind.

It is in 1983, then, that Derrida publishes the first of his so-called *Geschlecht* essays, an essay devoted to the question of sexual difference in Heidegger. If Derrida does not yet refer in this essay to the 1929–30 seminar, his eventual approach to that text and even some of the themes he will treat in it are already apparent. Already there, Derrida follows the fate of a concept or term, here the word *Geschlecht*, through Heidegger's corpus, a German word, therefore, the first of many, that Derrida will hesitate to translate and so will often leave in German in an analysis that at once engages Heidegger's thought in German, contests certain claims made about the privileges of the German language, and attempts to translate or, better, displace Heidegger's idiom into Derrida's own idiomatic French.

Two years later, in March 1985, in *"Geschlecht II, Heidegger's Hand,"* it is the question of species difference rather than sexual difference that is central, the question of man in relation to the animal, of man as *opposed* to the animal, the question of whether only man has a hand or has speech and the question of man's relationship to technology. It is here that Derrida makes his first reference, in a footnote, to the 1929–30 seminar. Having briefly evoked the thesis according to which the animal is poor in world due to its lack of access to the *as such* of beings, Derrida promises, "elsewhere I will study, as closely as possible, the developments Heidegger devoted to animality in *Die Grundbegriffe der Metaphysik* (1929–30)." Derrida in this footnote of 1985 thus defers to another time and place a full or fuller analysis of this text, which has already appeared to him to merit close attention.[4]

Two years later again, on March 14, 1987, in a lecture first given at the International College of Philosophy in Paris and later published as *Of Spirit*, Derrida follows the changing role of *Geist*, along with *geistig* and *geistlich*— yet another untranslated, untranslatable nexus of words—in Heidegger's work. Derrida there notes the relative absence of *Geist* in Heidegger's early works, its mention but not really its use in Heidegger's works of the late 1920s, its appearance in quotation marks in *Being and Time*, Heidegger's skepticism, therefore, with regard to it, and then, finally, in the *Rectorship Address*, the lifting of the quotation marks and Heidegger's apparent rehabilitation or resuscitation of the term.[5] It is in section VI, then, of *Of Spirit* that Derrida offers, as he had promised in "Heidegger's Hand," a closer and fuller reading of the three theses of the 1929–30 seminar in the context of this reading of *Geist*. To the question, "What do we call the world?" Derrida answers for Heidegger, or with Heidegger's words, "The world is always a *spiritual* world," that is, a *geistig* world (*OS* 47). Putting later claims about *Geist* into the context of the 1929–30 discussion of the three theses regarding the stone, the animal, and man, Derrida concludes that, for Heidegger, the animal has no world or is poor in world because it has no spirit, because it is not spiritual, because it is not *of spirit*, and it is not of spirit because it has no access to the *as such* of beings (*OS* 47–57). While the animal has a relationship to the beings with which it interacts, the bee to the flower, the lizard to the stone, it does not have a relation to these beings *as such* (*OS* 51). This claim about the animal, together with Heidegger's not unrelated claim that the animal is also deprived of the *as such* of death, of death *as such*,[6] ultimately betrays, according to Derrida, "the axioms of the profoundest metaphysical humanism" (*OS* 12), despite

Heidegger's own trenchant critique of humanism. Derrida concludes: "These difficulties—such at least is the proposition I submit for discussion—never disappear from Heidegger's discourse" (*OS* 57). They never disappear from Heidegger, and they never disappear from Derrida's work on Heidegger, as if Derrida would never—could never—be done with these theses and the difficulties they raise.

Two years after *Of Spirit*, at a conference organized by John Sallis in Chicago, Derrida presents the final installment in the *Geschlecht* series, "*Geschlecht IV*: Heidegger's Ear." It is this text, written, it seems, in 1989 and published in 1993, that brings us closest to some of the issues that will be central to the second year of *The Beast and the Sovereign* seminar. Derrida will continue to pursue in this last *Geschlecht* essay the questions he had developed in the previous ones and in *Of Spirit*, the question of why, for Heidegger, the animal has no world, no language, no experience of death, no relation to the *as such* of beings, no hand, and, as a result, no ear—no ear capable of hearing and carrying the voice of the friend ("G 4" 172). But Derrida is already oriented in this essay of 1989 toward the question of what I called at the outset a kind of originary or pre-originary violence, a violence that can be summarized by or gathered under the term *Walten*, a term, says Derrida, that is "very marked," "always very actively overdetermined by Heidegger" ("G 4" 205, 203), and that "will have long commanded all the thought of the Heraclitean *polemos* as Heidegger interprets it" (in texts such as the *Introduction to Metaphysics*) ("G 4" 169). Derrida thus writes of this word *Walten*, which, as we will see, plays such a central role in the second volume of *The Beast and the Sovereign*:

> The word that Heidegger privileges to say this originary unity of two contraries is *Walten*: to govern, to rule . . . [to] prevail, exercise in any case a power or a force, and not without a certain violence. Very difficult to translate, this word carries a weight all the heavier since, on the one hand, the word is inseparable from a certain *polemos*, preparing and thus legitimating the citation of Heraclitus, and since, on the other hand, Heidegger makes of this word quite simply, at a certain point, the synonym of *An-Wesen*, in two words, of presence, indeed of *aletheia*. The *An-* of *An-Wesen*, what makes come to presence this unfolding of a *physis* remaining however in itself, is the force or the violence of this *Walten*. ("G 4" 207)

Heidegger would have thus associated *Walten* with both a kind of originary strife or *polemos* and an originary understanding of *physis*, *physis* before its determination as mere nature. As the "originary unity of two contraries," this *Walten*, this originary violence or originary prevailing, identified already with Heraclitean notions of *physis* and *polemos*, is also not incompatible, says Derrida following Heidegger in a later text from 1955, with a pre-Aristotelian, pre-Platonic hearing of *logos* and even with a pre-Platonic, pre-philosophical notion of *philein* or *philia* ("G 4" 172). In other words, Heidegger's thinking of *Walten* as the originary prevailing of world or as the appearance of beings in their totality gathers together in *logos*, as *logos*, *polemos* and *philia*, the one and the other, the one as the other. Combining claims by Heidegger from 1935 in *An Introduction to Metaphysics* with others from 1955 in *What is Philosophy?* Derrida concludes: "If *philia* and *logos* are the same in 1955, if *polemos* and *logos* are the same in 1935, are not *philia* and *polemos* always the same?" ("G 4" 197) In a word, to cite the subtitle of "*Geschlecht IV*," Heidegger will have tried to lend an ear and thereby give voice to a sort of originary "Philopolemology."[7]

If Derrida still sees in this Heideggerian discourse of *Walten*, *polemos*, *philia*, and *logos* a tendency to favor an originary gathering or originary oneness of contraries, a gathering within strife rather than a dissemination or "dispersion" ("G 4" 214), the difference or the distance between Heidegger's determination of *Walten* and Derrida's own understanding of originary violence seems more and more difficult to maintain. For Heidegger will have insisted in the texts Derrida is citing that this notion of *polemos* as conflict or even as *Kampf*, as a *waltende Streit*, must be thought *before* everything human and divine ("G 4" 204), as the reigning or prevailing of "a conflict that is not a war in the human manner" ("G 4" 209). It is thus hardly surprising that this notion of *Walten* as a pre-onto-theological conception of "sovereign power" would interest Derrida, who never tired of trying to locate the limits of all onto-theological or theologico-political determinations of sovereignty.

Hence Derrida in 1989, six years after the first *Geschlecht* essay, continues his critique of Heidegger regarding the human/animal distinction, arguing that, for Heidegger, the animal is deprived not only of a hand but also of an ear for hearing this originary *polemos*, this originary philopolemology. Yet Derrida's attention is already beginning to shift, away from the distinction itself and toward the significance of this originary *Walten* in Heidegger's work of the early 1930s. What remains, then, and what in retrospect might have been predicted, is Derrida extending this interest in *Walten* to earlier texts, and particularly to Heidegger's 1929–30 lecture course.

Finally, in July 1997, eight years after *Geschlecht IV*, a decade after *Of Spirit*, Derrida delivered at Cerisy-la-Salle a long lecture on the question of the animal that would be published in its entirely only after his death as *The Animal That Therefore I Am*. The lecture took place on July 15 (Derrida had an unusual way of celebrating his birthday), and it would run more than nine hours over two days. Derrida makes numerous references in the course of this lecture to Heidegger's views on the animal. In the early chapters of the work, Heidegger's name appears on almost every other page.[8] But already from the outset of *The Animal That Therefore I Am*, Derrida promises a more sustained reading of Heidegger's 1929–30 seminar, either later in the lecture or at a later date. Having evoked, for example, the question of whether the animal has time, Derrida says he "must put off until later a patient reading and interpretation of the systematic and rich text that, in 1929–30, following *Being and Time*, Heidegger devoted to the animal" (*ATT* 22). Just a few pages later, Derrida speaks of *Of Spirit* as a "short book [that] deals abundantly and directly with the Heideggerian concept of the animal as 'poor in world' (*weltarm*), an analysis I would like to pursue further tomorrow, looking closely at the seminar of 1929–30)" (*ATT* 38).[9]

Derrida thus anticipates returning later in the lecture to a fuller analysis of Heidegger's 1929–30 seminar. But this is not what happened. While Heidegger is mentioned throughout, Derrida never gets to the fuller treatment of the 1929–30 volume that he had promised. At the request, therefore, of the participants of the Cerisy conference, an improvised session with Derrida was arranged a few days later, at the end of the conference, to discuss Heidegger's views on the animal. Recorded and transcribed, this session is included as the final chapter of *The Animal That Therefore I Am*, and it constitutes Derrida's last attempt to address Heidegger's 1929–30 seminar before the autumn of 2002 in *The Beast and the Sovereign*.

Derrida begins this improvised session, which has been given the title of Derrida's opening phrase, "I don't know why we are doing this," by promising yet again to return in a more formal way to the issues he is simply going to "outline" (*ATT* 141). To do justice to these issues, he says, he would have "to write a very long text, which is what I hope to do one day" (*ATT* 141). Derrida recalls, as we might have predicted, his previous readings of Heidegger, particularly in *Of Spirit*, on the stone, the animal, and man in their different relationships to the world (*ATT* 143). But instead of repeating those analyses, Derrida says he wishes to approach those three theses with different concerns in mind, several of which will be taken up in greater detail some five years later in *The Beast and the Sovereign*. Derrida thus looks at the animal's supposed lack of access to the *as such* of beings (*ATT* 142), the animal's *Benommenheit*, its encirclement or captivation (*ATT* 156), and, especially, Dasein's putative access to this *as such* (*ATT* 156, 160). He will also underscore, as he will five years later, that Heidegger's three theses concerning the stone, the animal, and man seem more intent on saying something about world than about these three kinds of beings.

Finally, Derrida points to Heidegger's reference to the nonapophantic discourse of prayer in Aristotle, a reference that, Derrida claims, has the potential of disrupting Heidegger's entire argument regarding the as-structure in its relation to apophantic discourse and to Dasein's exclusive access to the *as such* of beings and its exclusive ability to let beings be as they are (*ATT* 157–159). These are just a few of the most prominent themes raised by Derrida during this improvised session.[10] Noteworthy in its absence is any treatment of *Walten*, a term that is not uttered during this session either in relation to the 1929–30 seminar or any other Heidegger text.

These remarks from 1997 thus seem to be situated in both time and emphasis somewhere between *Of Spirit* of 1987 and *The Beast and the Sovereign* of 2002–2003. Hence, Derrida continues to express his skepticism with regard to Heidegger's drawing of the line between the human and the animal based on this having or not-having access to the *as such* of beings. He will even claim that, despite Heidegger's own critique of Descartes, "Heidegger's discourse is still Cartesian" (*ATT* 146). And yet there can also be heard throughout these remarks an expressed admiration for Heidegger's seminar that seems to go beyond what we heard earlier. Derrida credits Heidegger for taking "into account a certain ethological knowledge" (*ATT* 143), even if the conclusions he draws from it would not be Derrida's, and he says that in this seminar of 1929–30 Heidegger pursues the questions of world and the animal "with a breadth and rigor of analysis that I find incomparable" (*ATT* 143). He shows admiration for Heidegger's willingness to admit, two years after *Being and Time* where a full and rigorous rethinking of the phenomenon of world had been undertaken, that in the end we still do not know what the world is (*ATT* 151). Finally, Derrida attributes to the seminar a "grand pedagogical theatrical strategy" that might account for Heidegger's method of returning week after week to certain questions and that might explain why Heidegger says "*deliberately* contradictory things" (*ATT* 156; my emphasis). To really understand Heidegger's thesis regarding the animal, Derrida thus admits, one would really have to reconstitute the entire context surrounding it (*ATT* 144), something Derrida says he could not do there but that we might think *The Beast and the Sovereign* seminar was finally able to attempt.

Of Spirit, the *Geschlecht* essays of the 1980s, and these improvised remarks from 1997 are thus essential preparation for reading the second volume of *The Beast and the Sovereign* seminar, which, we now know, will be Derrida's last attempt to provide that fuller and more rigorous treatment of Heidegger's 1929–30 seminar he had promised some twenty years earlier. Let me try now to follow, then, the fate of this *Walten* in Derrida's seminar, which is far from the only thing, as we have seen, that Derrida treats in the seminar but which nonetheless comes to occupy a singular place within it, and right down, as I said, to its last word. To be clear, my interest here is not first and foremost historical or biographical; it is, rather, to follow this seminar from one week to the next in order to account for the way in which it will have been marked in its themes, its cadence, and its pathos by world events that were, so to speak, beyond its control, the death of Maurice Blanchot, for example, in February 2003, or the beginning of the war in Iraq just a couple of weeks later, or else, if I can put it this way, the event of this *Walten*—both the thing and the word, both its force and its signification—as it comes to sign and seal this final seminar.

Derrida lays out in the first of the seminar's ten sessions on December 11, 2002, the general trajectory—the heading—of the seminar to come: the two texts to be read, the question of the animal and of sovereignty in those two texts, and, of course, the themes of world, finitude, and solitude as they arise out of Defoe's novel and Heidegger's seminar *The Fundamental Concepts of Metaphysics*. The three theses concerning the stone's, the animal's, and man's access to the world, along with all the questions they provoke, are again also recalled in the opening pages of the seminar. But this time, says Derrida, he wishes to "relaunch all these questions" and, in order "to link them with the question of sovereignty," dwell "on the word *walten* (to rule violently) which we can rightly say dominates the beginning of the seminar and everything in it that concerns *physis*" (*BS 2* 30/60). *Walten*, a certain domination or violent rule, will thus itself *dominate*, says Derrida, the beginning of Heidegger's seminar, though its reign, as we shall see, will extend much further into Heidegger's corpus, and it will, as I have suggested, come to occupy or dominate Derrida's seminar as well.

Near the beginning of the Second Session, Derrida returns to the theme or word *Walten* that was simply announced in the First Session. *Walten*, says Derrida, is "a recurring word that in my opinion is given too little attention in Heidegger in general" (*BS 2* 32/62), a word that Heidegger makes use of "everywhere, really everywhere, more insistently than has ever been noticed, to my knowledge" (*BS 2* 32/63). Now, it is worth noting here that Derrida does not just point out the theme he wishes to follow but remarks that it is a theme no one else has noticed, a claim that would seem to presuppose a certain familiarity not only with Heidegger's corpus but also with the secondary literature on Heidegger. If Derrida would have no doubt considered himself a close and attentive reader of so many figures, from Plato and Aristotle to Kant and Hegel, Levinas and

Blanchot, I am not sure there are many other figures, apart from, perhaps, Husserl and Rousseau in the 1960s, for whom Derrida would have cast himself as, so to speak, a *scholar*, someone who will have surveyed the scholarship and noticed what others have missed. This gesture could easily be written off were it not found in almost *every* work of Derrida on Heidegger. In *Of Spirit*, for example, Derrida speaks of what Heideggerians have not noticed or have actually "avoided," namely, the importance of spirit and "the silent play of the quotation marks" around *Geist* (*OS* 66, see 3–4). In "Heidegger's Ear" Derrida remarks on the fact that so few scholars have noticed the voice of the friend in *Being and Time*, the notable exceptions being Jean-Luc Nancy, Jean-Francois Courtine, and Christopher Fynsk ("G 4"165). And in *Rogues* Derrida says as he is about to reread the famous *Der Spiegel* interview: "I think I know just about everything that has been said or could be said about this declaration, along with everything else in the *Der Spiegel* interview, everything about what is revealed there and what is kept silent. I think I know rather well the program, the irony, the politics, and the caustic responses to which such a provocation might give rise. Trust me on this" (*R* 110). Such claims, it has to be said, are rather rare in Derrida, who is much more apt to say that he lacks the competence to give an authoritative reading of some text or figure. And the gesture is all the more curious in light of Derrida's scathing remarks in the first volume of *The Beast and the Sovereign* with regard to Agamben's penchant for making similar types of claims (see *BS 1* 330–333/438–442).

Beginning here, then, in the Second Session, Derrida will follow the role of *Walten* in Heidegger's 1929–30 seminar and other, later texts. The path will hardly be straightforward or without detour, with long analyses of *Robinson Crusoe* on questions of prayer, technology, death, the unity of the world, and so on, interrupting the itinerary, but it will continually lead back to the question of what can be gathered—or not—under this word *Walten*. After underscoring, therefore, the general neglect of this term in the scholarship on Heidegger and after criticizing the common French translation of *Walten* as simply "*régner, gouverner*," that is, "to reign or to govern" in the sense of a silence that "reigns" in a room, a translation that "banalizes, neutralizes and muffles," says Derrida, the notions of "force and imposed violence," of power and "sovereign potency in *Walten* or *Gewalt*," Derrida turns to an early passage of *The Fundamental Concepts of Metaphysics* where Heidegger links *Walten* to a conception of *physis* before its determination as *nature* or *natura*.[11] We saw this earlier in "Heidegger's Ear," where Derrida remarked on the very same association of *Walten* and *physis* in Heidegger's 1935 *Introduction to Metaphysics*. Here, in *The Fundamental*

Concepts of Metaphysics of 1929–30, Heidegger relates *Walten* to a more originary notion of "physics" in "metaphysics," a notion of *physis* as what reigns in a sovereign fashion over the totality of beings. Derrida writes— parsing Heidegger:

> *Physis* is the *Walten* of everything, which depends, as *Walten*, only on itself, which forms itself sovereignly, as power, receiving its form and its image, its figure of domination, from itself. *Walten* as *physis, physis* as *Walten* is everything; *physis* and *Walten* are synonyms of every- thing, or everything that is, and that is, then, as originarily sovereign power. (*BS 2* 39/72)

Physis and *Walten* would thus be synonyms—or quasi-synonymous substitutes—for a notion of self-formed sovereignty and autarchic force that would precede *both* the political determination of violence *and* the determination of *physis* as natural growth. When Heidegger goes on to speak of *physis* in terms of growth, blooming, and emergence, but also in terms of "the changing seasons, the passage from night to day and recip- rocally, the movement of the stars, the storms, and weather, and the raging of the elements"—a truly "Robinsonian landscape," as Derrida remarks (*BS 2* 39–40/72–73)—it is clear that *physis* is better translated, "translated more clearly and closer to its originary sense, as *Walten* than as *Wachstum,* as prevailing violence rather than as increase, growing, growth" (*BS 2* 40/74). *Walten* rather than *Wachstum,* sovereignty and prevailing violence rather than growth, *physis* as what reigns or imposes itself before the deter- mination of biological life, *physis* before the opposition between nature and culture, before the political and the theological: what Derrida seems to find in Heidegger's 1929–30 seminar is what looks rather like a *decon- structive* use of the term *Walten,* as Heidegger takes the notion of a "a reign- ing and sovereign potency that is often emphasized in the political order" and transforms it into a "the general and quite indeterminate, in any case quite open sense of *Walten,*" a quasi-transcendental sense, it might even be said, that would exceed in a way that must be determined its "properly socio-political sense" (*BS 2* 32/63). Through this rewriting or reinscrip- tion, this double reading, so to speak, *Walten* would come to name a sort of archi-originary violence before all natural, political, or theologi- cal determinations.

The translation of *physis* by a prepolitical and pretheological notion of sovereignty and a prescientific notion of natural growth could thus not but interest Derrida, who was relentless in ferreting out the traces of onto- theology in such seemingly diverse notions as world, cosmopolitanism, literature, religious tolerance, the death penalty, the concept of religion itself, and first and foremost the concept of sovereignty. As for Heidegger's claim that *Walten*—the German word *Walten*—comes closer than other words to this prephilosophical, pre-Socratic notion of *physis*, Derrida lets it pass more or less in silence, though, as we will see, he will later discreetly propose his own—more French—translation of it.

But now we come to what is to my eyes the most powerful—most powerful because the most self-dispossessing—"reason" for Derrida's emphasis here on *Walten*, a reason that Derrida remarks upon already in the Second Session of the final seminar but that will return with even greater insistence and a quite different pathos near the very end. Derrida writes:

> The sense of sovereign and superhuman violence of *Walten,* of the all-powerful reign of *physis* appears the most clearly in Heidegger's elucidation when he makes clear that humans themselves are dominated, crushed, under the law of this sovereign violence. Man is not its master, he is traversed by it, "gripped" . . . dominated, seized, penetrated through and through by the sovereign violence of the *Walten* that he does not master, over which he has neither power nor hold. (*BS 2* 41/74)

It is this final "reason" for Derrida's interest in *Walten* that interests me most here, one for which Derrida himself could not have wholly answered insofar as he will have been—and more and more so as the seminar progresses—invested, subjected, gripped, and traversed by it. Rather than being a concept to be grasped, *Walten* is a term and a force, a word and a power that would always come to have a hold on the one who would try to grasp or get a hold on it.

Following the same penchant on display in the *Geschlecht* essays and *Of Spirit* of finding a word, here *Walten*, there *Geist* or *Geschlecht*, that plays either no role or a different role in Heidegger's work *before* the early 1930s than it does *afterwards*, Derrida underscores the fact that the word *Walten* is more or less absent from Heidegger's vocabulary through *Being and Time*, or at least it does not play the role of an "operational or thematic concept." Beginning with this seminar of 1929–30—dates, let me mention in passing, that could not but interest Derrida for other reasons—the term *Walten* and related terms such as *durchwalten, mitwalten*, and so on, become absolutely central and dominant in Heidegger's work. This is especially true in the period around *An Introduction to Metaphysics*, "a political period that is not just any period," as Derrida puts it (*BS 2* 94/147). It is during this politically "very marked time" that "the vocabulary of *Walten* is not only confirmed, but extends, differentiates, grows richer, and becomes invasive, especially around *physis* and *logos*" (*BS 2* 43/77–78). As in the *Geschlecht* essays and *Of Spirit*, Derrida attempts to follow the discontinuities and, especially, the *continuities* in Heidegger's thinking by means of the continuities and, especially, the *discontinuities* in his language.[12] He will thus trace the term *Walten* from the 1929–30 seminar through *An Introduction to Metaphysics* of 1935 before jumping ahead, much later in the seminar, to 1957 and *Identity and Difference*, where *Walten* is said to initiate or hold reign over the ontological difference but where, it seems, it is less circumscribed or defined by—less under the sway of—an explicit lexicon or rhetoric of violence.

As a reading of Heidegger, this analysis can and surely should be at once extended and nuanced, for it may be that the term *Walten* comes to have a much less marked relation to sovereign power and violence much earlier than Derrida had thought. Indeed, Krzysztof Ziarek has argued in a recent essay that as early as 1938–40 Heidegger proposes "to think *Walten* as released or freed from violence: as *gewalt-lose*."[13] If it is really the case, then, as Derrida claims, that the lexicon of *Walten* is virtually absent up through *Being and Time* in 1927 but becomes pervasive soon thereafter, and if it is the case, as Ziarek claims, that the lexicon is present but already transformed by the late 1930s, then we would need to sharpen our focus in order to explain the appearance, role, and significance of this very particular determination of *Walten* during the years 1929 to 1938, not just any years, as Derrida would have said, for Heidegger.

Derrida begins Session Four of the seminar by raising once again the central problem of *Aporias*, namely, the question of death *as such*, the question of whether the animal might not simply perish, as Heidegger seemed to think, but actually die, and then the more profound question of whether human Dasein *can* really die or have a relationship to death *as such*.[14] But Derrida in this session will quickly link the question of the *as such* to *Walten* and to what Heidegger characterizes, again in the 1929–30 seminar, as a kind of *Heimweh*, a sort of nostalgia drive, as we saw in Chapter 4, that pushes man to recover not just some particular place in the world, not just to return to some determined place called home, but to become at home everywhere in the world. This notion of drive adds a very new dimension to Heidegger's characterization of *Walten* and, thus, to Derrida's interest in it. It is as if this quasi-concept of *Walten*, which Derrida says is to be found everywhere in Heidegger beginning in 1929, cannot stop proliferating, growing, metamorphizing, and self-differentiating. Whereas *Walten* was related earlier to a notion of *physis* that would precede its determination as nature, it is here related to a notion of *Trieb* that precedes its determination as a merely subjective or psychical drive. In order to understand the scope of this *Trieb*—and thus its relation to

Walten—in Heidegger, Derrida devotes several pages to the notion of *Trieb* in Freud.[15] An ambiguous, borderline concept in Freud, *Trieb* is at once life drive, ipseity drive, ego drive, sexual drive, self-preservation drive, as well as a destruction or death drive. On the border between the psychic and the somatic, the province of both biology or even physics and psychology, *Trieb* would have to be thought in relation not just to *Walten* but to *physis* in its pre-Socratic sense, that is, to the growing or reigning, the domination, of beings in their totality. Inasmuch as *Trieb* as the drive to self-preservation, the drive to sustain and immunize the self from everything that seeks to destroy it, is inseparable from *Trieb* as the drive to self-destruction, Derrida will even speak here of *Trieb*—and thus of *Walten*—in terms of auto-immunity. This will not be the last time in the seminar that Derrida will come to find one of his own philosophemes in Heidegger, as if the best way to understand Heidegger's 1929–30 seminar were to translate it into Derridean French. Listen to how Derrida parses *Trieb*—and thus *Walten*—in its relationship to *physis*:

> On the one hand, *Trieb,* the drive, also designates in German pushing up, in the sense of what grows, of the growing (*phuein*) of *physis,* primarily in the vegetable sense, but also in the sense of the growth of what is born, the offspring, the bud, the child, etc. And so to speak of everything that is, of that totality of entities as *physis* in general, as pushing or pushing up, before any other distinction between nature and its others, between the vegetable and its others, is to speak of what *is* in general, and therefore of the world. The push of this pushing up, this drive or this pulse [*la poussée de cette pousse*], is a force, but a force the sense of which remains absolute, and thus indeterminate, as much a psychic, symbolic, spiritual, etc., force as a physical or corporeal force. (*BS 2* 103–104/158)

Between the French verbs *pousser* as pushing and *pousser* as growing or pushing up, between the French nouns *poussée* as pressure, push, or thrust, and *pousse* as shoot or growth, Derrida is here pushing without exactly forcing the French language in order to describe a force that does not yet belong exclusively to plants or animals as opposed to material objects, a force that can be understood in terms of either inner drive or external compulsion, spontaneous, self-acting growth or external movement and causation.

Walten thus seems to drive Derrida, following Heidegger, to a pre-Socratic notion of *physis*, and then, in the company of Freud, to a post-psychoanalytic notion of *Trieb*. Once again Freud is brought together with Heidegger, a strategy deployed early and often by Derrida, who first writes in *The Post Card* and then recalls in the final footnote to *Specters of*

Marx: "Freud and Heidegger, I conjoin them within me like the two great ghosts of the 'great epoch.' The two surviving grandfathers. They did not know each other, but according to me they form a couple, and in fact just because of that, this singular anachrony" (*SM* 196 n. 39; *PC* 191).

Walten thus "signifies," Derrida argues, "not something or someone, neither man nor God, but the exercise of an archi-originary force, of a power, a violence, before any physical, psychic, theological, political determination," "before any ontic or ontological determination" (*BS 2* 103–104/158; see 94 n. 2/147 n. 1). It is "both foreign or heterogeneous, excessive even, with respect to this ontic and therefore theological or theologico-political sovereignty," "an ontological super-sovereignty, at the source of the ontological difference" (*BS 2* 208/293). But when readers of Derrida, and particularly readers of Derrida's texts on negative theology, hear *Walten* characterized as a kind of "super-sovereignty" or "hyper-sovereignty" (*BS 2* 123/184), they are licensed to wonder in which of two ways Derrida is thinking this excessive sovereignty, this hyperbolic sovereignty, that is, to parse it rather tersely, whether it is a hypersovereignty that tends in the direction of a Good beyond Being, a sovereignty so sovereign that it exceeds all the determinations of what is called sovereignty, or a sovereignty that, perhaps like *chōra*, relinquishes all sovereign power, a retreat or withdrawal from sovereignty that gives place to but does not itself exercise sovereign violence. When Derrida extemporizes at one point during the seminar, "This is not the sovereignty of God, it is not the sovereignty of a king or a head of state, but a sovereignty more sovereign than all sovereignty," he seems to nudge *Walten* a little closer to the Good beyond Being (*BS 2* 123 n. 17/184 n. 2).[16] But when he speaks of *Walten* as "a force, a power, a dominance, even a sovereignty unlike any other—whence the difficulty that we have in thinking it, determining it and, of course, translating it" (*BS 2* 123/184), he seems to leave open the possibility of thinking *Walten* not just as another, more sovereign sovereignty but as the other of sovereignty, as a sovereignty in withdrawal or as the withdrawal of sovereignty, as that which makes way or gives place to the ontological difference and the violence of Being and beings.

In Session Five of *The Beast and the Sovereign*, this relationship between sovereign power and dispossession, between the power of a sovereign subject and a certain passivity or receptivity, takes a rather odd turn. We looked at this moment of the seminar in some detail in Chapter 3, but it is worth returning to it here in order to underscore the role played by *Walten*. After a brief reference to Heidegger's 1954 "Das Ding" and the question of whether the cadaver can be considered a thing, Derrida asks about the decision, the supposedly sovereign decision, that a large and growing number of people in the developed world now have with regard to how their remains will be disposed of, namely, whether they will buried or cremated. It is, in large part, a thinking of *Walten* that seems to lead Derrida from a thinking of the sovereign decision as what is mine to a thinking of the passive decision or a decision *of the other*, that is, from a thinking of Dasein as the sole entity with a relation to death *as such* to a thinking of the other as the one who will survive me and so must dispose of my remains (*BS 2* 126/187–188). Derrida asks:

> What is the other—or what are the others—at the moment when it is a matter of responding to the necessity of making *something of me,* of making of me some thing or their thing from the moment I will be, as people say, *departed,* i.e. deceased, passed, passed away? (*BS 2* 126/187–188)

It is just after this strange turn in the seminar, which we looked at from a different perspective earlier, that Derrida in effect adds one more term to translate or parse *Walten*, and this time it is a French term, a quasi-French word, one that Derrida himself will have—through his own generous *Walten*—imposed upon the French language. Still meditating on this definition of the other as the one who must take care of my remains, Derrida says that this relation to self and other involves both nature and law, both *physis* and *nomos*. We are thus, writes Derrida, "already either in the opposition of *nomos, tekhnē, thesis* to *physis* in the late and derived sense, or else in that différance (with an *a*) of originary *physis,* which takes the forms of law, thesis, technique, right, etc." (*BS 2* 126/188)

Derrida thus speaks of that "différance (with an *a*) of originary *physis*": but if *différance* is identified with *physis*, and *physis*, as we have seen, is identified with *Walten*, then Derridean *différance* would seem to be identified with, if not actually be another name for, Heideggerian *Walten*. For what is *Walten* but this *différance* of an originary *physis* before the ontological difference?[17] As Derrida wrote already back in 1965 in the early pages of *Of Grammatology*, and already in relation to Heidegger:

> The ontico-ontological difference and its ground (*Grund*) in the "transcendence of Dasein" . . . are not absolutely originary. Différance by itself would be more "originary," but one would no longer be able to call it "origin" or "ground," those notions belonging essentially to the history of onto-theology, to the system functioning as the effacing of difference. (*OG* 23)

Walten would thus seem to be a quasi-synonym of *différance*; it will have preceded *différance* and opened up the space for its appearance, and it will have been reinscribed in turn by Derrida in an economy that includes such terms as *dissemination, supplementarity, autoimmunity,* and so on. *Walten,* like *différance,* will have thus been open from the start to its own reinscription and replacement, a quasi-master term destined from the start to give way to the other, that is, to the movement of *différance,* to the reign or sway of the other's *Walten.*

The tenth and final session of the seminar—we are moving more quickly now—takes place on March 26, 2003. Derrida begins the session with a long meditation on Paul Celan's line *"Die Welt ist fort, ich muss dich tragen,"* "The world is far away, I must carry you," a line he had often cited and analyzed as a way of thinking both death as the end of the world and my ethical obligation toward the other in light of that end. He begins in this way because events of the previous few weeks have beset or besieged the seminar, forcing Derrida to respond on an almost weekly basis to them. Just a couple of weeks earlier, there was the death of Maurice Blanchot, and then, just a few days before this final session, the American-led coalition's invasion of Iraq, yet another world war that portends not just the end of the world with the death of every individual but, as Derrida puts it, "the absolute end of the world . . . the destruction of the world, of any possible world" (*BS 2* 259–260/359). It might appear that what we blithely call "world events" have taken us pretty far away from a reading of Heidegger, and yet Derrida's comments on these events continue to echo much of what has already been said about *Walten.* In the final dozen or so pages of the seminar, therefore, Derrida returns one more time to this word *Walten,* which he has been insisting on and following from the 1929–30 seminar onward because it seems, he says, to appeal to "a sovereignty so sovereign that it exceeds the theological and political—and especially onto-theological—figures or determinations of sovereignty" (*BS 2* 278/382). It is this word *Walten,* it seems, this significant but unnoticed or unemphasized term in Heidegger, that has caused Derrida to rethink the very nature and meaning of sovereignty itself. Derrida thus confesses here in this final seminar session:

As you see, late in my life of reading Heidegger, I have just discovered a word that seems to oblige me to put everything in a new perspective. And that is what happens and ought to be meditated on endlessly. If I had not conjoined in one problematic the beast *and* the sovereign, I wager that the force and organizing power of this German word that is so difficult to translate, but that informs, gives form to the whole Heideggerian text, would never have appeared to me as such. Any more than it has appeared, to my knowledge, to others. (*BS 2* 279–280/383)

Inasmuch as the importance of *Walten* had already been noted back in 1989 in *Geschlecht IV*, Derrida's claim that he has "just discovered" this word is not quite right. Regardless, it was, it seems, the *detour* of "the beast and the sovereign" that led Derrida back to Heidegger's *Walten*, though also, perhaps, the question of *Walten* in Heidegger that allowed Derrida to think or frame otherwise the question of the beast and the sovereign. For Derrida continues throughout the seminar to criticize what he considers to be Heidegger's undue confidence in the distinction between the human and the animal based on this supposed access to world or based on an access to death *as such*, Heidegger's "unjustifiable decision"—his *Walten*, precisely (*BS 2* 61/101)—to start out with Dasein in its relation to world. But as the seminar progresses, this critique recedes more and more into the background as Heidegger's discourse on *Walten*, even Heidegger's idiom of *Walten*, comes to take center stage.

As the seminar thus draws to a close, Derrida focuses yet again on the "superabundant use [that] is made of the vocabulary of *Walten*," the "untranslatable" vocabulary of *Walten* (*BS 2* 280/383), this time in *An Introduction to Metaphysics*. It is in this text of 1935 that Derrida seems to detect beneath or behind a *Walten* that continues to precede all theologico-political determinations a *structural configuration* that links it in Heidegger's thinking to world and to spirit and then to poetry and, especially, to German poetry. Heidegger writes, for example, and Derrida cites: "in poetry [*in der Dichtung*] (the poetry that is authentic and great) there reigns [*waltet*] an essential superiority of the spirit with respect to all that is purely science" (*BS 2* 280–281/384).[18] Derrida then comments: "So, let us paraphrase with prudence and restraint: what in poetry rules and affirms its superiority, and thus its sovereignty, is *spirit;* and the sovereignty of spirit *waltet,* imposes itself, prevails, affirms itself above science, any simple science" (*BS 2* 281/385). Returning, it seems, to the concerns and language of *Of Spirit*, Derrida wonders whether this spiritual sovereignty of poetry, this "sovereignty already determined as spiritual," is not still "caught up in metaphysical or onto-theological oppositions" (*BS 2* 281/385). But rather than pursue this critique, this identification of sovereignty with the spiritual and this spiritual sovereignty with poetry, and particularly German poetry, that is, rather than pursue the *Auseinandersetzung* of *Of Spirit*, Derrida comments instead on a *gesture* of Heidegger's, that is, on Heidegger's unique and idiomatic reinscription of *Walten* in his own writing.

The fold that must be re-marked here is that this poetic and spiritual sovereignty of language, as Heidegger will make clear immediately afterward, itself *signs*, in a sense, the untranslatable and idiomatic use of the word *walten* itself. It is a word and above all a writing gesture, a singular pragmatic use, *signed* by Heidegger who, presenting himself as a faithful thinking inheritor of the German language, is going ceaselessly to affirm and refine the vocabulary and syntax of *walten,* in defiance of all translatability, to designate what is most difficult and necessary to think, to know, namely . . . Being, the Being of beings . . . the *Unter-Schied* between Being and beings . . . (*BS 2* 282/386; my emphasis on *signs* and *signed*)

Derrida here detects in Heidegger's language a signature or a countersignature, one that will give us pause when, just a few pages later, at the very end of the seminar, Derrida will himself come to countersign—which is not the same thing as to endorse—this Heideggerian countersignature.[19] Already back in *Geschlecht IV,* Derrida had drawn attention to this notion of the signature or the seal in *An Introduction to Metaphysics.* Speaking of what Heidegger calls in that text "the three creative 'Gewalten' of historical Dasein," Derrida writes:

These three creators carry this unheard, they carry it first in themselves, close by themselves . . . like a mute voice and to which they respond by taking responsibility for it. They open in this responsibility. This work is theirs, since they carry the unheard in themselves and take responsibility for it. But this work is not theirs, since they only hear the unheard. Their work carries only the seal or the signature of the originary *polemos* that has projected and developed the unheard. ("G 4" 211)

It is, to be sure, more than curious that in this final session of his final seminar Derrida would turn to this high-water mark, so to speak, in Heidegger's lexicon of *Walten.* For *An Introduction to Metaphysics* is the place, recall, where, as Derrida says, "the vocabulary of *Walten* is not only confirmed, but extends, differentiates, grows richer, and becomes invasive, especially around *physis* and *logos*" (*BS 2* 43/78). After citing, therefore, the passage from *An Introduction to Metaphysics* on the spiritual superiority of poetry, Derrida turns briefly to Heidegger's much commented-on interpretation of the second choral ode in Sophocles' *Antigone* (*BS 2* 285–286/391–392). When he comes to the interpretation of *deinon* as *unheimlich*, Derrida says that Heidegger's text can today be read, in the light of the invasion of Iraq that has just begun, "as a discourse on terror, terrorism, and even state terrorism," a discourse on "shock and awe" (*BS 2* 286/391). Insofar as this violence extends over the totality of beings, there is, he says, "no longer any limit to this definition of *Walten* as *Überwältigende.* It is as if *to be beings* and *Walten* were the same thing" (*BS 2* 287/392). As for man or Dasein in this "powerful, super- powerful Heideggerian appropriation-translation" of Sophocles, he is "doubly *deinon*," at once "exposed to the violence of *Walten,* of beings," and "in a position to exercise this violence himself, to do violence" (*BS 2* 287/392). Man is at once a being that perpetrates violence and one that is surrounded, circumdominated (*umwaltet*), gripped by it, traversed by a superviolence that makes everything—earth, sea, fire, and animals—appear or "burst open in the Open" (*BS 2* 287 n. 59/393 n. 1). While "the violence that grips man is indeed that of the *as such* of beings that Dasein is and that he must take upon himself, in its *Walten*" (*BS 2* 288/394), what Derrida stresses here, in the spring of 2003, is less the fact that, for Heidegger, this *as such* "distinguishes man from the animal" (*BS 2* 288/395) than the fact that man is first of all "seized, gripped, *durchwalten* by the *Gewalt* of this *Walten*," and that man then tends to *forget* this fact and so begins to attribute this power to himself. Derrida writes:

> Because he believes he is the author, the master and possessor, and the inventor of these powers, he ignores the fact that he is first of all gripped, seized, that he must take them on, and he then becomes basically a foreigner—this is the whole story—to his own *Unheim-lichkeit.* (*BS 2* 288/394)

This would be, it seems, one of the profound "lessons" toward which this seminar points, a lesson without lesson insofar as this knowledge or quasi-knowledge cannot, it goes without saying, allow one to master or know this preeminent or originary violence.

Derrida had begun *The Beast and the Sovereign* seminar by questioning the line that has been drawn throughout the history of philosophy between the human and the animal on the basis of a power or ability that is possessed by man but not the animal, the power of the *as such*, the ability to accede to world, the capacity to die and not just perish, and so on. If Derrida's first gesture to counter such a claim is typically to suggest that we extend such capacities or powers to the animal by questioning, for example, whether the animal or some animals may not just perish but may actually die, or mourn, or have technology or language, his second and much more powerful gesture is, as we have seen, always to ask whether *man* can really be said to have these powers or capacities that he has denied the animal and attributed to himself. Derrida's emphasis on *Walten* as a power that seizes man rather than being seized or possessed by him would simply confirm that in the end man does not have possession of, or power over, this power either.

If the subtitle of Derrida's *The Beast and the Sovereign* could well have been, as the title of this chapter suggests, "World, Finitude, Solitude," then the title of Heidegger's 1929–30 seminar could just as well have been "the beast and the sovereign," for central to it is not only the question of the relationship between the animal and man but the beast and the sovereign, as well as the question of sovereignty or *Walten* itself. But there is *Walten* and then there is *Walten*, the *Walten* that Heidegger made or imposed and the *Walten* to which he too was subject—the one coming always to haunt or hold sway over the other. To follow Heidegger as faithfully or as "loyally" as possible (*BS 2* 92/142), as Derrida himself says he wishes to, is thus to lay oneself open to this *Walten* or these *Waltens*, to the *Walten* that will have been the subject of the seminar and the one that would have been, as we will see, its ultimate signatory.

It is more or less at this point that Derrida breaks off his reading of *An Introduction to Metaphysics*, encouraging his students to read it on their own and to focus on the way Heidegger, much as he did in 1929–30, links *Walten* to *physis* and to *logos*, to *eidos* or *idea*, to the domination of the idea and of idealism in Western metaphysics, to the imposition of names and the violence of ideology.[20] And then Derrida adds these two final paragraphs to his seminar, two paragraphs that, in three moments, introduce, cite, and then comment on a final line from Heidegger. Here's how Derrida begins:

> I would like to end, if you'll give me one more second, on a single final quotation from Heidegger that could be given many readings and that I leave you to appropriate as you wish as you watch the war on television, in Iraq, but also closer to us. Heidegger writes this, which seems to mark the absolute limit of *Gewalt* or of *Gewalttätigkeit*. It's about what will basically have been besieging this seminar, behind the cohort of cremators and inhumers of every order, and other guardians of the mourning to come: death itself, if there be any, was our theme. (*BS 2* 290/396)

It was thus apparently not the beast and the sovereign that was the central theme of the seminar but death, says Derrida. *Death* will have been their theme, his theme. Heidegger will thus be cited one final time on this theme as well, even if, Derrida hastens to add, he would perhaps interpret this line differently than Heidegger would have. He continues:

Heidegger writes this, but I'm not sure that I will read it as he writes it or interpret it as he auto-interprets it—we would have to reconstitute the whole passage: "(There is only *one* thing against which all violence-doing, violent action, violent activity [all *Gewalt- tätigkeit*], immediately shatters [*scheitert*])" . . . "That is death [*Das ist der Tod*]." (*BS 2* 290/397)

Bringing death together with *Walten* or with *Gewalt*, Derrida then adds—and this is the third and final moment of this final passage—and thus of the entire seminar:

The question, that was the question of the seminar, remains entire: namely that of knowing who can die? To whom is this power given or denied? Who is capable of death, and, through death, of imposing failure on [*mettre en échec*] the super- or hyper-sovereignty of *Walten*? (*BS 2* 290/397)

Derrida thus ends the seminar with a series of questions: who can die, who is capable of death, who has the power of death, which is the only thing, says Heidegger, against which all violence-doing *scheitert*, that is, shatters, founders, gets shipwrecked. But what kind of power is death if it is able to thwart or cause to founder all activity, all violent activity? Is it simply that which puts an end, sets a limit, to all activity, or is it a strange disempowering power, not a counterpower but a counter to power and to violence, the only thing, then, on which all activity finds no hold, no grasp, no grip, and so founders or shatters? Derrida does not answer this question, and he does not return to it, as he had hoped to, the following year. He simply leaves us with this question—but in the form, which makes all the difference, of a *countersignature*.

If the seminar begins with *Je—Je suis seul(e)*—it ends with *walten*. But why *walten*? That is exactly the question Derrida asks himself near the very end of Session Nine. Just after parsing a line from *Identity and Difference*, he asks, "Why *walten*? Why this word which so often goes unnoticed? We shall continue asking ourselves this question for a long time" (*BS 2* 256/355).[21] To this question, there would or could be no definitive answer—not for us and not even for Derrida. But it is worth noting that in "Force of Law" in 1990 Derrida had already read and interpreted this word *walten* in relation to Walter Benjamin and had already identified it as a kind of seal or signature. After arguing in the section of "Force of Law" titled "The First Name of Benjamin" that "it is always necessary that the other sign and it is always the other that signs last. In other words, first,"

Derrida cites and underscores these concluding words from Benjamin's *Critique of Violence*: "Divine violence, which is the sign and seal but never the means of sacred execution, can be called sovereign violence [*die waltende heissen*]." Of this final line, Derrida then goes on to write: "Not only does it sign, this ultimate address, and very close to the first name of Benjamin, Walter. It also names the signature, the sign and the seal, it names the name and what calls itself *die waltende*."[22]

By ending the second year of *The Beast and the Sovereign* with *Walten*, it is as if Derrida were not just citing the language of the other but signing or countersigning in the name of the other—somewhere between Heidegger's *Walten* and Benjamin's. As Derrida writes elsewhere in a text entitled, precisely, "Countersignature," one must at once "respect the absolute, absolutely irreducible, untranslatable idiom of the other" and "countersign the other's text without counterfeit" ("CS" 29). That is, one must respect the untranslatable idiom of the other and one must translate it, displace, reinscribe, and countersign it. In "Living On: Border Lines," one of the texts most responsible for bringing Derrida's thought to the English-speaking world, Derrida brings together this necessity both to translate and not to translate with the possibility of survival and, thus, with the notions of trace and the archive that we have been following throughout this work:

> A text lives only if it lives *on* [*sur-vit*], and it lives *on* only if it is *at once* translatable *and* untranslatable. . . . Totally translatable, it disappears as a text, as writing, as a body of language. Totally untranslatable, even within what is believed to be one language, it dies immediately. Thus triumphant translation is neither the life nor the death of the text, only or already its living *on*, its life after life, its life after death. The same thing will be said of what I call writing, mark, trace, and so on. It neither lives nor dies; it lives *on*. ("LO" 82–83)

If everything in Derrida's seminar of 2002–2003 relating to Heidegger will have been in some sense foreseeable, on the program, everything from Heidegger on the animal and on world to the reinscription of *Walten*, this signature or this countersignature could have never been predicted, not even, I would venture to say, by Derrida himself, this countersignature that is haunted at once by the vocabulary of Heidegger's seminar of 1929–30, by Derrida's own translations of *Walten* throughout the seminar, and by the proper name of someone else about whom Derrida will have already written—and precisely in relation to Heidegger and the question of violence—and whose birthday he will have shared.[23] How else could he have signed this final seminar, this final very autobiographical seminar that he will have himself given, to be sure, but to which, in the end, he will have also been given over? How else but in the name of another? Or in the name of an originary or elementary violence that effaces all these names?

Conclusion: *Désormais*

... at stake from now on [*désormais*] is an end of the world ...

The Beast and the Sovereign, **vol. 2**

... the adverb *désormais* is for me one of the most beautiful, and one of the most untranslatable, words, in a word, in the French language.

Demeure

From *Je* to *Walten*, from French to German, from the first-person pronoun to a verbal noun that borders on a proper name that had already been marked and analyzed in "Force of Law" as a sort of signature, Derrida seems to sign with the name and in the language of the other as the sign of an identity or an ipseity that necessarily inscribes itself in the world and, in an autoimmune fashion, loses itself in the world. The countersignature of this sovereign *Walten* would thus seem to suggest that there can never be a sovereign or master term, that deconstruction must always pass through history and through the language of the other, that there can be no sovereign last word to put an end to the violence or the endless discussion. It suggests that this sovereignty beyond all sovereignty, this sovereignty that has perhaps, just perhaps, been divested of all sovereign power, can go by the name of *différance*, or autoimmunity, or *physis*, or indeed, *Walten*.

"How does one impose names?" asks Derrida near the very end of the seminar, "that is one of our great questions" (*BS 2* 289/396). To answer that question, one might begin by citing Derrida's "Letter to a Japanese Friend," a short text of 1983, the year of that first "Geschlecht" essay:

The word "deconstruction," like any other, acquires its value only from its inscription in a chain of possible substitutions, in what is so blithely called a "context." For me, what I have tried and still try to write, the word has interest only within a certain context, where it

167

replaces and lets itself be determined by so many other words such as "writing [*écriture*]," "trace," "*différance*," "supplement," "hymen," "*pharmakon*," "margin," "cut [*entame*]," "*parergon*," and so on. By definition, the list can never be closed, and I have cited only nouns, which is inadequate and done only for reasons of economy. ("LJF" 5–6)[1]

"By definition," says Derrida, "the list can never be closed." What this means, it seems to me, is that the list is always open to the supplement of the other. Signing or countersigning in the name and in the language of the other is thus not simply a choice or a possibility among others but the necessity to which thinking, speaking, and writing must always yield. Signing with the name of the other, speaking in the language of the other, appears not to be the gesture of mastery, erudition, or worldliness we are often tempted to attribute to the scholar, the cosmopolitan, or the seminar leader. It is, rather, already the sign of a certain dispossession, the desperate attempt to protect oneself against the anxiety of a certain *Walten* by saying to another in their language: *Je suis seul(e)*, but perhaps also *Je suis seul(e) avec toi*—a certain experience, then, of world, solitude, and finitude, and the intimation of the event against which all sovereignty shatters.[2]

I am reminded of the story told by Nathalie Sarraute of the last words of Russian playwright Anton Chekhov, who, in 1904, suddenly sat up in his deathbed to say, "not in Russian, not in his own language, but in the language of the other, in the German language, speaking loudly and clearly, *Ich sterbe*, before falling back dead into his bed."[3] *Ich sterbe*, then, as if this exile into another language were already a sign or signature of death, of the world that is far away. *Ich sterbe* as the sign of a world that is going away, a speech act within the world that would contest the stability and unity of the world, a speech act that would contest the very notion of an *act*. This *ich sterbe* would be, as it were, the other face of that other impossible performative for traditional speech act theory, *je suis mort*, "I am dead": an impossible performative for a first person subject.[4] *Ich sterbe/ je suis mort*: though these are impossible performatives for a subject whose possibilities must remain his or her own, such performatives—such events—happen, and happen all the time, in literature or in the archive. As I have suggested throughout, the archive says perhaps only this, which means that everything needs to be rethought—everything from life and death to survival and world.

But then there is this strange example of survival in the archive, this line that is not exactly a part of *The Beast and the Sovereign* seminar, since it is not dated and was never spoken during it, though it prefaces, frames, and perhaps even signs in its own way the entire seminar from front to back. The line comes to us in a note to the "Editorial Note" that precedes the seminar of 2002–2003. After remarking—in good archival fashion—that the reference text for the edition of the seminar that is being published is "the printout of the seminar as kept by Derrida in his files," and after then informing us that there are two copies of the seminar, one in a yellow folder that is now deposited in the Jacques Derrida archives at IMEC and one in a red folder that "Derrida used for this American seminar," the editors note the following of this second:

> On the cover of the folder, along with the abbreviated title, "BS— 2002–03 (3)," and an illegible crossed-out word, is this handwritten phrase: "ma peur de la mort, désormais sa souffrance [my fear of death, henceforth his or her suffering]." The word "sa" is circled. (*BS 2* xvn7/16n5)

There is no further commentary on this enigmatic phrase, which was found in the archives of Jacques Derrida and made public by the editors of the seminar, even though it does not belong, strictly speaking, to the seminar itself.[5] It is not unlike the reporting of that strange prayer found sewn into Pascal's garment after his death; and even though this line was not concealed like that one was, having been left open to view, laid bare right on the surface of the folder, like an open message or a postcard, it remains no less secret or cryptic. It is a single line, not even a complete sentence, a fragment on the cover of the American copy of the seminar, which all by itself raises so many of the questions we have confronted here: questions of the archive, of life and death, of mourning, and of self and other.

My fear of death, *ma peur de la mort*, says Derrida, is *désormais*, henceforth or from now on, *sa souffrance*, his or her suffering. His fear of death, the line seems to say, Derrida seems to say, has now become or will be from now on the other's suffering, his or hers, those who will remain, we might speculate, who will be there to watch over his death and who will be charged with mourning, with burying or cremating, with disposing of his remains in one way or another. Instead of a fear of death that would still be his own, still his ownmost possibility, as Heidegger would have said, he would be given over to the hands of the other—corpse and corpus alike, and right down to a phrase like this one. From his fear to his or her suffering: the fear he feels or will have felt has now become or is now giving way to the suffering of the other, the suffering he or she will now undergo. As Derrida said during the seminar, "That's what is meant, has always been meant, by 'other'"—the one who or those who "might survive me, survive my decease and then proceed as they wish, sovereignly, and sovereignly have at their disposal the future of my remains, if there are any" (*BS 2* 126–127/188–189).

But there is yet another interpretation of this enigmatic line, one that would read not some other (he or she) into the second part of the phrase but the self as other, the self that must now undergo what it had previously only feared. My fear of death, *ma peur de la mort*, from now on, *désormais*, its suffering, *sa souffrance*, that is, the suffering, my suffering, of it, of death. Whereas I once feared death, had a fear of death, whereas I once kept death at bay, at a distance, mastering it even through this fear, from now on all I can do is suffer it, yield to it, undergo it: *ma peur de la mort, désormais sa souffrance*. My fear of death, my fear of a future death, has now become, through its imminence, my suffering of it, something I can only undergo, await, wait out. *My* fear of death, from now on *its* suffering.

This enigmatic line on the cover of the folder of the American copy of the seminar is not, as I said, a part of the seminar strictly speaking. It is neither the seminar's first line nor its last; it is not dated like all the other lines of the seminar. It was not written or recorded as everything else was. And yet it remains, a line that now frames the entire seminar and so by itself poses all the questions of life, death, mourning, survival, and the archive that we have pursued throughout this work. It is perhaps no coincidence, then, that this line is open to multiple interpretations and multiple selves, that self and other here get confused, that it is in the depths of a self that *can* still act, read, fear, that we might find an other, or else the suffering of what has previously been kept at bay. Everything gets played out here between *ma* and *sa*, *ma peur*, my fear, *sa souffrance*, his, her, or its suffering; between *ma* and *sa*, *ma/sa*, another *Masafuera*, perhaps, another deserted island, like the *sa* that is circled, as the editors note, on the cover of the American copy of the seminar. Circled, enclosed like an island, (*sa*) like an image of *Savoir Absolu* (Absolute Knowledge)—or of who knows whatever other encrypted name from *Glas* or *The Postcard*—an image of ipseity, perhaps, but one that has now given way to a suffering that opens the self to what is outside it, to death, to the other, to a suffering that is from now on not even wholly one's own. Through a simple play of possessive pronouns, everything in this seminar that begins with *Je* and ends with *Walten* can be read in the alternation or alternative between *ma* and *sa*, between what is me or mine and what is his, her, or its. This is what it means, perhaps, to entrust *my* archive to the hands of the other, what it means to write and to choose, to designate one's heirs and make decisions, to exercise one's will, and to have this will executed, as we say, always by the other. This is what it means to give oneself over, to be oneself given over, to the other, whether this be the human other or the animal, vegetal, or elemental other, given or given over, in the end, to the *Walten* to which everything is subject.

Walten, then, and not just any *Walten*, but the one that pushed up, that grew, that emerged in and came to dominate Heidegger's seminar from the autumn of 1929 into the spring and summer of 1930, a seminar that would have been like a period of gestation for Derrida himself—"like a still unborn child, to be born, to be carried to term in the uterus of the origin of the world" (*BS 2* 259/358).[6] It is as if, through this *Walten*, Derrida were unwinding his seventy-three years, bringing himself in the course of the seminar back to the origin, back to this *Walten* that will have come to beset or besiege his final seminar as the last quasi-synonymous supplement, the last disseminative iteration, the last autoimmune inscription, the last "proper name," for what Derrida once called—called and signed, marked and remarked in a quasi-sovereign gesture at the limits of the French language that he so loved—*différance*, or else, from the beginning and *désormais, la déconstruction*.

Notes

Introduction: Derrida's Other Corpus

1. Roughly speaking, the seminars of 1960–69 were handwritten, those of 1969–87 typed, and those of 1987–2003 composed directly on a word processor or computer.

2. Many of these seminars or sessions from these seminars were repeated, sometimes with significant changes and sometimes improvised in English, at various universities in the United States, including Johns Hopkins University, Yale University, the University of California at Irvine, New York University, and the University of Chicago.

3. Though Derrida often expressed a certain reticence about the publication of the seminars, there is ample evidence to suggest that had he been assured of the right editorial oversight he would not have opposed their eventual publication. Also, while the seminars were indeed, as I say, "nearly publishable" in their existent form, the editors did have to track down and insert quotes, which Derrida would often read in the seminar directly from the text being cited. A number of small editorial changes were also necessary to make the text more readable. See the "General Introduction to the French Edition" (*BS 1* ix–xi, *BS 2* ix–xi).

4. The current plan is to begin by publishing the first ten or so years of the seminar in reverse chronological order. After the two volumes on "The Beast and the Sovereign," there will thus be two volumes on the death penalty, two on perjury and pardon, two on hospitality, and two on testimony.

5. To take just a single example, Derrida appears to have used the Cerisy conferences devoted to his work (in 1980, 1992, 1997, and 2002) as occasions, in part, to reread himself, to retrace his own steps, to pick up the scent of

themes scattered here and there throughout his corpus in order to bring them together and lead them in new directions. After thus presenting in 1980 a reading of Kant and the question of an apocalyptic tone in philosophy (in relation, in part, to the theme of the conference, "The Ends of Man," and in part in relation to *La carte postale*, which had just been published) and in 1992 a reading of Heidegger on the question of death or being-toward-death (with references to his many previous readings of Heidegger along the way), Derrida at the Cerisy conference in 1997 entitled "The Autobiographical Animal" begins by recalling his many previous works on the question of the animal, and in 2002, in what would become the first part of *Rogues*, his many previous allusions to democracy and the democracy-to-come. Moreover, there appears to be, at least in retrospect, a certain trajectory to the themes of the conferences themselves, the question of apocalypse and of the ends of man in 1980, the question of borders in 1992, of the animal in 1997, and the question of sovereignty and democracy, and particularly the question of the relationship between the beast and the sovereign, in 2002. Derrida himself writes in 1997 of the first three Cerisy conferences: "I move from 'the ends of man,' that is, the confines of man, to 'the crossing of borders' between man and animal. Passing across borders or the ends of man I come to surrender to the animal" (*ATT* 3). If I recall here the conferences at Cerisy-la-Salle, it is also because the two years of *The Beast and the Sovereign* seminars also seem to be looking or referring back to previous works, to works on Heidegger, on the animal, on violence and on sovereignty, and on death. If each of the Cerisy conferences I mentioned rereads one aspect or theme of Derrida's work—humankind's relationship to death, the relationship between the human and the animal, and, finally, the relationship between the animal and sovereignty—it seems as if *this seminar* actually returns to *all* these themes, bringing them into proximity to one another and binding them to one another. Derrida is very clear about this theme of return. He says in the first line of the Fifth Session, "Every week, as you've noticed, and every year, we return." As we will see, this seminar, what turned out to be Derrida's final seminar, moves forward by looking back in a unique and often rather uncanny way.

6. For example, in the second volume of *The Beast and the Sovereign* there is an extraordinarily lyrical four-page passage on two lines of John Donne (*BS 2* 50–54/86–91). Though the passage certainly contributes something to the seminar and makes sense within it, it is the sort of passage that Derrida might well have edited out of a published text.

7. Derrida's teaching at the École Normale Supérieure was determined in large part by the program for the *agrégation* exam, for which Derrida had the responsibility of preparing his students. Derrida would thus enjoy a great deal more freedom at the École des Hautes Études en Sciences Sociales. This can be seen already in the titles of the seminars. Beginning in 1984, Derrida embarked on a series of multiyear seminars on "Philosophical Nationality and Nationalism" (1984–88), "Politics of Friendship" (1988–91), and then an even longer series

entitled "Questions of Responsibility" (1991–2003)—with multiyear seminars on the secret, testimony, hospitality, perjury and pardon, the death penalty, and the beast and the sovereign.

8. While many of the seminars were on topics that would eventually be reworked by Derrida into essays and books, very few of the seminar sessions have been published in the form in which they were delivered in Paris or elsewhere. Among the very few seminar sessions that have seen the light of day in anything like their original form, there is *Politics of Friendship*, which is based on a couple of sessions of the seminar of the same name given in Paris in 1988–89, and two sessions on hospitality from 1996 published in *Of Hospitality* and one from 1997 included in the collection *Acts of Religion*. The first volume of *Beast and the Sovereign* is somewhat unique in that it includes a couple of sessions that more or less reproduce, with only minor modifications, parts of what was presented at the 1997 conference at Cerisy-la-Salle devoted to Derrida's work and published posthumously in *The Animal That Therefore I Am*.

9. Derrida even returns in the first volume of *The Beast and the Sovereign* to the very same passages from Pascal on the relationship between justice and force that he had treated in "Force of Law" (*BS 1* 7–8).

10. Of course, a case could be made for the exceptional status of *every* seminar. For instance, it might appear that each of the seminars gathered under the general title "Questions of Responsibility" (1991–2001) treats a very restricted, local, and localizable theme within the more general field of ethics or philosophy (e.g., hospitality, perjury and pardon, the death penalty, and so on). But, as always in Derrida, that which appears to be contained turns out to contain that which contains it. Hence, each of these seemingly limited themes becomes in the course of Derrida's analysis nothing less than an interrogation of the entire matrix of terms and concepts that we might have thought could be taken for granted in analyzing the more restricted theme. The publication of the two-year seminar on the death penalty will suffice to make this very evident. Rather than assuming that we know what sovereignty, punishment, law, and death are, so as then to ask how the death penalty is a moment or example of these, Derrida demonstrates that the question of the death penalty provides unique access for asking about the very nature of sovereignty, death, punishment, and law, though also history, the human, reason, and so on. In short, there will be no "minor" seminars in the series. Moreover, if each of these seminars bears the general title "Questions" of Responsibility, one can be certain that each will pose at some point the question of the question. Hence, every seminar is unique—just like this last one—and each asks the most fundamental questions possible, including the question of what response or responsibility might mean be *before* the question.

11. *Die Grundbegriffe der Metaphysik. Welt—Endlichkeit—Einsamkeit* (Frankfurt am Main: Vittorio Klostermann, 1983); *The Fundamental Concepts of Metaphysics: World, Finitude, Solitude,* trans. William McNeill and Nicholas Walker (Bloomington: Indiana University Press, 1995).

1. Derrida's Flair (For the Animals to Follow . . .)

1. See, for example, *Sophist* 218c and 287c or *Phaedrus* 265d–e. Of course, for Derrida there are no such "natural joints" between concepts, no place outside language and thought from which the conceptual "animal" might be surveyed from above and then cut up by following the natural lines of division.

2. The full publication history of this work is rather complex. Of Derrida's long ten-hour lecture at Cerisy, two sections or chapters were published separately before being published together in *The Animal That Therefore I Am*. The first of these two chapters, "L'animal que donc je suis," was first published in French in the conference proceedings of Cerisy, *L'animal autobiographique: Autour de Jacques Derrida*, ed. Marie-Louise Mallet (Paris: Éditions Galilée, 1999), 251–301; these pages correspond to *L'animal que donc je suis* (Paris: Éditions Galilée, 2006), 15–77. It was then published in English as "The Animal That Therefore I Am (More to Follow)," trans. David Wills, *Critical Inquiry* 28, no. 2 (2002): 369–418; these pages correspond to *ATT* 1–51. The second of the two chapters was published first in English as "And Say the Animal Responded," trans. David Wills, in *Zoontologies: The Question of the Animal*, ed. Cary Wolfe (Minneapolis: University of Minnesota Press, 2003), 121–146; this material corresponds to *ATT* 119–40 as well as to *BS 1* 111–135; it was then published in French as "Et si l'animal répondait?" in *Cahier de l'Herne* 83, *Jacques Derrida*, ed. Marie-Louise Mallet and Ginette Michaud (Paris: L'Herne, 2004), 117–129; this material corresponds to *L'animal que donc je suis* 163–191, as well as to *La bête et le souverain* (2001–2002), 1:158–187. These two chapters were then published as part of the book *The Animal That Therefore I Am*, which includes all the other previously unpublished sections of Derrida's 1997 Cerisy talk as well as a transcription of Derrida's improvised session on Heidegger from later in the conference.

As for the title *The Animal That Therefore I Am* (L'animal que donc je suis), it is, of course, to be heard as a deformation of Descartes' famous "I think therefore I am" (*Je pense donc je suis*), but where the first person singular form *suis* can be heard not only as *am* (from *être*), but as *follow* (from *suivre*), as in to *follow after* or *track* or else to *follow upon* or *come after*. The phrase thus suggests at once the animal that therefore I am, the animal I therefore follow after, the animal I come after and so follow (see *ATT* 10).

3. In addition to the formal talk on July 15, 1997, Derrida gave an improvised session later during the conference where he comments at some length on Heidegger's claim in his 1929–30 seminar that the stone is worldless, the animal poor in world, and the human world-building. This discussion is taken up in much greater detail—as is promised at *ATT* 141—in 2002–2003 in the second and final year of *The Beast and the Sovereign* seminar.

4. Derrida writes: "I won't go back over the arguments of a theoretical or philosophical kind, or in what we call a deconstructive style, arguments that for a very long time, *since I began writing, in fact*, I believe I have dedicated to the

question of the living and of the living animal. For me that will always have been the most important and decisive question" (*ATT* 34; my emphasis).

As for this notion of *flair*, Derrida writes in *The Animal That Therefore I Am* of the way in which he has doubled back on this theme of the animal throughout his work, such that his trajectory would "resemble the running of an animal that, finding its way on the basis of a scent [*au flair*] or a noise, goes back more than once over the same path to pick up the traces, either to sniff [*flairer*] the trace of another or to cover its own by adding to it, precisely as though it were that of another, picking up the scent [*flairant*], therefore, of whatever on this track demonstrates to it that the trace is always that of another, demonstrating also that in following the consequence or direction of this double arrow (it is a matter of the scent [*il y va du flair*], and the scent one smells is always the trace of another), the animal becomes inevitable" (*ATT* 55; see also *ATT* 33, 78, 92).

Indeed, Derrida had attempted from as early as *Of Grammatology* in 1967 to rethink the very concept of the trace or the sign in relation not only to humans but animals by means of this trope or quasi-concept of flair: "We must begin *wherever we are* and the thought of the trace, which cannot not take the scent [*flair*] into account, has already taught us that it was impossible to justify a point of departure absolutely. *Wherever we are*: in a text where we already believe ourselves to be" (*OG* 162).

In the first year of *The Beast and the Sovereign* seminar, this theme of the *flair* returns with some frequency. For example: "If God is the model of sovereignty, saying 'God *like* the beast' puts us again on the same track, sniffing out [*flairer*] everything that might attract the one to the other" (*BS 1* 50/82). Derrida had thus long been tracking this theme of the animal, and he had been doing so while tracking and using one of the tropes of the animal, namely, scent, *flair*, as opposed to, or in addition to, the sight of *theoria*—even though, as Derrida often reminds us, *theoria* means not only vision but "procession" (see *ATT* 39). Finally, Kelly Oliver has reminded me of a passage from the second year of *The Beast and the Sovereign* where Derrida speaks of having a certain flair for what one cannot see coming, "anticipating without anticipating, sensing in the sense that one says that animals sense, and do better with scent and with noses, than we humans, when animals sense catastrophes coming that we do not see coming, for example earthquakes that certain animals register long before we do, even before the earthquake breaks surface, if I can put like that" (*BS 2* 173/249).

5. One might wish to juxtapose this rather large claim with another equally large one on a seemingly disconnected theme. In *Rogues*, a work written in 2002 and first published in 2003, Derrida writes, "we would do well to recall that there are in the end rather few philosophical discourses, assuming there are any at all, in the long tradition that runs from Plato to Heidegger, that have without any reservations taken the side of democracy. In this sense democratism in philosophy is something rather rare and, in the end, very modern. And perhaps not even very philosophical" (*R* 41).

6. On the word *animot* as a chimera, see *ATT* 41, 47–48.

7. On the theme of being shamed or embarrassed before the animal gaze, see *ATT* 3–5, 11. Derrida writes of this absolute origin in the other: "It has its point of view regarding me. The point of view of the absolute other, and nothing will have ever given me more food for thinking through this absolute alterity of the neighbor or of the next(-door) than these moments when I see myself naked under the gaze of a cat" (*ATT* 11).

8. When, for example, Alice in Lewis Carroll's *Alice in Wonderland* seems to conclude that an animal cannot reply, that it might seem to reply but never really does, Derrida questions less this explicit claim regarding the animal than Alice's implicit assumption that we humans can respond and that we can determine what a human really means when he or she responds. "[Alice] seems, at this moment at least, to believe that one can in fact discern and decide between a human *yes* and *no*" (*ATT* 9). But, Derrida asks, can one really decide in all rigor when a human is saying *yes* or *no*?

9. "One of the questions to be raised, therefore, would be to know whether man does that. In other words, in order to indicate the governing principle of the strategy I would like to follow, it would not simply consist in unfolding, multiplying, leafing through the structure of the 'as such,' or the opposition between 'as such' and 'not as such,' no more than it would consist in giving back to the animal what Heidegger says it is deprived of; it would obey the necessity of asking oneself whether man, the human itself, has the 'as such'" (*ATT* 159–60).

10. See *ATT* 94–95, where Derrida rearticulates this strategy with regard to the capacity of the human to refer to itself by means of an autoaffection that would exclude all heteroaffection.

11. Penelope Deutscher and Kelly Oliver are two scholars who have been pursuing this aspect, among others, of Derrida's seminar. See, for example, Oliver's recent work *Technologies of Life and Death: From Cloning to Capital Punishment* (New York: Fordham University Press, 2013), where questions arising out of Derrida's seminars with regard to the relationship between the human and the animal, the masculine and the feminine, life and death, and so on, are thoughtfully and fruitfully conjoined with reflections about contemporary technologies of life and death (e.g., cloning, surrogate motherhood, genetic engineering, autopsy, the human treatment of animals, the death penalty).

12. This is precisely the itinerary Derrida will follow in the second year of *The Beast and the Sovereign* as he questions Heidegger's claims regarding the animal. He begins by questioning Heidegger's too rapid dismissal of scientific discourses on the animal, even though Heidegger is, Derrida admits, much more sympathetic than most philosophers to such studies. But what Derrida is then most intent on questioning is the *confidence* with which Heidegger will then attribute an ability he has denied the animal—for example, access to the *as such* of beings—to man.

13. Élisabeth de Fontenay, *Sans offenser le genre humain: Réflexions sur la cause animale* (Paris: Éditions Albin Michel, 2008), 19.

14. The first volume of *The Beast and the Sovereign* in fact ends with some reflections on the universality of phonocentrism as opposed to logocentrism, reflections that bring us right back to some of the concerns of *Of Grammatology*.

15. As Derrida writes in *The Animal That Therefore I Am*: "It was in order to name that sacrificial scene that I spoke elsewhere, as though of a single phenomenon and a single law, of *carnophallogocentrism*" (*ATT* 104).

16. Derrida writes elsewhere in *ATT*: "All the philosophers we will investigate (from Aristotle to Lacan, and including Descartes, Kant, Heidegger, and Levinas), all of them say the same thing: the animal is deprived of language. Or, more precisely, of response, of a response that could be precisely and rigorously distinguished from a reaction" (*ATT* 32).

17. And this is the case from the very first word on—*bête*, which, taken as a noun, can be translated not too problematically as *beast* (though *animal* is in many cases a more natural translation), but, as an adjective, means not so much beastly as ignorant, stupid, or, as David Wills often translates it, asinine.

18. The theme of sacrifice runs throughout *ATT*, from its Greek and biblical origins to Kant, for whom the animal can never be an end in itself but only a means to an end and thus, lacking the dignity or *Würde* of an end in itself, can be sacrificed (*ATT* 100; see 91–92).

19. Derrida writes again: "That would be the law of an imperturbable logic, both Promethean and Adamic, both Greek and Abrahamic (Judaic, Christian, and Islamic). Its invariance hasn't stopped being verified all the way to our modernity" (*ATT* 21).

20. Derrida also detects in Lacan's treatment of the animal not just an insidious anthropocentrism but a latent *fraternalism*, a Christian ethic of the fellow or the brother that can be fruitfully compared with what Derrida says about fraternalism in *Rogues* and *Politics of Friendship*, as well as in several seminars of the 1980s that were given under the general title "Philosophical Nationality and Nationalisms." This critique of fraternalism, indeed of any ethics based on some supposed or "phantasmatic" identification through family, nation, race, culture, or religion, leads Derrida to suggest at one particularly poignant moment in *The Beast and the Sovereign* that ethics has to do not with the similar but the dissimilar, that it begins only in relationship to what is *not* like me, and so perhaps in relation to the animal even more than the human.

21. Derrida identifies other common traits among them. None of them, he writes, "evoke the possibility of being looked at by the animal that they, for their part, observe," none of them "evoke or take into account the problem of nakedness or modesty operating between animal and human," none of them "think to distinguish animals from one another," and so all of them "speak of 'the animal' as of a single set that can be opposed to 'us,' 'humans'" (*ATT* 90).

22. Derrida also provides us with an extended reading of Deleuze on animality, psychoanalysis, and *bêtise*, as well as a development of his brief critique in *Rogues* of Agamben's distinction between *bios* and *zōē* and his claims regarding the novelty of biopolitics.

23. Derrida writes: "I think that Cartesianism belongs, beneath its mechanistic indifference, to the Judeo-Christiano-Islamic tradition of a war against the animal, of a sacrificial war that is as old as Genesis. And that war is not just one means of applying technoscience to the animal in the absence of another possible or foreseeable means; no, that violence or war has until now been constitutive of the project or of the very possibility of technoscientific knowledge within the process of humanization or of the appropriation of man by man, including its most highly developed ethical or religious forms" (*ATT* 101).

2. "If you could take just two books . . .": Derrida at the Ends of the World with Heidegger and Robinson Crusoe

1. Simon Glendinning has reminded me of the popular British radio program *Desert Island Disco*, which regularly asks its guests just this question.

2. Derrida himself heard the very same thought experiment in this alternative. He asks his audience during the second session of the seminar, just before the holiday break in December: "Which book would you take to a desert island, the Bible or a Heidegger seminar about the concept of world?" (*BS 2* 48/83)

3. Derrida will indeed keep his promise of focusing throughout the year on these two texts of Defoe and Heidegger, though many other figures will emerge in a more abbreviated or punctual manner in the course of the seminar. In addition to Joyce, Rousseau, Marx, Woolf, Deleuze, and Tournier as commentators on *Robinson Crusoe* in the First Session, there are references to Coetzee, Donne, and Kant (in the Second Session), Rousseau and Bergson (in the Third Session), Novalis, Levinas, Aristotle, and Freud (in the Fourth Session), Husserl (in the Fifth Session), Freud, Hegel, and Joyce (in the Sixth Session), Blanchot and Celan (in the Seventh Session), Pascal, Aristotle, and Genet (in the Eighth Session), La Fontaine, Lacan, and Bentham (in the Ninth Session), and Kant and Abū Bakr ibn Tufayl (in the Tenth Session). For a complete list of the figures and texts treated in each chapter, see again the first two chapters of David Krell's *Derrida and Our Animal Others* (Bloomington: Indiana University Press, 2013); hereafter abbreviated as DOA.

4. Derrida even says that *Robinson Crusoe* is not just another book within the world but "the world itself" (*BS 2* 18/44).

5. Derrida makes this point already in the improvised reading of Heidegger included at the end of *The Animal That Therefore I Am* (*ATT* 151).

6. On Kant and the idea of the world, and particularly his essay "What is Called Orientation in Thinking," see *BS 2* 97–100.

7. Derrida writes, at once commenting on Heidegger and setting up his own subsequent analysis: "We think we know what the world is, what we mean when we say 'world,' and that everything is the world, everything is in the

world or of the world, that there is nothing outside the world, and therefore we are unable to specify, to determine a question bearing on the world, as it would bear on this or that, on a determinable being. A question about the world is a question about everything and nothing" (*BS 2* 58/97).

8. This *not* having, it should be said, is central to Heidegger's seminar as well.

9. As Derrida notes, "everything is in threes" in Heidegger's seminar (*ATT* 149).

10. Derrida argued something similar in "Heidegger's Ear" when he suggested—and again in relation to Heidegger—that before this *Kampf* or this *polemos* "there is no world, there is nothing" ("HE" 210).

11. On this notion of death as the end of the world, see Geoffrey Bennington, *Not Half No End: Militantly Melancholic Essays in Memory of Jacques Derrida* (Edinburgh: Edinburgh University Press, 2011), xiii, 8, 40.

12. As Derrida puts it in *Aporias*, "*death* is always the name of a secret, since it signs the irreplaceable singularity" (*AP* 74).

13. In remarks made during a roundtable discussion at the American Academy of Religion and the Society of Biblical Literature, Derrida extends this faith or trust to animals: "to be true to science, knowledge, and to be true to faith, we have to find in our experience, each as a living being, the experience of faith far beyond any received religious tradition, any teaching. That is why I constantly refer to the experience of faith as simply a speech act, as simply the social experience; and this is true even for animals. Animals have faith, in a certain way. As soon as there is social bond there is faith, and there are social bonds in animals: they trust one another, they have to. . . . This trust, this bond, this covenant within life, is the resource to understand the heterogeneity between faith and knowledge. Both are absolutely indispensable, but they are indissociable and heterological. That's the ground of our experience of faith as living beings" ("EF" 45).

14. In the second year of the death penalty seminar (the session of January 10, 2001), Derrida makes it clear that this end of the world in death is not limited to the death of a human being. He argues that "the death one makes or lets come in this way is not the end of this or that, this or that individual, the end of a who or a what *in the world*. Each time something dies [*ça meurt*], it's the end of the world. Not the end of a world, but of the world, of the whole of the world, of the infinite opening of the world. And this is the case for no matter what living being, from the tree to the protozoa, from the mosquito to the human, death is infinite, it is the end of the infinite. The finitude of the infinite [*le fini de l'infini*]." My thanks to Geoff Bennington for drawing my attention to this passage.

15. Derrida later characterizes this as a "quasi-final session" because it was followed by a couple of sessions of student presentations (*BS 2* 277/380).

16. The line from Novalis that Heidegger cites near the beginning of his seminar, and that I look at in Chapter 4, is: "Philosophy is really homesickness, an urge to be at home everywhere" (*Fundamental Concepts of Metaphysics*, 5).

17. Derrida earlier relates the Heideggerian notion of *not* being at home in the world, of being driven *toward* the world without dwelling *in* it, to this line from Celan (*BS 2* 104–105/159–160).

18. Jeffrey Nealon has recently written a remarkable piece on this aspect of the seminar. In a chapter of *Plant Theory* (Durham, N.C.: Duke University Press, 2014), Nealon returns to *Glas* and the contrast between a kind of animal desire (in the Hegel column) and a plant desire (in the Genet column) in order then to highlight Derrida's references to plant life in relation to the lexicon of *Walten* in *The Beast and the Sovereign* seminar.

19. Derrida also argues here, as elsewhere, that the end of *a* world or of *a* history, the end of an individual world, is indistinguishable from the end of *the* world or the end of *history itself.* There is thus an interesting slippage in several places of the seminar between *histoire* as *story* and *histoire* as *history* (see *BS 2* 161–162/234, 164/237, and 224/312–313).

20. "If man becomes an animal again, his arts, his loves, and his play must also become purely 'natural' again. Hence it would have to be admitted that after the end of History, men would construct their edifices and works of art as birds build their nests and spiders spin their webs, would perform musical concerts after the fashion of frogs and cicadas, would play like young animals, and would indulge in love like adult beasts." Alexandre Kojève, *Introduction to the Reading of Hegel: Lectures on the Phenomenology of Spirit* (Ithaca, N.Y.: Cornell University Press, 1980, 159 n. 1).

21. In his description of this performative, Derrida appears to make a veiled reference to the famous Courbet painting *The Origin of the World*, once owned by Lacan and Sylvia Bataille. He speaks of a "performative lodged like a pearl in the oyster of a constative, like a still unborn child, to be born, to be carried to term in the uterus of the origin of the world as it is" (*BS 2* 259/358).

22. How are we to hear Derrida's invocation of "poetically" here? To understand what Derrida has in mind, we would have to look at Derrida's use of this word elsewhere in the seminar, in the previous year of the seminar, and in other works (see, for example, *BS 1* 271–272/364–365 and *BS 2* 169–170/244). We would see, for example, that Derrida often refers to poetry or poetics when it is a question of negotiating between contradictory imperatives, for example, the contradictory imperatives of hospitality. He thus speaks in "The Principle of Hospitality" of "a difference both subtle and fundamental, a question that arises on the threshold of the 'home,' and on the threshold between two inflections. An art and a poetics, but an entire politics depends on it, an entire ethics is decided by it" (*PM* 67). It would also be worth looking at the distinction Derrida makes in "Istrice 2: Ick bünn all hier" between the poematic and the poetic; while the latter is related to the "setting to work of truth" and to a certain *Versammlung* or gathering (particularly in Heidegger's *The Origin of the Work of Art*), the former is related to the "aleatory," to the nonsemantic and the nonsubstitutable, to the learning by heart of language (*P* 304–305).

I am also tempted to hear behind this invocation of poetry Derrida's own analyses in "Heidegger's Ear" of *An Introduction to Metaphysics*. Derrida there follows Heidegger on the question of the work of art and, especially, of poetry, and he asks "How does the *unheard* originarity of the unaccomplished make itself heard *then*, outside of itself in itself, in a sort of heterotautology, through historical works and events?" Heidegger's answer is that "the originary struggle is then carried on (*getragen*) by those that open (creators), poets, thinkers, statesmen" ("HE" 211). These are, in short, "the three creative 'Gewalten' of historical Dasein" ("HE" 211). Derrida concludes: "These three creators carry this unheard, they carry it first in themselves, close by themselves . . . like a mute voice to which they respond by taking responsibility for it. They open in this responsibility. This work is theirs, since they carry the unheard in themselves and take responsibility for it. But this work is not theirs, since they only hear the unheard. Their work carries only the seal or the signature of the originary *polemos* that has projected and developed the unheard" ("HE" 211). Given Derrida's many references to Heidegger throughout this seminar, it would be important to consider to what extent this word *poetically* is also marked by Heidegger's discourse, and even by his 1929–30 seminar, which begins with a line from Novalis and ends with a passage from Nietzsche's *Zarathustra*.

But perhaps the most interesting path to follow here would be to read Derrida's analysis of Celan in terms of what in *Politics of Friendship* he calls—initially in relation to Nietzsche—*teleiopoesis*. Peggy Kamuf makes a very convincing case for this in a remarkable paper, "Teleiopoetic World," published in a special issue of *SubStance* on *The Beast and the Sovereign*, no. 1 (2014).

23. Peter Szendy, in a fascinating unpublished essay, relates this lack or end of the world to what he calls an *acosmic* cosmopolitanism, a cosmopolitanism where "cosmonauts" do not relate to one another against the backdrop of a world but, precisely, bear one another into the void.

24. Derrida writes in "Shibboleth," "The crypt takes place (it is a passion, not an action, of the poet) wherever a singular incision marks language. As one might engrave a date in a tree, burning the bark with the ciphers of fire. But the voice of the poem carries beyond the singular cut" (*SQ* 48).

25. In a series of improvised remarks from 2002 published under the title "Trace and Archive," Derrida argues something similar about the necessity of living with phantasms, in this case, the phantasm (or illusion) of the self. After arguing that "one cannot live without 'the illusion of the essentialization of the I' or 'of the self,'" he goes on to suggest that "there is a considerable difference between not being able to live without the illusion of the essentialization of the I and saying 'there is an essential I'" ("TA" 17). Hence the difference between believing and then claiming that there is a world and knowing that there is not but making nonetheless as if there were, like the difference between believing and claiming that there is an essential self and knowing that there is not but recognizing the necessity of living as if there were, is a difference of knowledge, of belief, and no doubt ultimately, of how to live a life.

26. The island was renamed after Alejandro Selkirk in 1966. In an article from 2011 in the *New Yorker*, Jonathan Franzen recounts going to this small island—about as close as one can get these days to the ends of the world—in order to try to come to terms with the death of his friend David Foster Wallace. It is an article—yet another one—about world, finitude, and solitude, and about death as a certain end of the world. "Farther Away," *New Yorker*, April 18, 2011. My thanks to James Griffith at DePaul University for suggesting this article to me.

3. To Die a Living Death: Phantasms of Burial and Cremation

1. Derrida often spoke of this power of the voice and of the phantasm attached to it, that is, the phantasm of a voice that would still be attached to the life or life-source that produces it. In "Trace and Archive," Derrida argues that "the voice is what is most identifying or identifiable for the others, it is in the voice that one recognizes me the best no doubt, better than in the image and in what I say. [But] . . . if there is one thing that one cannot reappropriate, even less than one's image, it's one's voice" ("TA" 31).

2. The actual web address is DeadSoci.al.

3. Geoffrey Bennington phrases this very nicely in *Interrupting Derrida* (London: Routledge, 2000), 27: "On this view, decisions are taken *by the other*, my decisions, my most sovereign decisions, cannot be decisions if they are taken by some self-coincident agency, but are decisive only if there is a diremption between 'me' and the decider (in me)."

4. See *BS 2* 325 n. 2. See also my "History's Remains: Of Memory, Mourning, and the Event(s) of 9/11," in *Derrida From Now On* (New York: Fordham University Press, 2008), 167–186.

5. Robinson Crusoe imagines giving himself up without defense, in his body, to the elements, to wild animals, or to other men, three forms of the other that correspond, it seems, to Heidegger's three modalities in *Fundamental Concepts of Metaphysics*: stone, animal, and man. Of these three forms of destruction, the worst would be, for Crusoe, being destroyed and consumed by other men. In cannibalism, that which is seemingly closest—the other human being—becomes most distant, cannibalism being a sort of self-destruction or self-devouring, indeed an autoimmunity, of the species (*BS 2* 138–143/203–209). As Derrida develops the paradox, the cannibal is *more* other because *less* other (*BS 2* 142/208).

6. James Joyce, *Ulysses* (New York: Vintage Books, 1990), 373.

7. On this "logic of the phantasm," a logic that is strictly speaking not a logic insofar as it exceeds or resists the *logos*, a logic that thus contests a certain phantasm of the *logos*, see *BS 2* 262–263.

8. As Derrida argued earlier, Robinson Crusoe wants to deny the existence of phantasms (or ghosts) but he cannot. He wants to believe that he doesn't believe in them, but he cannot (*BS 2* 136/200). That is the power of the phantasm: even if it is not real, perhaps because it is not real, it has an *effect*

over us. "So the fantasy is really [*effectivement*] more effective, more powerful, it is really [*en effet*] more powerful than what is opposed to it—let's say, good sense and reality, perception of the real" (*BS 2* 137/201).

9. Derrida also notes that, for Freud, it is in times of war that primitive man is reawakened (*BS 2* 158/229). This reference to war is hardly fortuitous; it's February 12, 2003, just weeks before the American invasion of Iraq.

10. What Derrida says about the phantasm of an *individual* imagining life after death, the individual dying a living death, has a correlate in the phantasm of an apocalypse where humanity itself would be extinguished. Back in 1984 in "No Apocalypse, Not Now," Derrida argued that those who contemplate the possibility of a nuclear war imagine—phantasize—a sacrifice of life in the name of something greater than life, a sacrifice of the living that nonetheless leaves the one who phantasizes this catastrophe intact, surviving, so to speak, over the smoldering ruins of the earth. "Today, in the perspective of a remainderless destruction, without symbolicity, without memory and without mourning, those who contemplate setting off such a catastrophe do so no doubt *in the name* of what is worth more in their eyes than life ('Better dead than red'). . . . Nuclear war, at least as a hypothesis, a phantasm, of total self-destruction, can only be waged in the name of what is worth more than life. What gives life its worth is worth more than life" ("NA" 407–408).

11. Krell reminds us that "inhumation is the site of Freud's three irremediably uncanny elements: the dark, the quiet, the aloneness" (*DAO* 60).

12. As Derrida writes, "Ashes do without the body [*Les cendres font l'économie du cadavre*" (*BS 2* 168/242). Ashes are, of course, everywhere in Derrida's work, from *Glas* to *Cinders* to *Of Spirit*, which begins," I shall speak of ghost, of flame, and of ashes." David Krell has reminded me of Derrida's phantasm in *The Post Card* of drowning and then being cremated (*DAO* 61; see *PC* 211).

13. Notions such as being buried alive or dying a living death—notions that contest the very limits of life and death—are central to all of Derrida's work. To give just a single example, Derrida writes in "*Fors*" in his reading of Abraham and Torok: "the inhabitant of a crypt is always a living dead, a dead entity we are perfectly willing to keep alive, but *as* dead, one we are willing to keep, as long as we keep it, within us, intact in any way save as living" ("FOR" xxi).

14. In "Justices," Derrida evokes the alternative between burning and burying in relationship to writing or texts: "According to a Jewish tradition that Levinas discusses, when a mistake in spelling or transcription of the name of God comes to alter a manuscript, this manuscript must be neither destroyed or burned (for one does not annihilate the name of God) nor preserved (for one does not keep the trace of such a blasphemy). The parchment must in that case be buried. One must hide it and put it in a safe place, but keep it at the same time invisible and illegible" ("J" 710).

15. Derrida recalls in a similar way during the first year of the *Death Penalty* seminar that the "moment" or "instant" of death is defined quite differently in different cultures and periods of history.

4. Reinventing the Wheel: Of Sovereignty, Autobiography, and Deconstruction

1. This chapter was initially prepared for the conference "Coming Home," the Twenty-Fifth Annual Stony Brook English Graduate Conference, held at Stony Brook University in Manhattan on March 16, 2013. Let me thank here Eduardo Mendieta, chair of the Department of Philosophy, along with Allison Tyndall Locke and Laura James, the two principal organizers of the conference. The line from Maya Angelou with which I begin was cited on the conference's homepage.

2. Angelou's first album was, curiously and coincidentally, entitled *Miss Calypso*.

3. Novalis, too, it should be said, was a pen name for Georg Philipp Friedrich Freiherr von Hardenberg.

4. The novel as a whole also begins with the person singular pronoun: "I was born in the year 1632," the first words of the first chapter "I Go to Sea."

5. If Derrida will express his admiration for the potter and compare himself to a potter, it will not be insignificant, perhaps, that he later casts Heidegger in the role of potter (*BS 2* 97/150).

6. It was precisely this freeing of the hands, often considered to be the proper of man, that Derrida in *Of Grammatology* tracked through the work of Leroi-Gourhan in relationship the human's erect posture and the development of writing. Derrida thus commented there on the way in which "Leroi-Gourhan describes the slow transformation of manual moticity which frees the audio-phonic system for speech, and the glance and the hand for writing" (*OG* 84). Derrida recalls in *The Beast and the Sovereign* his prior work both on Leroi-Gourhan and on Heidegger's "*humainisme*" (*BS 2* 83/130).

7. Derrida writes of both the wheel and of prayer: "The nearest and the farthest, the same and the other, touch each other and come into contact in the circle, on the island, in the return, in the wheel and in the prayer. Everything happens as though, on this fictional island, Robinson Crusoe were reinventing sovereignty, technology, tools, the machine, the becoming-machine of the tool, and prayer, God, true religion" (*BS2* 78–79/124).

8. It is perhaps no coincidence, then, that Plato in the *Seventh Letter* chooses as an example of an object of knowledge nothing other than a *kuklos*, that is, a circle, or perhaps—since the word can be translated in both ways—a wheel. As Plato argues in that letter, there corresponds to every existing and knowable object five things: (1) a name, a conventional name, in this case, *kuklos*; (2) a definition made up of nouns of verbs, in the case of *kuklos*, "that which is everywhere equidistant from the extremities to the center"; (3) the image or representation of the object; (4) knowledge of the object; and, finally, (5) the

object itself. Now as for the image or representation of the object, what Plato calls an *eidōlon*, it is the object "in course of being portrayed and obliterated, or of being shaped with a lathe, and falling into decay" (*Seventh Letter* 342 b–d). It thus appears that the *eidōlon* covers both two dimensional circles that are drawn or portrayed and then erased as well as three-dimensional objects fashioned on a lathe or in some other way, a *kuklos* made of wood or some other material that will last for a time and then fall into decay. From the singular *kuklos* that is not in time or space, from the circle itself that belongs to being, thus comes the *kuklos* that is in time and space, the *kuklos* of becoming, or, better, the multiple *kukloi*, the many circles or wheels that can be drawn or constructed and then erased or destroyed on the basis of the singular *kuklos*. Plato, *Seventh Letter*, trans. R. G. Bury (Cambridge, Mass.: Harvard University Press, 1981).

9. According to Liddell and Scott, the Greek noun *kuklos* can be used to describe any number of circular bodies or configurations, from a place of assembly, an amphitheater, or a crowd gathering in a circle or ring, to the vault of the sky, the orb or disc of the sun or moon, heavenly bodies themselves as well as their circular motions or orbits, the circle or wall around a city, a round shield, eyeballs, a cycle or collection of poems, the revolution of the seasons, a circular dance, the cycle of rebirth, and, finally, a wheel, such as the wheels of a chariot or the golden wheels that Hephaestus fastens beneath the base of tripods so that "of themselves [*automatoi*] they might enter the gathering of the gods at his wish and again return to his house, a wonder to behold." *Iliad* 18.378, trans. A. T. Murray (Cambridge, Mass.: Harvard University Press, 1934).

10. This passage continues: "In this logic of iterability are found the re-sources both to cast into doubt oppositions of the type *physis/tekhnē* (and therefore also *physis/nomos, physis/thesis*) and to begin to analyze, in a different domain, all the fantasmatics, all the ideologies or metaphysics that today encumber so many discourses on cloning, discourses both for and against cloning" (*BS2* 75/120). A couple of pages later, Derrida defines the machine as "what works on its own by turning on itself" (*BS 2* 78/123); the machine thus combines mechanization and spontaneity (*BS 2* 78/123–124).

11. Derrida returns to Poll some 180 pages later, when he says that he does not want to "insult Poll, Robinson Crusoe's parrot (*psittakos*), first victim of the humanist arrogance that thought it could give itself the right to speech, and therefore the right to the world as such" (*BS 2* 260/360).

12. Derrida says in a conversation with Jean-Luc Nancy: "In Ovid, as you know, Echo is forbidden by the jealous goddess to do anything other than repeat the last words of Narcissus. But, in repeating the last words, or rather the last syllables, in order to obey and at the same time disobey the law, that is, in order to say something in her own name by playing with language, she manages to produce a totally unforeseeable event for Narcissus. And for the forbidding goddess. That indeed is the problematic of narcissism . . ." (*FS* 64).

13. As Krell argues with regard to Heidegger: "The two dangers of thinking are that one may err and therefore never find one's way back, or that one may go in circles and find one's way back forever" (*DAO* 51–52).

14. See *BS 2* 34/65–66; 36–38/68–71; 51/88; 63/105; 73/117; 119/179; 126/187; 143/209; 170/245; 216/302; 231/323. During the seminar, such detours are often occasioned by Derrida's reading of Heidegger. After asking at the beginning of the Fifth Session, "What is a thing? What is the other?" Derrida says to his audience, "Leaving these questions to wait for a moment, suspended for *the time of a detour*, I naturally invite you to read or reread Heidegger's two great texts on the thing, beginning with . . . (*BS 2* 119/179; my emphasis).

15. For this relationship between pottery and philosophy, see my own "Derrida at the Wheel," in *Derrida From Now On* (New York: Fordham University Press, 2008), 112–121.

16. From *La trace de l'autre*, cited in Jacques Derrida, "Violence and Metaphysics," in *Writing and Difference*, trans. Alan Bass (Chicago: University of Chicago Press, 1978), 320 n. 92. Levinas says something very similar in "Meaning and Sense," in *Basic Philosophical Writings*, ed. Adriaan T. Peperzak, Simon Critchley, and Robert Bernasconi (Bloomington: Indiana University Press, 1996), 48: "The itinerary of philosophy remains that of Ulysses, whose adventure in the world was only a return to his native island—a complacency in the Same, an unrecognition of the Other."

17. As David Krell notes, "Heidegger's emphasis on restiveness brings him close to the Celan who says, 'The world is gone, I'll have to follow you'" (*DAO* 56).

18. It is tempting to want to end this chapter, as it began, with the words of a great American poet, not Maya Angelou, this time, but Robert Hunter, the principal lyricist of the Grateful Dead. In a song written for the Dead entitled "The Wheel," Hunter gives voice to the ineluctable law of the wheel in words that just could have been inspired by *Robinson Crusoe* as read by Derrida: "Round, round, Robin run around / Gotta get back where you belong / . . . / Every time that wheel turn round / Bound to cover just a little more ground."

5. Pray Tell: Derrida's Performative Justice

1. J. Hillis Miller, *For Derrida* (New York: Fordham University Press, 2009), 133–173.

2. Miller even asserts, "I hold that it would be a catastrophe to blur different meanings of *performativity*." Ibid., 134.

3. Ibid., 135.

4. Miller writes: "'Performativity theory' and current 'performance studies,' I suggest, are somewhat later hybrids combining speech act theory, Foucault, and the original performance studies" (ibid., 136). "'Performativity,' it now appears, means, among other things, the assumption that human beings have

no innate selfhood or subjectivity but become what they are through more or less forced repetition of a certain role" (ibid., 146).

5. The quotations here are from ibid., 138 and 151.

6. Ibid., 152.

7. Ibid.

8. Ibid., 153.

9. Ibid., 154–155. Miller says that this is the only use of the word *performativité* he has found in Derrida's work.

10. Derrida will ask five weeks later, in the Eighth Session, "And can this experience of prayer be true or false, authentic or inauthentic, as Robinson Crusoe wondered . . . when he confessed having only slowly and painfully learned to pray again, and then to pray with a prayer that was authentic and worthy of the name?" (*BS 2* 204/287)

11. "There is suspension of any expectation, any economy, any calculation. I am not expecting, I am not hoping: my prayer is hopeless, totally, totally hopeless. I think that hopelessness is a part of what prayer should be. Yet I know there is hope, there is calculation. There is economy, but what sort of economy? Is it the economy of the child or my economy now, as an old man?" ("EF" 31).

12. Derrida says earlier: "I know that the most authentic believers know that they are very close to pure atheism because they know that in using the word 'God' they may be merely mentioning it" ("EF" 38).

13. This would be the case, says Derrida, "even if what I'm doing is not simply benevolent and beneficent, generous, giving (one can give love, but one can also give blows): the torturer also prays his victim to receive and to be present, to be aware of the blows he is giving him" (*BS 2* 203/287).

14. In "Ulysses Gramophone," Derrida evokes the "perfume of discourse" in relationship to an originary or elementary affirmation that would precede all discourse (*AL* 297). On this "perfumative force," see Diane Davis's excellent essay, "Performative Perfume," in *The Performative After Deconstruction*, ed. Mauro Senatore (New York: Bloomsbury Press, 2013), 70–85.

15. David Krell, in *Derrida and Our Animal Others*, also speaks of an "I pray you" and "a silent prayer or plea [that] precedes every constative, every statement of fact, every assertion, even the most coolly and confidently scientific protocol sentence" (*DAO* 162). "I pray you," "pray tell," but then also, as Derrida will go on to remark, "do not forget": "I cannot speak to someone without praying him or her, at least implicitly, not only to pay attention, but by that very fact to retain the memory of what I am saying to him or her, be it only from the beginning to the end of the sentence. By praying the other to listen, from the start, I'm praying him or her to retain the memory, to retain in memory; and perhaps every prayer, to whomever addressed, comes down to, or begins, by saying or letting be understood: 'remember, retain the memory, and first of all remember me, remember what I'm saying to you'" (*BS 2* 204/287–288).

16. "It is thus with reference to the *als-Struktur,* to the ability to perceive beings as such, that Heidegger says that he is interpreting man as *zōion logon echon* and the animal as a *zōion alogon*" (*BS 2* 218/305).

17. Insofar as all *logos,* according to Heidegger, signifies and has an intelligibility that comes from convention rather than nature, every *logos* is a *logos semantikos. Logos* is thus what is proper to man. But there is within this *logos semantikos* a kind of *logos* that seems even more proper to man as the sole being with full access to the *as such* of being. This is the apophantic *logos* (the *logos apophantikos*), that is, "the *logos* capable of showing, of showing that toward which it is directed as such" (*BS 2* 216/302). Only this *logos* has, for Heidegger, "the value of an enunciative proposition (*Aussagesatz*)"—the kind of proposition that Heidegger claims to be most proper to man. In order thus to elucidate this apophantic or enunciative *logos,* Heidegger will contrast it with the nonenunciative, nonapophantic *logos* of prayer, a *logos* that, according to Aristotle in *On Interpretation,* is neither true nor false.

18. Derrida credits Miller with something similar in "Justices," namely, the discovery of a speech act theory avant la lettre: "There is here a typically Millerian gesture, even if, in 1963, one did not yet have recourse to the lexicon of Austinian speech act theory and, above all, to the problematization of the categories of performative and constative" ("J" 695). Derrida will also find in Miller a deconstruction avant la lettre: "One recognizes the taste of it in what he says about the singularity of taste, the limits of language, *logos,* thus logocentrism, and especially about what exceeds and divides presence" ("J" 705).

19. Derrida thus accuses Heidegger of a kind of haste or "precipitation" with regard to faith and philosophy. But as Geoffrey Bennington has recently argued, this is perhaps more Derrida's precipitation than Heidegger's. Indeed, Derrida suggests that it is *Heidegger* who is making this exclusion, though Heidegger seems simply to be quoting Aristotle's *De interpretatione.* The "brutal exclusion" would thus seem to be Aristotle's, not Heidegger's. See Geoffrey Bennington, "Pseudos," in *L'a-venire di Derrida,* ed. Gianfranco Dalmasso, Carmine DiMartino, and Caterina Resta (2014).

20. Hence, Derrida can argue, as we saw earlier, that "animals have faith in a certain way," that "as soon as there is a social bond there is faith, and there are social bonds in animals" ("EF" 45).

21. Derrida admits not knowing how to interpret this single word, which seems to oscillate "between the fire of glory and the fire that reduces to ashes or that still smolders under the ashes of some cremation (*Aschenglorie*)" (*BS 2* 212/298).

22. "This is the whole history of relations between faith and prayer, on the one hand, and onto-theology on the other. I think it was, from the beginning, a focal point of the Millerian meditation. As Heidegger notes in *Identität und Differenz,* to the God of the philosophers, to the God of onto-theology, to the *Causa Sui,* to the Ground of what is, one can address neither prayers, nor

sacrifices, no music, nor dance. I would add: nor a poem, nor literature in general" ("J" 709).

23. What Derrida says about the singularity of *selftaste* in his reading of Hillis Miller's analysis of Gerard Manley Hopkins resembles the third of the three theses that Derrida develops in the First and Tenth Sessions of the seminar and that I have considered in some detail in Chapter 2. Miller's claims regarding the "univocity of being" would, says Derrida, "constitute an exception" to traditional ontology "as soon as no taste of self resembles any other, neither from one man to another, nor from one living being to another, nor from a finite living being to God. There is only the unique" ("J" 704).

24. Derrida continues: "It is a little as if we were asking ourselves: how can one be as alone as God? How to endure this uniqueness? And what can be the selftaste of God the Just?" ("J" 702)

25. As Derrida writes again in "Justices," "To respond faithfully, to obey loyally the text's demand. . . . I must sign a new text, issue another pledge that, however faithful it may be, will still signify something else as well and thus will risk betraying the demand, betraying it out of fidelity, in order to exert an unforeseeable and, by definition, improvident 'performative force' on readers" ("J" 716).

6. Derrida's Preoccupation with the Archive

1. "The archive is a violent initiative of authority, of power; it's a taking power for the future, it *pre-occupies* the future; it confiscates the past, the present, and the future. We know very well that there are no innocent archives" ("CF" 85; my translation).

2. As Derrida argues in *Echographies*: "The impression that the horizon is closed, that there is no future, etc. may just as well be a sign of the power of archivization as the contrary. Of course, the power of or drive to archivization may open to the future, to the experience of the open horizon: anticipation of the coming event and of what one will be able to keep of it by calling it in advance. But by the same token, this increase, this intensification of anticipation may also nullify the future. This is the paradox of anticipation. Anticipation opens to the future, but at the same time, it neutralizes it. . . . A single movement extends the opening of the future, and by the same token, by way of what I would call a *horizon effect*, it closes the future off, giving us the impression that 'this has already happened.' I am so ready to welcome the new, which I know I'm going to be able to keep, capture, archive, that it's as if it had already happened and as if nothing will ever happen again" (*Echographies* 105–106).

3. The question of the survival or inheritance of his own thinking or archive was clearly on Derrida's mind in his final interview of August 2004, published under the title *Learning to Live Finally*: "This question is more relevant today than ever before. It preoccupies me constantly [*Elle m'occupe sans cesse*]. But the time of our techno-culture has radically changed in this regard. The people of

my 'generation,' and *a fortiori* those of previous ones, had been accustomed to a certain historical rhythm: one thought one knew that a particular work might or might not survive, based upon its own qualities, for one, two, or, perhaps, like Plato, twenty-five centuries. Disappear, then be reborn. But today, the acceleration in the forms of archivization, though also use and destruction, are transforming the structure, temporality, and duration of the legacy. When it comes to thought, the question of survival has taken on absolutely unforeseeable forms. At my age, I am ready to entertain the most contradictory hypotheses in this regard: I have simultaneously—I ask you to believe me on this—the *double feeling* that, on the one hand, to put it playfully and with a certain immodesty, one has not yet begun to read me, that even though there are, to be sure, many very good readers (a few dozen in the world perhaps, people who are also writer-thinkers, poets), in the end it is later on that all this has a chance of appearing; but also, on the other hand, and thus simultaneously, I have the feeling that two weeks or a month after my death *there will be nothing left*. Nothing except what has been copyrighted and deposited in libraries. I swear to you, I believe sincerely and simultaneously in these two hypotheses" (*LLF* 33–34/34).

4. I look at this same passage from a different perspective and with a different intention in *Miracle and Machine: Jacques Derrida and the Two Sources of Religion, Science, and the Media* (New York: Fordham University Press, 2012), 168–169.

5. Transposing, as it were, the terms of revelation and revealability, of *Offenbarung* and *Offenbarkeit*, into a rethinking of the archive, Derrida writes in "Typewriter Ribbon": "There is the event one archives, the *archived* event (and there is no archive without body—I prefer to say 'body' rather than 'matter,' for reasons that I will try to justify later), and there is the *archiving* event, the archivization. The latter is not the same thing, structurally, as the archived event, even if, in certain cases, it is indissociable from it or even contemporary with it" (*WA* 113).

6. As Derrida writes in *Archive Fever*, "the concept of the archive cannot but carry in itself, like every concept, the weight of what is unthought" (*AF* 29). This unthought might be understood negatively, in terms of what is repressed or suppressed, but it is also, argues Derrida, that which "engages the history of the concept, it inflects desire or the archive fever, opening them to the future . . . everything that links knowledge and memory to the promise" ("AF" 29–30; translation slightly modified).

We might thus say, as Jean-Luc Nancy argues in a little text on the archive published by IMEC—this great repository of archives of contemporary French thought—that plural archives open onto or give access to the singular archive, that is, onto that which cannot be repeated. Jean-Luc Nancy, *Où cela s'est-il passé?* (Paris: Institut Mémoires de l'édition contemporaine, 2011). As Nancy notes, Derrida will have in effect introduced or reintroduced the singular "archive" into a French language that almost always uses the plural *archives*

(12–13). It is thus through archives, in the plural, that the archive, in the singular, opens up (29–31). One must then think, argues Nancy, "the 'impossible' enveloped in the archive" as "that which will have not arrived" (12). Nancy's book is one in a series that goes under the title "The Place of the Archive." In addition to Nancy's book, there is Gwenaëlle Aubry's *L'extase de l'archive* (Paris: Institut Mémoires de l'édition contemporaine, 2012), another very sensitive exploration of the notion of the archive that takes much of its inspiration from Perec and Sebald. Aubry writes, for example, in a passage on Sebald: "The living are the archives of the dead" (17). See also J.-B. Pontalis, *Oublieuse mémoire*, published in 2011 in the same collection.

7. Derrida writes elsewhere in *Archive Fever*, "A spectral messianicity is at work in the concept of the archive and ties it, like religion, like history, like science itself, to a very singular experience of the promise. And we are never far from Freud in saying this. Messianicity does not mean messianism" (*AF* 36). And again: "The condition on which the future remains to come is not only that it not be known, but that it not be *knowable as such*. . . . It is a question of this performative to come whose archive no longer has any relation to the record of what is, to the record of the presence of what is or will have been *actually* present. I call this the *messianic*, and I distinguish it radically from all messianism" (*AF* 72).

8. See "*Comment donner raison*? 'How to Concede, with Reasons?'" where Derrida follows another of Heidegger's admissions in his 1942 seminar on Hölderlin (*P* 191–195).

9. As Derrida writes in the context of a reading of a line by John Donne that might be understood in terms of what Derrida in *Politics of Friendship* calls *teleiopoesis*: "All the *Umwege*, all the detours of the race are outplayed by a death that precedes me, that is ahead of me, before me—since yesterday. Always anterior, in its very futurity, like what remains to come, affecting itself in advance from the nostalgia of its own archive—its very light affecting itself without delay with photography, autobiophotography. Or affecting itself in advance, via what in photography is called a delay mechanism, with its own photograph, a photograph that is itself not reappropriable. Everything begins with the archive or with archive fever" (*BS 2* 51/88). One would also need to think the "paradox of the 'forget me'" in both Pascal and Blanchot in relation to this question of the archive (*BS 2* 210/295).

10. Another interesting example of a living, walking archive would be the prayer of Pascal's that we looked at in the previous chapter, the prayer Pascal had copied out on a piece of paper and then sewn into his garment to be discovered on his person after his death. Though all writing, as we saw, is *posthumous*, indeed even when the writer is still living, this strange document would be exemplary in this regard, a written prayer—a moment of the archive—that would continue speaking, as it were, close to him, on his very body, even after the animating breath of his body will have left him (*BS 2* 209–214).

11. The discussion took place after a screening of Safaa Fathy's *D'ailleurs, Derrida*.

12. Derrida makes this odd comment in a discussion with Jean-Luc Nancy and Philippe Lacoue-Labarthe: "I don't believe in immortality. But I know that there is an *I*, a *me*, a living being who is related to itself through autoaffection, who might be a bird and who will feel alive like me, and who might thus say, in silence, *me*, and who will be *me*! There will be some living being who will continue to say me and this will be a me, this will be me! I could give other examples. But I don't take much comfort in this" (*FS* 26).

13. As Derrida said in those spoken comments of 2002: "[the trace] is something that parts from an origin but that just as soon separates itself from the origin and remains as trace to the extent that it is separated from the tracing, from the tracing origin. It is there that there is trace and the commencement of archives. Every trace is not an archive, but there is no archive without trace. The trace thus always parts from me and separates itself from me" ("TA" 18).

14. "The trace remains, but that does not mean that it is, substantially, or that it is essential; but it's the question of remaining [*restance*] that interests me, remaining of the trace beyond all ontology" ("TA" 18). Derrida elaborates on this in several places, among them an interview with Maurizio Ferraris from 1990: "The way I write it, the word 'rest' is closer to the German *Rest*, in the sense of residue, refuse, or trace than to *bleiben* in the sense of permanence. The rest 'is' not, because it is not what remains, in the stance, substance, or stability. What I call *restance* no longer comes to modify Being or the presence of Being. It indicates a repetition, an iterability rather, which no longer takes shape only on the basis of Being or beingness. Whence the question of cinders, of the cinder without spirit, without phoenix, without rebirth, and without destiny. . . . The rest 'is' always what can radically disappear, without remainder [*reste*] in the sense of what would remain permanently (memory, a memory, vestige, monument). The rest can always not remain [*rester*] in the classic sense of the term, in the sense of substance. This is the condition for there being any remainder. On the condition that it remain, that it can happen to it not to remain. A remainder is finite—or it is not a remainder" (*P* 322–323).

15. Pepperberg recounts her long relationship with Alex the parrot in *Alex & Me* (New York: HarperCollins, 2009).

7. "World, Finitude, Solitude": Derrida's *Walten*

1. The parenthetical *e* of *seul(e)* suggests that the speaker could be either masculine or feminine.

2. As Hillis Miller colorfully phrases this relation in *A Companion to Derrida* (Cambridge, Mass.: Blackwell, 2013), "Heidegger was for Derrida what King Charles' head was for Mr. Dick in Dickens's *David Copperfield*." Miller also claims that Derrida once told him he had probably written some ten thousand pages on Heidegger over the course of his many books and seminars.

3. It might be argued that this book would have benefited from a more independent assessment of Heidegger's seminar, that is, a more critical reading of Derrida's reading of Heidegger, but that has not been my objective here. I have tried to follow Derrida's reading of Heidegger, whether fair and accurate or forced and idiosyncratic, because of what it teaches us about Derrida and his work. Fortunately, there are a couple of excellent works—both by colleagues at DePaul—that provide this more neutral assessment of Heidegger's seminar, the one more or less independently of Derrida's reading and the second in conversation with it. For a superbly detailed analysis of Heidegger's patient and complex mise-en-scène of the question of life in his 1929–30 seminar, see the first chapter of Will McNeill's *The Time of Life: Heidegger and Ethos* (Albany: State University of New York Press, 2006), 1–51. I am very grateful to Will both for this published work and for everything I was able to learn from him in a 2011 seminar at DePaul University on Heidegger's 1929–30 seminar.

As I have hinted throughout, this book been informed and enriched from start to finish by David Krell's own masterful book on Derrida's final seminar, *Derrida and Our Animal Others: Derrida's Final Seminar, "The Beast and the Sovereign"* (Bloomington: Indiana University Press, 2013). The opening pages of the first chapter of Krell's book argue much more eloquently and persuasively than anything found in the present work for the significance of Derrida's seminars for contemporary thought. In his final chapter, Krell also provides us with a long list of "directions for future research," an entire research agenda, really, on Derrida and Heidegger, Schmitt, Lacan, Merleau-Ponty, and Nietzsche, though also Descartes, Schelling, and even Melville, on questions of the animal, solitude, life-death, poetry, and so on. If anyone is at a loss for an original dissertation subject, essay or book project, on Derrida, he or she would do well to begin here.

In *Derrida and Our Animal Others*, Krell reads Derrida's analysis of Heidegger's seminar both on its own terms and with an eye to several elements in Heidegger that Derrida does not emphasize or, in some cases, does not even mention. Krell shows, for example, how the question of death as what Heidegger called "the touchstone of all philosophy" (*DAO* 103–107) complicates Derrida's claim that only Dasein is capable of death. "In his best moments," Krell can thus argue, Heidegger "break[s] down the monolithic barrier between humans and other living beings" (*DAO* 118). Krell shows, for example, the great proximity between humans and animals in Heidegger in their mutual relation to *Benommenheit*, that is, in relation to a "bedazzlement" that characterizes the animal in 1929–30 but that in *Being and Time* describes both Dasein's being bedazzled by worldly concerns and the anxiety or uncanniness—a certain relation to "ecstatic time" (*DAO* 89)—that would allow Dasein to discover its proper self. Even in 1929–30, Krell shows, there are places where Heidegger seems to grant all life—animals as well as plants—a certain openness to world (*DAO* 107–109), and he notes Derrida's surprising neglect of Heidegger's reference in 1929–30 to Romans 8:19 and "the suffering and longing that pervade all forms of life" (*DAO* 115). Krell also demonstrates the importance of non-apophantic discourse in Heidegger, from the significance of the hermeneutic-as in *Being and Time* (*DAO* 91, 112–114) to a consideration of language in the "Logos" essay that is decidedly "beyond assertion and assertiveness" (*DAO* 121).

Krell also makes some invaluable remarks on the use and scope of the lexicon of *Walten* in Heidegger and in German more generally. He asks whether Derrida might not have overestimated or overtranslated the language of *Walten* as violence in the 1929–30 seminar, or whether Derrida might have detected something in this early seminar that became palpable only later, for example in *Introduction to Metaphysics* (see *DAO* 52). He also demonstrates a certain ambivalence in Heidegger's use of *Walten*—as well as of *Austrag*—in 1957 in *Identity and Difference*, where it is related at once to the clearing and to the "onto-theological constitution of metaphysics itself" (*DAO* 67–68). Finally, Krell supplements Derrida's reading of "the beast and the sovereign" with a long analysis of Merleau-Ponty's 1942 *The Structure of Behavior* and some reflections on Nietzsche as "the 'autobiographical animal' par excellence" (*DAO* 3). If one thus wants a more objective assessment of Heidegger on the question of the relationship between the animal and the human, a less partisan perspective on Derrida's reading of Heidegger, then one should begin with Krell's *Derrida and Our Animal Others* and then return to McNeill's *The Time of Life*.

4. My suspicion is that this footnote was added after the fact, perhaps after a series of exchanges with David Krell (see note 3), then at the University of Essex, who either brought Heidegger's 1929–30 seminar to Derrida's attention in the first place or else convinced him of its importance for his work.

5. As for the missing or as-yet-unpublished "*Geschlecht III*," it would have apparently developed in some detail the reading of Trakl's poetry that Derrida was pursuing at the time in his seminar in Paris. Derrida appears to summarize some of this material in the final fifteen pages of *Geschlecht II* and in the latter sections of *Of Spirit*. When Derrida first delivered *Geschlecht II* at a conference in March 1985 in Chicago, he handed out to the participants an additional thirty-three typewritten pages, in French, on Heidegger's reading of Trakl. Derrida concludes these typewritten pages: "The transcription of the seminar had to end here, for lack of time. Five sessions [i.e., seminar sessions] still need to be transcribed, about a hundred pages. Please do not circulate this rough draft of an outline—provisional and incomplete!" For an excellent summary of these pages, see David Farrell Krell's "Marginalia to *Geschlecht III*: Derrida on Heidegger on Trakl," *New Centennial Review* 7, no. 2 (2007): 175–199. A good deal of what would have been *Geschlecht III* is thus available in some form, but there is still much that has never been published.

6. *OS* 119–120 n. 3. Derrida develops this argument in much greater detail in *Aporias* (see *AP* 21, 71, 75–76).

7. It is tempting to want to draw political conclusions from this chronology, that is, from this shift in emphasis on the sameness of *logos* and *polemos* in 1935, that is, *before the war*, to an emphasis on the sameness of *logos* and *philia* some ten years *after the war*. While such interpretations are certainly not illegitimate, prudence would be required here more than ever.

8. See *ATT* 14, 19, 22, 27, 32, 36, 38–39, 40, 45, 47, 48, 54, 59, 70–71, 79–80, 81, 84, 87, 88, 89, 90, 91, 93, 96, 110, 111, 127, 129.

9. There are several other places where Derrida promises this reading of the 1929–30 seminar. He says, for example, that he will explore Heidegger's claims about the *Benommenheit* of the animal "in a text that later I would like to read closely" (*ATT* 19; see also 48, 79, 93, 129).

10. Derrida also underscores Heidegger's attempts in *Being and Time* to distance himself from all "biologism" (*ATT* 144). This then raises, for Derrida, the whole question of *life* in Heidegger. As Derrida points out, Heidegger will wish to approach the question of the relationship between Dasein and the animal on the basis not of life or of consciousness but of a fundamental attunement (*ATT* 148–49) or else of "existence": if the animal *lives*, it is only man or Dasein that *exists* (*ATT* 158). Derrida also raises "the question of the animality of *Dasein*," a question, he claims, "Heidegger, naturally, leaves aside or in suspense—I would say from one end to the other of his life and his thinking" (*ATT* 155). He also points out places in the 1929–30 seminar that imply a shared "finitude" of the animal and man (*ATT* 150–51), a "claim" that seems to be in conflict with what Heidegger says elsewhere about the animal's inability to die (*ATT* 154). On the topic of life in Heidegger, and particularly in *The Fundamental Concepts of Metaphysics*, see, once again, Will McNeill's *The Time of Life: Heidegger and Ethos*.

11. Derrida admits that this neutralization or banalization can happen in German as well, so that one risks missing or neglecting "what exactly Heidegger imprints on it, insistently and strangely, but clearly explicitly and deliberately, at the beginning of the seminar" (*BS 2* 32/63).

12. It is thus by means of this "interpretation of both *physis* and *logos* on the basis, let's say, of the hidden or revealed sovereignty of *Walten*" (*BS 2* 43/77), by means of an analysis of these shifts in vocabulary in Heidegger, that Derrida is able to suggest without developing a political reading of Heidegger, one that would neither simply accuse nor vindicate Heidegger but try to think at once the *Walten* that Heidegger will have exercised and the one he will have thought. Derrida's strategy in reading Heidegger is similar in the *Geschlecht* essays, *Of Spirit*, and *The Beast and the Sovereign*. In each case he tries to demonstrate the changes in valence or simply in the appearance of a word from the 1920s through to the 1950s, with the mid-1930s being, for obvious reasons, the place where Derrida will focus the majority of his attention.

13. Krzysztof Ziarek, "*Das Gewalt-lose Walten:* Heidegger on Violence, Power, and Gentleness," in *Proceedings of the Forty-Fifth Annual Meeting of the*

Heidegger Circle (2011): 145–163; http://antihumaniste.files.wordpress.com /2011/07/2011proceedings.pdf.

14. See Andrew Mitchell's essay "Heidegger's Later Thinking of Animality: The End of World Poverty," *Gatherings: The Heidegger Circle Annual* 1 (2011): 74–85.

15. "What interests me," says Derrida, "is the relation between this *Trieb* and *Walten*" (*BS 2* 102 n. 20/156 n. 2).

16. Derrida himself seems to hesitate throughout the seminar about this point: "Before the theologico-political, unless one says that, precisely, there is something theologico-political here because there is some *Walten* which is both theological and political, opening everything. But it is not a category: if I translate *Walten* as sovereignty, obviously this does not have a narrowly political or narrowly theological sense because it covers both the political and the theological. Now, one can also say the opposite—one can say that it is the foundation of the theologico-political" (*BS 2* 41 n. 16/75 n. 1).

17. Derrida goes on to suggest a kind of resemblance between *Walten* and the neuter in Blanchot. Insofar as this latter is "situated before or beyond that difference between Being and beings," it resembles a thinking of *différance* (*BS 2* 190/269). Heidegger's *Walten* would thus resemble Blanchot's neuter, which would resemble Derrida's *différance*.

18. Ralph Manheim not only neutralizes the force of *Walten* in his translation but actually reads the phrase differently: "the spirit of poetry (only authentic and great poetry is meant) is essentially superior to the spirit that prevails in all mere science." Manheim attaches the "prevailing" to science rather than to "poetry." *An Introduction to Metaphysics* (New Haven: Yale University Press, 1959), 26. Gregory Fried and Richard Polt have it right in their retranslation of this important text: "in comparison to all mere science, an essential superiority of the spirit holds sway in poetry (only genuine and great poetry is meant)," *Introduction to Metaphysics* (New Haven: Yale University Press, 2000), 28.

19. Derrida speaks earlier of the "very poetic and singular" use Heidegger makes of the word *Austrag* in *Identity and Difference*. He argues that *Walten* would sign or be the signature of this poetic sovereignty (*BS 2* 282/387). Between the bearing of *Austrag* and the violence of *Walten*, Heidegger's writing will have signed this poetic sovereignty, and Derrida's seminar will have remarked on and, as we will see, countersigned this signature.

20. If he had just a few more hours, says Derrida, he would "be able to deduce from all that both the superarmament of ideology and idealism, and its inseparability from the televisual image relayed by satellite. Think about it when you're watching television" (*BS 2* 290/396). "It is through war that idealism too imposed its interpretation of Being, a war for the victory of an idea, of the idea of idea, of the intelligible as *eidos*, i.e. as visible object" (*BS 2* 290/396).

21. As for *Identity and Difference*, I cannot do justice here to Derrida's close reading of a few passages from that text, so let me instead summarize in just a

few sentences Derrida's arguments with regard to it and the reasons for his interest in it. Still concerned with what distinguishes human Dasein from the animal, with what gives Dasein access to the *als-Struktur*, to the *as such* of beings, to the difference between Being and beings, Derrida turns to a passage from *Identity and Difference* (1957) where what is at stake is the supervening or the event of this difference and the according of a certain power (*Vermögen, Verhalten*) to man or to Dasein in relation to it. Once again, it is *Walten* that characterizes this event or this supervening, a *Walten* that, Derrida remarks yet again, has been "scarcely noticed by all the readers of Heidegger I think I know" (*BS 2* 252/350). In this text of 1957, *Walten* would be at once "the event, the origin, the power, the force, the source, the movement, the process, the meaning etc.—whatever you like—of the ontological difference, the becoming-ontological-difference of the ontological difference, of the supervening of Being and of the arrival of beings?" (*BS 2* 256/355; see 283/387).

22. In a "Post-Scriptum" to "Force of Law," Derrida brings Benjamin together with Heidegger, arguing that "this text [i.e., "Critique of Violence"], like many others by Benjamin, is still too Heideggerian, too messianico-Marxist or archaeo-eschatological for me" ("FL" 298).

23. Both Walter Benjamin and Derrida were born on July 15, the former in 1892, the latter in 1930.

Conclusion: *Désormais*

1. The title "Letter to a Japanese Friend" alone already resonates with Heidegger's "A Dialogue on Language: Between a Japanese and an Inquirer," in *On the Way to Language*, trans. Peter D. Hertz (San Francisco: Harper & Row, 1971), 1–54.

2. Derrida had referred to Benjamin's first name much earlier in the seminar: "So much for *Walten*, and for those who are called—we know at least one of them—Walter" (*BS 2* 41–44/75–78). Moreover, Derrida begins his "Post-Scriptum" to "Force of Law": "*This strange text is dated. Every signature is dated, even and perhaps all the more so if it slips in among several names of God and only signs by pretending to let God himself sign. If this text is dated and signed (Walter, 1921) . . .*" ("FL" 293–294).

3. Nathalie Sarraute, *L'usage de la parole* (Paris: Gallimard, 1980), 12; my translation. Cathy Caruth's reading of an English phrase in a letter from Freud to his son in 1938, that is, about sixteen months before Freud's death, seems to move in a similar direction. She writes in *Unclaimed Experience: Trauma, Narrative, and History* (Baltimore: Johns Hopkins University Press, 1996), 23–24: "In the line he writes to his son, the last four words—'to die in freedom'—unlike the rest of the sentence, are not written in German, but rather in English. The announcement of his freedom, and of his dying, is given in a language that can be heard by those in the new place to which he brings his voice, to us, upon whom the legacy of psychoanalysis is bestowed. . . . I would like to suggest that it is here, in the movement from German to English,

in the rewriting of the departure within the languages of Freud's text, that we participate most fully in Freud's central insight, in *Moses and Monotheism*, that history, like trauma, is never simply one's own, that history is precisely the way we are implicated in each other's traumas. For we—whether as German- or as English-speaking readers—cannot read this sentence without, ourselves, departing. In this departure, in the leave-taking of our hearing, we are first fully addressed by Freud's text, in ways we perhaps cannot yet fully understand. And, I would propose today, as we consider the possibilities of cultural and political analysis, that the impact of this not fully conscious address may be not only a valid but indeed a necessary point of departure."

4. *Je suis mort* is, of course, the phrase from Baudelaire's translation of Edgar Allan Poe's "The Facts in the Case of M. Valdemar" that Derrida cites as an exergue to *Speech and Phenomenon*.

5. See David Krell's comments on this enigmatic line at *DAO* 62.

6. As we saw in Chapter 3, Derrida much earlier in the seminar associates the island with the womb and then, as if to close a certain circle, the womb with inhumation or the tomb: "We shall also come back to everything that is at stake, as to the island, in these terrified desires or desiring terrors of being swallowed alive or buried alive—in their relation to insularity, of course, but also to the maternal womb, and also to the alternative of mournings and phantasms of mourning: between inhumation and cremation" (*BS 2* 92/143).

Index

Abraham, 101, 122, 129
Abraham, Nicolas, 185n13
Abrahamic religions, 34, 69–71, 79–80, 179n19
Abū Bakr ibn Tufayl, 180
Agamben, Giorgio, 143, 151, 180n22
Agrégation exam, 3, 144, 174n7
Alex (the parrot), 141, 194n15
American Academy of Religion, 110, 181n13
Angelou, Maya, 83–87, 101, 183, 186nn1–2, 188n18
Animals, animality, 3–11, 13–14, 17–40, 43–48, 52, 55–58, 65, 75, 80, 83, 88, 91, 95, 97, 104, 107, 116–18, 129–31, 138, 140–41, 143, 145–50, 154–55, 159, 161–62, 164, 171, 174n5, 176nn1–3, 176–77n4, 178nn7–9, 11–12, 179nn13, 15–18, 20–21, 180nn22–23, 181n13, 182nn18, 20, 184n5, 190nn16, 20, 195–96n3, 197nn9–10, 198n14, 199n21; animal faith, 52, 117, 181n13, 190n20; animal-machine, 32, 34–35, 131; animal suffering, 33; animals in philosophy, 6, 8, 17–28, 30–34, 36–39, 43, 91, 107, 161, 176n4

Apocalypse, 50, 126, 174n5, 185n10
Archives, 7, 9, 12–16, 65, 81–82, 96, 103, 104, 119, 121–23, 125–41, 164, 168–70, 191nn1–3, 192nn5–6, 193nn6–7, 9–10, 194n13
Ariès, Philippe, 81
Aristotle, 4, 18, 19, 32–34, 38, 41, 42, 93, 113, 116–17, 143, 147, 149–50, 179n16, 180n3, 190nn17, 19
Atheism, 110–12, 114–16, 123, 189n12
Aubry, Gwenaëlle, 193n6
Augustine, 100, 124
Austin, John, 105–7, 118, 119, 190n18
Autobiography, 7, 10, 11–12, 20–21, 83, 87, 89, 92, 96, 99, 100–3, 104, 114, 131, 138, 165, 174n5, 176n2, 196n3
Autoimmunity, 71–72, 89, 93–95, 99, 102–3, 128–29, 137, 155, 158, 167, 171, 184n5

Balibar, Étienne, 134
Bataille, Sylvia, 182n21
Baudelaire, Charles, 200n4
Benjamin, Walter, 100, 163–64, 199nn22–23, 2
Bennington, Geoffrey, 18, 56, 181nn11, 14, 184n3, 190n19

201

Perspectives in Continental Philosophy

John D. Caputo, series editor

John D. Caputo, ed., *Deconstruction in a Nutshell: A Conversation with Jacques Derrida*.

Michael Strawser, *Both/And: Reading Kierkegaard—From Irony to Edification*.

Michael D. Barber, *Ethical Hermeneutics: Rationality in Enrique Dussel's Philosophy of Liberation*.

James H. Olthuis, ed., *Knowing Other-wise: Philosophy at the Threshold of Spirituality*.

James Swindal, *Reflection Revisited: Jürgen Habermas's Discursive Theory of Truth*.

Richard Kearney, *Poetics of Imagining: Modern and Postmodern*. Second edition.

Thomas W. Busch, *Circulating Being: From Embodiment to Incorporation—Essays on Late Existentialism*.

Edith Wyschogrod, *Emmanuel Levinas: The Problem of Ethical Metaphysics*. Second edition.

Francis J. Ambrosio, ed., *The Question of Christian Philosophy Today*.

Jeffrey Bloechl, ed., *The Face of the Other and the Trace of God: Essays on the Philosophy of Emmanuel Levinas*.

Ilse N. Bulhof and Laurens ten Kate, eds., *Flight of the Gods: Philosophical Perspectives on Negative Theology*.

Trish Glazebrook, *Heidegger's Philosophy of Science*.

Kevin Hart, *The Trespass of the Sign: Deconstruction, Theology, and Philosophy*.

Mark C. Taylor, *Journeys to Selfhood: Hegel and Kierkegaard*. Second edition.

Dominique Janicaud, Jean-François Courtine, Jean-Louis Chrétien, Michel Henry, Jean-Luc Marion, and Paul Ricoeur, *Phenomenology and the "Theological Turn": The French Debate*.

Karl Jaspers, *The Question of German Guilt*. Introduction by Joseph W. Koterski, S.J.

Jean-Luc Marion, *The Idol and Distance: Five Studies*. Translated with an introduction by Thomas A. Carlson.

Jeffrey Dudiak, *The Intrigue of Ethics: A Reading of the Idea of Discourse in the Thought of Emmanuel Levinas*.

Robyn Horner, *Rethinking God as Gift: Marion, Derrida, and the Limits of Phenomenology*.

Mark Dooley, *The Politics of Exodus: Søren Kierkegaard's Ethics of Responsibility*.

Merold Westphal, *Overcoming Onto-Theology: Toward a Postmodern Christian Faith*.

Edith Wyschogrod, Jean-Joseph Goux, and Eric Boynton, eds., *The Enigma of Gift and Sacrifice*.

Stanislas Breton, *The Word and the Cross*. Translated with an introduction by Jacquelyn Porter.

Jean-Luc Marion, *Prolegomena to Charity*. Translated by Stephen E. Lewis.

Peter H. Spader, *Scheler's Ethical Personalism: Its Logic, Development, and Promise*.

Jean-Louis Chrétien, *The Unforgettable and the Unhoped For*. Translated by Jeffrey Bloechl.

Don Cupitt, *Is Nothing Sacred? The Non-Realist Philosophy of Religion: Selected Essays*.

Jean-Luc Marion, *In Excess: Studies of Saturated Phenomena*. Translated by Robyn Horner and Vincent Berraud.

Phillip Goodchild, *Rethinking Philosophy of Religion: Approaches from Continental Philosophy*.

William J. Richardson, S.J., *Heidegger: Through Phenomenology to Thought*.

Jeffrey Andrew Barash, *Martin Heidegger and the Problem of Historical Meaning*.

Jean-Louis Chrétien, *Hand to Hand: Listening to the Work of Art*. Translated by Stephen E. Lewis.

Jean-Louis Chrétien, *The Call and the Response*. Translated with an introduction by Anne Davenport.

D. C. Schindler, *Han Urs von Balthasar and the Dramatic Structure of Truth: A Philosophical Investigation*.

Julian Wolfreys, ed., *Thinking Difference: Critics in Conversation*.

Allen Scult, *Being Jewish/Reading Heidegger: An Ontological Encounter*.

Richard Kearney, *Debates in Continental Philosophy: Conversations with Contemporary Thinkers*.

Jennifer Anna Gosetti-Ferencei, *Heidegger, Hölderlin, and the Subject of Poetic Language: Toward a New Poetics of Dasein*.

Jolita Pons, *Stealing a Gift: Kierkegaard's Pseudonyms and the Bible*.

Jean-Yves Lacoste, *Experience and the Absolute: Disputed Questions on the Humanity of Man*. Translated by Mark Raftery-Skehan.

Charles P. Bigger, *Between* Chora *and the Good: Metaphor's Metaphysical Neighborhood.*

Dominique Janicaud, *Phenomenology "Wide Open": After the French Debate.* Translated by Charles N. Cabral.

Ian Leask and Eoin Cassidy, eds., *Givenness and God: Questions of Jean-Luc Marion.*

Jacques Derrida, *Sovereignties in Question: The Poetics of Paul Celan.* Edited by Thomas Dutoit and Outi Pasanen.

William Desmond, *Is There a Sabbath for Thought? Between Religion and Philosophy.*

Bruce Ellis Benson and Norman Wirzba, eds., *The Phenomenology of Prayer.*

S. Clark Buckner and Matthew Statler, eds., *Styles of Piety: Practicing Philosophy after the Death of God.*

Kevin Hart and Barbara Wall, eds., *The Experience of God: A Postmodern Response.*

John Panteleimon Manoussakis, *After God: Richard Kearney and the Religious Turn in Continental Philosophy.*

John Martis, *Philippe Lacoue-Labarthe: Representation and the Loss of the Subject.*

Jean-Luc Nancy, *The Ground of the Image.*

Edith Wyschogrod, *Crossover Queries: Dwelling with Negatives, Embodying Philosophy's Others.*

Gerald Bruns, *On the Anarchy of Poetry and Philosophy: A Guide for the Unruly.*

Brian Treanor, *Aspects of Alterity: Levinas, Marcel, and the Contemporary Debate.*

Simon Morgan Wortham, *Counter-Institutions: Jacques Derrida and the Question of the University.*

Leonard Lawlor, *The Implications of Immanence: Toward a New Concept of Life.*

Clayton Crockett, *Interstices of the Sublime: Theology and Psychoanalytic Theory.*

Bettina Bergo, Joseph Cohen, and Raphael Zagury-Orly, eds., *Judeities: Questions for Jacques Derrida.* Translated by Bettina Bergo and Michael B. Smith.

Jean-Luc Marion, *On the Ego and on God: Further Cartesian Questions.* Translated by Christina M. Gschwandtner.

Jean-Luc Nancy, *Philosophical Chronicles.* Translated by Franson Manjali.

Jean-Luc Nancy, *Dis-Enclosure: The Deconstruction of Christianity.* Translated by Bettina Bergo, Gabriel Malenfant, and Michael B. Smith.

Andrea Hurst, *Derrida Vis-à-vis Lacan: Interweaving Deconstruction and Psychoanalysis.*

Jean-Luc Nancy, *Noli me tangere: On the Raising of the Body.* Translated by Sarah Clift, Pascale-Anne Brault, and Michael Naas.

Jacques Derrida, *The Animal That Therefore I Am.* Edited by Marie-Louise Mallet, translated by David Wills.

Jean-Luc Marion, *The Visible and the Revealed.* Translated by Christina M. Gschwandtner and others.

Michel Henry, *Material Phenomenology.* Translated by Scott Davidson.

Jean-Luc Nancy, *Corpus*. Translated by Richard A. Rand.

Joshua Kates, *Fielding Derrida*.

Michael Naas, *Derrida From Now On*.

Shannon Sullivan and Dennis J. Schmidt, eds., *Difficulties of Ethical Life*.

Catherine Malabou, *What Should We Do with Our Brain?* Translated by Sebastian Rand, Introduction by Marc Jeannerod.

Claude Romano, *Event and World*. Translated by Shane Mackinlay.

Vanessa Lemm, *Nietzsche's Animal Philosophy: Culture, Politics, and the Animality of the Human Being*.

B. Keith Putt, ed., *Gazing Through a Prism Darkly: Reflections on Merold Westphal's Hermeneutical Epistemology*.

Eric Boynton and Martin Kavka, eds., *Saintly Influence: Edith Wyschogrod and the Possibilities of Philosophy of Religion*.

Shane Mackinlay, *Interpreting Excess: Jean-Luc Marion, Saturated Phenomena, and Hermeneutics*.

Kevin Hart and Michael A. Signer, eds., *The Exorbitant: Emmanuel Levinas Between Jews and Christians*.

Bruce Ellis Benson and Norman Wirzba, eds., *Words of Life: New Theological Turns in French Phenomenology*.

William Robert, *Trials: Of Antigone and Jesus*.

Brian Treanor and Henry Isaac Venema, eds., *A Passion for the Possible: Thinking with Paul Ricoeur*.

Kas Saghafi, *Apparitions—Of Derrida's Other*.

Nick Mansfield, *The God Who Deconstructs Himself: Sovereignty and Subjectivity Between Freud, Bataille, and Derrida*.

Don Ihde, *Heidegger's Technologies: Postphenomenological Perspectives*.

Suzi Adams, *Castoriadis's Ontology: Being and Creation*.

Richard Kearney and Kascha Semonovitch, eds., *Phenomenologies of the Stranger: Between Hostility and Hospitality*.

Michael Naas, *Miracle and Machine: Jacques Derrida and the Two Sources of Religion, Science, and the Media*.

Alena Alexandrova, Ignaas Devisch, Laurens ten Kate, and Aukje van Rooden, *Re-treating Religion: Deconstructing Christianity with Jean-Luc Nancy*. Preamble by Jean-Luc Nancy.

Emmanuel Falque, *The Metamorphosis of Finitude: An Essay on Birth and Resurrection*. Translated by George Hughes.

Scott M. Campbell, *The Early Heidegger's Philosophy of Life: Facticity, Being, and Language*.

Françoise Dastur, *How Are We to Confront Death? An Introduction to Philosophy*. Translated by Robert Vallier. Foreword by David Farrell Krell.

Christina M. Gschwandtner, *Postmodern Apologetics? Arguments for God in Contemporary Philosophy*.

Ben Morgan, *On Becoming God: Late Medieval Mysticism and the Modern Western Self*.

Neal DeRoo, *Futurity in Phenomenology: Promise and Method in Husserl, Levinas, and Derrida.*

Sarah LaChance Adams and Caroline R. Lundquist, eds., *Coming to Life: Philosophies of Pregnancy, Childbirth, and Mothering.*

Thomas Claviez, ed., *The Conditions of Hospitality: Ethics, Politics, and Aesthetics on the Threshold of the Possible.*

Roland Faber and Jeremy Fackenthal, eds., *Theopoetic Folds: Philosophizing Multifariousness.*

Jean-Luc Marion, *The Essential Writings.* Edited by Kevin Hart.

Adam S. Miller, *Speculative Grace: Bruno Latour and Object-Oriented Theology.* Foreword by Levi R. Bryant.

Jean-Luc Nancy, *Corpus II: Writings on Sexuality.*

David Nowell Smith, *Sounding/Silence: Martin Heidegger at the Limits of Poetics.*

Gregory C. Stallings, Manuel Asensi, and Carl Good, eds., *Material Spirit: Religion and Literature Intranscendent.*

Claude Romano, *Event and Time.* Translated by Stephen E. Lewis.

Frank Chouraqui, *Ambiguity and the Absolute: Nietzsche and Merleau-Ponty on the Question of Truth.*

Noëlle Vahanian, *The Rebellious No: Variations on a Secular Theology of Language.*

Michael Naas, *The End of the World and Other Teachable Moments: Jacques Derrida's Final Seminar.*

Jean-Louis Chrétien, *Under the Gaze of the Bible.* Translated by John Marson Dunaway.

Edward Baring and Peter E. Gordon, eds., *The Trace of God: Derrida and Religion.*

Vanessa Lemm, ed., *Nietzsche and the Becoming of Life.*

Aaron T. Looney, *Vladimir Jankélévitch: The Time of Forgiveness.*